The Social Limits of Art

山水有清音得
者才心是寒泉
潄石根冷七諮心耳
向日我携宓畊釣
閒雲兼念乙小彌
戀春風吹月起
清湘大滌子畊心艸
山艿生揚笑

John Manfredi

# THE SOCIAL LIMITS OF ART

Mountain waters have clear sounds.
Those who hear them feel at home.
Cold springs, wash, stone, roots
All enlighten my heart, I listen
And think, "When can I bring my people
To farm and fish high in the clouds?"
I think and think and feel more sad,
As spring breezes blow and the moon rises.

---

Ching-hsiang Ta-ti-tze Keng-hsin Tsao-tang
given to Mr. Hsia-shan for a smile (1703)

The University of Massachusetts Press    Amherst, 1982

---

Perception and Culture. Priest Shih-t'oa Yuan-chi (1640–1707), *Album of Landscapes*, Ch'ing Dynasty, dated 1703. Album of twelve leaves, ink and color on 18¾-by-12⅓ inch paper.

Geometric perspective, the principal way of achieving depth in Western landscape, is entirely absent in this drawing. Depth is portrayed by varying the size of the objects and the contrast and dilution of the washes. The man in the boat is an incidental element rather than a central concern and demonstrates a practice in accord with the off-hand treatment of such matters in the "Book of People and Things" in *The Mustard Seed Garden Manual of Painting* (1679). A translation of the poem made by my valued colleague Ching-Mao Cheng has been rendered into verse by Arnold Kenseth and appears on the title page. The poem itself speaks of a longing to live within the stream of nature rather than in opposition to it. Such an objective is consistent with the absence of the tension that rational thinking imposes, with viewing the central fact of life as a felt continuum, and with the lack of the defined structure that Westerners have expected of poetry until very recently. The drawing itself is not less realistic than a comparable Western academic effort; it is a product of a culture that makes the mind give meaning to the felt, fluid aspects of the data of perception.

Courtesy, Museum of Fine Arts, Boston. William F. Warden Fund.

# Acknowledgments

Permit me to say for whom I have written this book. I have written it for my good wife whose concerned counsel I avoided until she read the galley sheets; for my son, Louis, and my daughter, Laurel; for the dear mentors and friends of my youth—the late psychologist and painter, Cheves West Perky, my junior-high-school English teacher, Mrs. Kathleen McCarthy White, my cronies Miles Davidson and Edwin Fiedler; for Baruch Sachs who gave me courage when I needed it. Finally, it is for my late father, mother, and Aunt Estelle.

There are those whom I must thank for more tangible help. Nancy Pride, Laura Martin, and Mary Louise Creekmore put their patient hands to typings of the manuscript. Professor Paul Norton unselfishly pinned down some questions for me that I could never have answered without his help. Professor Ching-Mao Cheng generously translated the poem on the frontispiece from its beautiful archaic script, and the Reverend Arnold Kenseth put the words into verse and gave them the music that belongs with the picture. Steven Owyoung and Naomi Johnson of the Fogg Art Museum and the Boston Museum of Fine Arts graciously helped assemble the illustrations. If it had not been for the comments of the unnamed readers at the University of Massachusetts Press, this book would have been a hopelessly involuted effort. They brought me into the stream of the concerns of others. Richard Martin, the acquisitions editor of the press, is to be thanked for his faith in my work, and for seeing it through various committees. Mary Mendell designed the book and made it pleasing to the eye. Finally, but hardly the least to me, are those who put their minds to the writing itself. Professor Russell K. Alspach, a wise man and distinguished Yeats scholar, commented carefully upon the first draft, and it saddens me that he did not live to see the book in print. Pamela Campbell edited it exactly. John T. Parkhill, a well-known librarian and whilom instructor in composition at Harvard College, "English A'd" it with Olympian wrath. My wife, Jean, helped with the index and looked wisely and well at the galley sheets and showed me how to correct some of the remaining affronts against the Queen's English. All of them brought home to me the truth of the dictum of the immortal Gertrude Stein to a young writer who did well later: "Hemingway, remarks are not literature."

Amherst, Massachusetts
June 28, 1982                                                        John Manfredi


VISSI D'ARTE; VISSI D'AMORE . . .

Floria Tosca

# Contents

# Introduction

IT is perhaps more appropriate to call this a postcomment rather than an introduction because it is written after I put down all that seemed straight in the path.

I must first note what I have omitted. The original outline included a section on those art forms whose existence depends more on the demands of a market than on the impulses of the artist. Many things prevented me from completing that section and the most important lie within me. I find it difficult to empathize with the tastes of that market and my bias often shows. The work to which I was taught to respond has never been popular with many people. My tastes run to the products of the studio, the conservatory, and the ivory tower. I am not to the manor born in my preferences, but the network in which my early life was spent was one in which there was a lively concern for the matters that follow. The kinsmen, friends, and teachers of my youth thought that certain books and paintings were especially good and that a "cultured" person was supposed to know something about them. Moreover, my teachers were not about to defer to the opinions of any young student, and it was perilous to reject what they considered best, although sometimes I thought their examples bad, and for the most part I still do. They did, however, force me to understand externally defined standards. Perforce I had to go to the art museums and the concert halls, but not to the movies, swing bands, and, most unfortunately, the ethnological collections. It is only in recent years that I have tried to separate the wheat from the chaff among these other genre. I also can claim some training as an artist as a background for the present effort. I studied to be a sculptor until I was eighteen; I then realized that no David waited for me to liberate him from the flawed block of marble.

There is, however, another reason for reserving popular art for a later study. As I tried to clarify my thoughts it became clear to me that "studio" and "conservatory" art is essentially different from work explicitly produced for sale in a predefined market—even when the buyers are well educated and sophisticated. When art is produced to satisfy a commercially defined audience, the compulsions of the artist are barely tolerated at best. The artist does not express himself but becomes part of a medium that acts as if it were an autonomous consciousness. The medium is indeed the message! It is as unthinkable for the artist who works in this matrix to follow his own bent as it would be for a worker in a beehive to try to be a drone, as the Beatles discovered some years ago when they evolved a music that could not be immediately understood. It is a sure way to get thrown out of the hive.

And there is another personal reason. I am so repelled by the social and commercial contexts of this market that I do not trust myself to be fair. Perhaps if I saw less of these ancillary activities, I would be able to respond to its products.

I have deliberately selected "safe" examples. I have tried to keep to work that is securely established by critics and historians. Often I have put aside things that I find very exciting because no strong consensus has yet arisen to support my response, e.g., Erik Satie's music and Edgar Degas's posthumously cast bronzes of race horses, not to mention much of the nonacademic sculpture of the last half century.

I have also avoided work produced for special markets as well as products of craftsmen whose works remain primarily adjuncts to special modi vivendi. I have not tried to consider, for example, jewelry, enamels, porcelains, or even simple mass-produced nineteenth-century cast-iron pots. I have also kept away from some artists when I doubt their craftsmanship. Piet Mondrian probably influenced the direction design took more than any other person in this century, but, if one believes that art necessarily involves good craftsmanship, keeping away from him is justified. A glance at his early objective paintings shows that he was certainly not a virtuoso craftsman, even though he was a careful draftsman. (René Magritte and Salvador Dali didn't think so either, for whatever their opinions may be worth. Still, I like his work.) Sometimes craftsmanship seems comparable, but somehow critics have given more attention to one artist than another—Fabergé less than

Cellini and the Clouets less than Holbein. Sometimes the reasons for such differences in recognition may be aesthetic, sometimes they are sociological, but to say they are only sociological means that one has already made a critical judgment.

Since I am both loath and unqualified to be an advocate, I have kept to established examples no matter where current enthusiastic opinion places them. There remained more than enough to talk about, perhaps there are even too many. The seeming lack of consensus in current canons of criticism has made many more different tastes acceptable than was true a generation ago. The present seller's market in exchangeable art brings much from the attic that might be better left there. Moreover, I have become less sure of my own tastes. As I have allowed immediate apprehension to guide me, rather than critical strictures, I am less sure, and I care less that my favorites are the right ones for chic society. For such reasons, it seemed better to keep to what is commonly given space in histories. Naturally, availability and common familiarity were important considerations. Finally, my own varying levels of knowledge of different art forms have governed my choice of examples. I know painting, sculpture, and architecture fairly well and discuss them more than music, dance, and literature, about which I know less.

A few words about the impetus for this study are appropriate. My first attempt to deal with these considerations was in my doctoral thesis, which I finished writing in 1951. It was called "The Relationship of Class-Structured Pathologies to the Contents of Popular Periodical Fiction, 1936–1940." At that time it was one of the most intensive (and perhaps even the longest) attempts at a content analysis of magazine fiction. Its assumptions were after Gregory Bateson's *Hitlerjunge Quex*, but avoided the psychoanalytic apparatus that characterized that work. I finished it convinced that such content analyses told more about the editors' assumptions about their readers than about readers themselves. I later realized that the rejection of much popular story writing by serious critics was justified in one essential respect: its publishers rarely challenge the right of the businessman and politician to force the product to conform to the demands of the market and the apologetics of administrative failure. In so-called serious art, the vision of the artist remains the central determinant of form and content no matter what concessions are made. Nevertheless, there remain a social matrix and cultural system that direct and often even inhibit the work of the artist. Much of the present book is concerned with the conflicts that arise in the perpetual attempt of artists to produce work that expresses their own tastes and inclinations amid ambient restraints.

I have tried to write this as a study about the dynamics of culture. Why did I take art rather than any number of other things that concern many educated people more? The answer is simple. The production of art has been a constant human activity and the influence of avant-garde art has had profound consequences for the evolution of collective consciousness. Moreover, it is a coherent, analytically distinct activity. It does not fall apart as a separate universe of discourse on analysis (as does, for instance, juvenile delinquency). In the high civilizations of the East and West the fine arts are produced within definable segments of social structures and have their own courses of development. Moreover, during the last six hundred years in the West the perceptions of artists have been bellwethers of the developments of the rest of our culture, and I have reasons to believe that this is sometimes true of other high civilizations as well, particularly China. Finally, the production of art has been a remarkably persistent activity even under the most disorderly conditions. The legendary notion of the instability of artists compared to the stability of people in other callings does not bear examination very well. There is no evidence that artists fly off the handle more often, or even more flamboyantly than politicians, physicians, clergymen, generals, or even businessmen. Artists are perhaps more stubborn, but it is likely that this very stubbornness helps them go on under conditions of sheer chaos. If one wishes to study the development of any cultural system without the distractions of transitory disorder, it is hard to find better subjects than the fine arts. Viewing the changes they have undergone has an added advantage, because their changes foreshadow developments in the rest of the cultural system.

I have meant this effort for liberally educated readers rather than for artists, critics, or sociologists. They should be aware of the main features of both Western civilizations and Chinese and Indian civilizations. I have not expected them to be aware of a wide range of ethnographic data because the sheer diversity of primitive societies does not allow even tentative generalizations about them. I have avoided Islam and its often glorious art because, as ibn-Khaldun saw five hundred years ago, its great civilizations have always lorded unsteadily over scores of intransigent barbarian tribal consciousnesses. I have shied away from Russia because it is hard to say what is really Russian other than European

Russia itself. (Can we call these scores of irredentist peoples—Armenians, Jews, Ukranians, and the like—Russians?) I have kept to cultures commonly studied in the English-speaking world. I also assume a familiarity with major Western periods and styles. I have kept away from terms that are peculiar to specialists in order to broaden my readership.

Finally, I have kept away from psychologizing and psychoanalyzing. This study deals with the social and cultural constraints that determine the forms of art, not with why a person with certain personality traits and life experiences would produce work of one character rather than another. It may be interesting to learn whether Eugene O'Neill wrote *Ah! Wilderness* to silence carping that he could not write a broad farce or to create a fantasy of a happy adolescence he never had in his crabby, lace-curtain family home, but it is not the type of question relevant to the present study.

The outline of this essay is simple enough. It begins and ends with art as an expression of the culture. It begins with the quality of appearances as the expression par excellence of the quality of communal life. It proceeds to outline the professional matrix in which the artist must operate. This includes schools and conservatories, the consensus of other professional artists, entrepreneurs, institutional watchdogs, and critics. From here, it goes on to the critical apparatus by which the artist is judged and by which he judges himself, and the assumptions as to the nature of reality that determine the form and quality of the cultural systems that art expresses.

It is also appropriate to say a word about the kind of sociology that I employed. A current prejudice among some social scientists is that "quantification" gives one a "hard" sociology. Unfortunately, as Sorokin's work showed many years ago when he tried to actualize such hopes in his *Social and Cultural Dynamics*, the result can be a very, very soft sociology, so soft, in fact, that Crane Brinton called the whole effort "socio-astrology." I understand why Brinton said it. I have found no substitutes for sitting among ruins and pondering, looking at pictures, buildings, and statues, going to theaters and concert halls, listening to records, and "looking things up." Hard data in a final sense are the intuitive judgments of what experts can agree upon and we ignore them at our peril.

This exercise, however, has taught me one thing that I have often been loath to allow. I find that it is not possible, at least for a man of my intellectual generation, to escape the way Max Weber analyzed problems in social dynamics. I have been long suspicious of the Weber cult but I cannot dismiss him as a "little tin God," as Georges Gurvitch did in a conversation, although he did not always use good first-hand sources and is rarely quoted by experts in some of the fields for which he wrote. However, the way he used the work of the scholars of his day deserves respect. He used it to construct ideal types—what the situation would be if a given set of values were followed through in action in a "logical" manner. The analysis here could not have been possible without implicitly assuming ideal types. Weber's methods enabled me to define my sociology in a way that freed it from naive psychologizing and dormitory psychoanalysis. I have thus preferred to start from scratch. Much of the literature in the area of the sociology of art has nothing to do with art, is often no more than self-contained quantifications that refer only to themselves, and, on a psychological level, confuses motive and meaning—a trap that never caught Weber.

# 1

## Art, Culture, and Professionalism

SPIRO AGNEW once re-marked that if one has seen one slum one has seen them all. This remark is not only callous, it is also only partially true of most American cities although it is, curiously enough, largely true of older Western European cities. The slums of the inner cities of Philadelphia and Baltimore seem to look alike, but neither looks like those of Washington, Detroit, or Chicago. New York is unique. It has not only the cast-off housing of the middle and upper classes that compose so much of the family slums of other cities, but the "old law" tenements as well as the badly policed, badly managed, unsuitably designed, public housing that figures so large in homilies about the condign miseries of the poor. The older American slums are more varied in appearance than those of Europe. The slums of each American city seem to have quality that sets them apart—except, of course, for some of our public housing projects. Popular terms call such differences "character"; the term used by the great students of cultural configurations of the early part of this century was "ethos," the qualitative aspect of culture. Gibbon was not the last man to sit among the shambles of what seemed an aesthetically coherent world that had fallen to ruin when its inheritors no longer really understood, knew, or cared about the purposes it had been built to serve. The inner-city slums of older American cities similarly recall styles of living that few of its present residents are part of, or would want to be part of even if they had the means and for which they feel no nostalgia. But educated people, who have participated in that older world vicariously through the study of history and literature and the recollections of older people, see it as having had charm, beauty, and a manageable scale. Indeed, it is easy to share such nostalgic illusions wherever the poor have been priced out of these old, decayed central urban areas by wildly expensive remodeling.

The locations of slums of old European cities in the countries that benefited from the Marshall Plan show a different pattern. They are not generally in the central city. In Rome, Paris, London, Vienna, Milan, and Munich, and other old world centers, the central city is still an expensive backdrop for "Society," the arts and professions, and whoever else can afford to affect the externals of elegance. The unique qualities of the appearances of these cities are as easy to tell apart as American ones when you keep to their old, central cores.

However, when one goes to what have become the slums of many European cities, Mr. Agnew's comment is appropriate. They are suburban. Each is a mixed world of the sheet-metal shacks and concrete apartment houses. It is a world of sweaty, overdressed women and their jealous men. Something here has led to uniformity, and whatever gave the core of these older cities individuality is absent. There is only sameness to the suburban slums in Europe, but the central cities are different. They each have their own underlying qualitative consistency that in some as-yet-undefined way seems to make the seemingly disparate aspects within each go together. It does not seem odd to find the grimy splendors of the Farnese and the Spada palaces in a Roman quarter that houses not only diplomats, patricians, and people rich and talented enough to be interesting, but sharp, clever, working people. When you live in Rome you discover that a common ethos and symbolic system enable these people to live together. You call it Roman because it seems only Roman. Each of the inner centers of other old European cities gives a sense of consistent, unique textures of local life that does not exist elsewhere.

But why do the ubiquitous suburban slums of these cities seem so much alike that they often can be barely told apart? The people who live in them are not part of the prefactory bourgeois culture of the inner city. Some are part of the large urban proletariat that has been created by industrialism; some are not even proletarians and seem only waiting for something to happen. The factory workers dwell in mile upon mile of concrete apartment houses; the others live in shacks of corrugated sheet metal and other scavenged materials. There is a sameness about these slums and it is easy to see why this is so. Factory workers needed housing quickly and cheaply, and it cannot be provided by the slow hand techniques of skilled craftsmen. In fact, the use of building machinery entails employing components that are standardized in function, dimensions, and design, and that leads, perhaps inevitably, to those block upon block of poured-concrete buildings with metal-framed windows. The process itself precludes individuality. It is no surprise that they were built by men in contractors' clumsy yellow iron giants that move like obese schoolboys. These are the barracks of the industrial armies, their women, and their camp-followers. Only their graffiti assert individuality.

The shacks have more individuality because each is custom made. Their occupants are those last ragged individuals who cannot accept the discipline of industrialism. They are not punished for this; they are simply ignored and relegated to corrugated sheet-metal shacks. It is poured concrete, the standardized metal windows, and the shacks that makes Mr. Agnew right about postwar European slums in a way that he could never be right about the decaying central city slums of the United States; it is at least true that if you have seen one slab of concrete and one sheet-metal shack, you have seen as many as you need to see, even if not all there are. Different ways of organizing a society and different symbolic systems produce different kinds of lives that are associated with different worlds of appearances in which each has its own underlying qualitative similarity. What really made many of our central cities into slums was the ways of life of the inhabitants, which did not belong with the configurations of technological and aesthetic systems that produced such areas. A vast literature explores the relationship of life styles to technological systems, but it is hard to see how any of it goes beyond the work of Karl Marx, Thorstein Veblen, William Graham Sumner, and E. Wight Bakke. When one begins to search out the relationship of social and aesthetic systems, the literature becomes blurred and confused. In the first half of the twentieth century A. L. Kroeber, P. A. Sorokin, F. S. C. Northrop, and Thorstein Veblen stand out as exceptions, and in the last century there is Friedrich Nietzsche and few others.[1] But the areas they dealt with are important because much art is incomprehensible if it is considered apart from the ethos of the culture and the intentions of the artist. Let us examine these questions briefly.

[1] I have never taken seriously attempts to show that artistic systems are an invariant expression of the tastes of elite strata of the society. As far as the work of major figures is concerned it has often been the other way. For every Haydn who bore the role of a court flunky patiently, there was a Beethoven who did not.

What has been said about slums also can be said about art museums. If you visit one, you have visited them all—unless you are a real connoisseur of the contents. Three of the four greatest American ones—the Metropolitan Museum of Art, the Philadelphia Museum of Art, and the Boston Museum of Fine Arts—look like one another.[2] All three have generic interior resemblances to the National Gallery in London, which in turn looks like other English museums. Many German and Austrian ones look like one another. Italian galleries provide more variety in their external physical characteristics. They are usually housed in palaces that have been abandoned to the pictures by their human occupants, and show more individuality because the country itself has never been culturally united enough for styles to be consistent from one area to another. (The officially approved nineteenth-century Italian academic style only shows in a minority of them—providentially!) Moreover, they were not all built within a fifty-year span; these cast-off palazzos span better than a millennium. But, in all cases, once inside, you know that you are in a museum. They are nearly always brothers under the skin. Where the best methods of showing things are used, nothing that is extraneous to the exhibits distracts you. The walls are nearly always white, the floors are always hard, and there are never enough places to sit down. Unless you decide to look at just a few things, you get museum feet and the images begin to coalesce. You not only have the experts' troubles in telling the work of the youths Titian and Giorgione apart, but a great many other problems as well.

In short, the museum—with its bare white walls and its high, sky-lighted galleries—turns out to be a very confusing place to view art. However, the objection can go further than that: they foster the idea that the work of the artist—art itself—exists in special vacuums that are apart from the rest of life. Sometimes this separation is what one wants, especially if one is a critic trying to compare and evaluate.

Let us make a simple comparison. The work of John Singer Sargent placed against the bare white walls of a gallery tells us that he was a very talented man who often seduced himself into being a society hack. We know from at least one of his letters that he considered the academic art of his time bad, but few intimations of such opinions show here. The museum pieces show he was cater-

[2] The Philadelphia Museum has more than an edge for site; Boston faces a mess; the Metropolitan is on the fringe of a park. All three are in the Corinthian style. The fourth is, of course, the National Gallery and is smaller than the others, an Ionic structure with a modern wing. The Boston Museum opened a new wing in 1981 that is also in a modern style.

ing to a clientele who wanted its women to be made of Parian marble, doing what was deemed appropriate no matter how they felt. As Mrs. Franklin Delano Roosevelt put it, they had a code that did not allow one to beg off because of a headache. Sargent knew how to put all this across. It is only the occasional and mainly late pictures—such as the four little girls wearing pinafores shown in the Boston Museum of Fine Arts[3]—that let us see that he was capable of transcending the lazy formula that kept caviar in the ice box, as well as groceries on the table. Comparing the work of James Abbott McNeill Whistler and Thomas Eakins in the same undistracting ambience tells us something about these artists. In Whistler's case, we can see a man who responded early to advanced tendencies but never carried them far—Post-Impressionism, adumbrations of Abstract Expressionism (in the nocturnes) and the gradual displacement of architectonic quality by an absorption with surface textures. It is not surprising that his relations with the critics were a perpetual Donnybrook Fair. Eakins (whom John Canaday has tried to return to a place that he has not lately enjoyed in the esteem of critics) presents us with a world that has been caught human. There are handsomely built young men rowing on what is recognizably the Schuylkill River at Philadelphia, confident, privileged physicians operating in the University of Pennsylvania Hospital, a singing young woman in a pink satin gown who is not at all pretty, and many other full-length portraits that hardly catered to their subjects' vanity.[4] A comparison made from the walls of a museum tells us that the three men were on a par as technicians and that they shared common Western aesthetic canons, but we cannot miss that the uses to which they put their skills and the voices to which each listened must have been very different indeed. Some of the differences can be taken to arise from the temperaments of the men themselves. Sargent was a sociable man who seemed to have had little trouble accommodating himself to a moneyed clientele in England and America; Whistler was an ebullient, colorful man who experimented in response to influences that were quite at odds with school-taught painting of his day; Eakins remained in a parochial, scholarly, prosperous world that was close to the University of Pennsylvania Medical School and the Jefferson Medical College. The paintings[5] we see on the walls of the museum make none of this surprising

---

[3] The Daughters of Edward D. Boit.

[4] Turning the Stake, The Clinic of Professor Agnew, The Concert Singer.

[5] In Whistler's case there are etchings as well. Joseph Pennell in Etchers and Etching regarded him as the greastest etcher after Rembrandt.

to read. We can see certain kinds of historical examples have been followed. Eakins obviously liked the way seventeenth-century Dutch painters handled light; the links of Whistler's visions with Japanese printmakers are pretty obvious; Sargent was all too often painting pictures that were intended to look like eighteenth-century English family portraits. However the similarities between the work these men admired and their own remain quite superficial. None of them was able to imitate such examples any more than Puccini was able to write Chinese or Japanese music (as he tried, although not too hard, in *Turandot* and *Madama Butterfly*). The impediment to Puccini was that he was a nineteenth-century Italian; for the three painters it was that they were nineteenth-century Americans.[6] For better or for worse, it not only imposed nineteenth-century technical training upon them, but conventions as to aesthetic canons and subject matter, as well.

So far, I have mentioned a number of the influences that operate upon the work of the creative artist. First, the temperament and intellectual orientation of the individual artist affect how he will use the techniques that he has learned. Moreover, the artist's national and cultural identity, as well as the available technology, influences his product. None of these influences is necessarily for the best from the standpoint of the "man of taste." What is apparent when one looks at the work of these men is that their art did not exist apart from the nineteenth-century Western culture that their society expressed. This brings us to the essential questions that one may ask in any prolegomenon to the sociology of art: Does any art actually ever exist as an activity that is parallel to but not part of its society? How much of what artists try to express and what is considered good is bound up in a social consensus that is determined by the culture?

Such questions only give trouble in the contexts of museums and critiques based upon what are considered absolute standards of good and bad. One may even, perhaps, make a good case for absolute standards based on the behavior of the artists themselves in that they have often grasped the value of exotic art forms well before either the scholars or the public at large.[7] But even in the

---

[6] All in fact lived in the twentieth century. Whistler died in 1903, Eakins in 1916, Sargent in 1925, and Puccini in 1924. They were all, however, born before 1860.
[7] A few well-known examples may be mentioned in this context. Italian painters of the fifteenth century respected and found examples in the work of Flemish painters; in the eighteenth century European architects and furniture and porcelain makers began a vogue for Chinese styles that often showed a good understanding of the aesthetics of their exemplars; nineteenth-century French painters were intensely interested in Japanese wood-block prints, while earlier in

museum and historical context the examples are almost always grouped by periods and styles. The focus generally remains on the objects themselves and subordinates the social and cultural configurations of which they are a part.[8] There is nothing wrong with it as a way of comparing the capacity to elicit responses from viewers that are not influenced by distracting social contexts. This may, in fact, be efficient for some purposes—as in making a preliminary ad hoc judgment. It takes but a five-minute viewing of a representative showing of nineteenth-century English academic painting to judge the justification of its new vogue. However, museums still foster the idea that art exists apart from life and the image of the artist as an alienated seer or a bohemian who lives outside the main currents of life. When one looks to other fields of study this prejudice is absent. In fact, the artistic remains of ancient societies engender curiosity as to what the societies themselves must have been like. Archeologists, for example, assume that Egyptian architects and craftsmen were logical products of their time and culture. Few archeologists ever seem to have doubted that the artistic output of the past provided reliable guides to the character of the entire society and culture. The reason that the material and artistic remains of a culture are seen as reliable indicators of total cultural configurations is that the most persistent part of the past is its art. Some of the character of the objects arises out of technical exigencies, but other aspects of their appearance seem to be easier to associate with the systems of taste we usually call style. Some years ago (1918) Alexander Goldenweiser wrote an often-quoted passage on why oars are always alike in shape. His argument is well known: oars have to be round on one end to make them easy to manipulate; they must be flat on the other to push against the water; they must be of a tough, resilient material. It continues in this vein through several pages, but Goldenweiser never tells why oars are so often embellished in ways that make it fairly easy for the expert to judge their prove-

---

the century some major Japanese artists (e.g., Hiroshige I) became interested in Western geometric perspective; in the first decades of this century artists began to look carefully at the examples of primitive art to be found in ethnological museums and curiosity shops; during the 1950s and '60s much music that came out of folk and primitive societies was studied intensively by professional musicians after portable high-fidelity tape recorders made it possible to bring it in from the field.

[8] The "new" museum curators are changing this. The cost, however, of changing any such conventional practices in a major museum is so prohibitive, that it is only fine, relatively small museums, like the Peabody in Salem, Massachusetts, that show a major portion of their collections with such considerations in mind.

nances. One of the things that seems necessary to examine is just why there are these distinctive consistencies of style within a given culture and society.

However, within the formation of the styles—the artistic forms—a process I should like to call segmental autonomy begins to operate. The division of labor involves the development of specialized knowledge and special skill. Max Weber stated that the difference between the professional and the dilettante was application. A usual consequence—not a logical one—of this application is that there is an increasing drift from the lay images and modes of analysis.

One must comment here in passing. The impression of the artist as a creature of feeling who never intellectualizes what he is doing is sheer nonsense historically. There is not a single major artist whose life is well documented who did not formulate the aesthetic of his work coherently from time to time, even if not in treatises. And this holds true of recent figures as well. Sir Herbert Read in his *Concise History of Modern Painting* makes this very clear. He felt that giving careful attention to such formulations was essential to the understanding of modern art even though he felt that a work of art had to stand alone without them. That artists should be able to formulate what they are doing is not implausible. If it were not so, the arts would be the only human activities that are developed as professions where what one is trying to do is not clearly formulated. There may be natural athletes but there are no natural baseball players; there is artistic talent but no really born artists. Both emerge from training. There are, unquestionably, people with a more intense capacity to feel than others, but expressing it as painting, sculpture, or any other art has to be learned and formulated. If one knows what he is doing, he necessarily must verbalize it clearly first. (He may train himself to a point where

---

1   The social determination of perception. Equal talents, a common culture, and different readings of it: a society portrait. John Singer Sargent, *Mrs. Fiske Warren (Gretchen Osgood) and her daughter.*

This is as slick a portrait as Sargent ever turned out. He knew how to convey what his clients wanted, and there is nothing in it to which Mr. Fiske Warren could have objected. It presents a mother and daughter of great beauty who know how to wear their clothes, yet, unlike Eakins's *Walt Whitman* (fig. 3), the picture tells us nothing about their psyches. Until his last years Sargent's sitters were people who lived by a code that demanded that women suppress personal feelings. When Sargent painted to please himself he did things that were quite different in spirit (see fig. 4).

Courtesy, Museum of Fine Arts, Boston. Gift of Rachel Warren Barton and the Emily L. Ainsley Fund.

such expressions become autonomic, but this always requires clear objectives.) In fact, such expertises can develop without respect to each other or to common collective lay opinions. In some cases it is obvious to almost everyone that this has occurred: most of us are content to leave relativity to physicists, chemistry to chemists, and networks to electrical engineers. Other things we give up jealously: nearly everyone practices some medicine in the strict sense of the term; on such issues as racial segregation, capital punishment, penal practice and other technical, legal, and social issues expert opinion often diverges markedly from many commonly held lay notions. The reason is simple: expertise involves isolation from amateur judgments and modes of analysis, it involves access to kinds of information that laymen lack, and finally, it involves always a vision of things that is markedly different from that of the person who has not lived with a subject apart from competing interests. Once one becomes a professional, he vows to follow truth wherever it takes him, and this often makes him an alien to his fellows. Sometimes he becomes odd in the eyes of the world. An identical process operates with the arts. As soon as the artist begins to operate as a specialist, he brings to his work the results of constant expert and thoughtful appraisal of what he is doing. It becomes a part of this process that he begins to perceive reality in a way that diverges from common perceptions of things. Here too there is no logical reason inherent in the process itself. It is simply a common concomitant of expertise. Any artistic calling that becomes a profession shows the same segmental autonomy that any other scholarly or professional study shows.

Different professions, however, enjoy different rates of lay acceptance of the work and outlook of the professional. One may wish to say that sooner or later truth triumphs over error and the work of the professional comes to be accepted and there is a consistent lag between professional reasoning and lay acceptance. Nothing of either sort occurs in any field with any consistency. Dynamic psychology has gone well beyond orthodox Freudian modes of thought, but I do not think it an exaggeration to say that even Freud himself never reached far into the boondocks, the dark Satanic mills, or, for that matter, Upper Montclair and county.[9] I suppose if one were really looking for a field that proceeds independently without ever being widely diffused into lay thinking, the case par excellence would be mathematics. There are still large ranges of mathematics that deal with issues that by-pass all but

[9] This is at least on a level of the overt assumptions on which collective life is based. We don't know to what extent sophistication is suppressed in our overt actions "because one has to live in society."

logicians and epistemologists and, of course, mathematicians. On the other end of the scale, there are the immediate, striking successes that are sometimes achieved in medicine in areas where practical successes are inescapably apparent.

The reasons are simple. First, the isolation of professionals with each other results in much of their work being produced for other professionals. Second, they may not really care very much what people who are not professionals think of their work and (as was indicated above) may see themselves simply as having better things to do than argue with lunatics and tyros, or perhaps they may simply be confused and hurt at the incomprehension of laymen. In any case the very code of professionalism itself demands that they only care about what other professionals think. However, this is pure speculation. It is only essential to note that the isolation of professionals and professions does indeed produce a segmental autonomy.

Once segmental autonomy has developed—by whatever process—there arises a consensus as to what is to be professed, to be practiced, and to be observed. The result is that the rest of the society becomes a public to be influenced.

Whatever may be the immediate intuitive response to any professionalized approach, sooner or later some persons or segments of the society either through desire, accident, or necessity achieve insight into how the professional reasons and come to accept it. Here again, one may wish for rules for how acceptance comes about, but one is again confronted with the simple difficulty that any rules would be hard to apply to all cases—or perhaps even enough cases to give the rules heuristic value. We do not, for instance, consistently seek out solidly based professional opinions when we are confronted with crises even in areas where there is agreement among professionals (e.g., the uselessness of capital punishment). However, to a greater or lesser degree there is acceptance and with acceptance comes influence. It should be pointed out that this influence does not need to take the form of mass acceptance. There are, in fact, in any complex society profound inequalities in authority, power, and influence. It is only really necessary to achieve acceptance with those persons and among those circles that can diffuse their outlook and taste easily by virtue of the fact that they are strategically placed within the larger social system—which is a long way of saying that only some can decide and make their decisions stick without respect to their actual numbers. This brings us to the second question to which these pages will be devoted. If indeed the artistic system does influence the entire society as the arts emerge as recognized professions, how does that influence come to be felt through the rest of society? It leads us to the central concerns of this essay: What is the role of the artistic system in the culture? What are the internal professional factors, as well as the external constraints, that determine how arts are practiced in a given society? How do they express the cultural system of the society of which they are a part? What have been their roles in changes in the society and culture?

## BACKGROUND NOTE

The most cogent exposition of the economic and social forces that determined the appearance and life of American cities is among the earliest: Robert Park and Ernest Burgess, *The City* (Chicago: University of Chicago Press, 1925). Harvey Zorbaugh's *The Gold Coast and the Slum* (Chicago: University of Chicago Press, 1929), an early classic, follows Park and Burgess. Lewis Mumford in *The City in History: Its Origin, Its Transformations and Its Prospect* (New York: Harcourt Brace, 1961), considers the broader cultural changes. Specialized studies of city planning theory carry back considerably. They range from Giorgio Vasari's *La Città Ideale, Piante di Chiesa (Pallazzi e ville) di Toscana e d'Italia* (Rome: Officina, 1970); Le Corbusier (Charles E. Jeanneret-Gris), *The City of Tomorrow and Its Planning* (London: J. Rooker, 1929); Eliel Saarinen, *The City, Its Growth, Its Decay, Its Future* (New York: Reinhold, 1965); Batty Langley, *The City and Country Builders and Workman's Treasury of Designs* (1756; reprint ed. Blom, New York, 1967); and Theodore S. Cook, *City Planning Theory: The Destiny of Our Cities* (New York: Philosophical Library, 1969). The literature on Western urban organization not only includes Mumford, but Max Weber, *The City* (Glencoe, Ill.: The Free Press, 1958), Emrys Jones and Eleanor Van Zandt, eds., *The City: Yesterday, Today, and Tomorrow* (London: Aldus, 1974); William Lowe, *City Life* (Rochelle Park, N.J.: Hayden Book Co., 1974); Henri Pirenne, *Medieval Cities* (New York: Doubleday, 1956); and Robert G. Anderson, *The City and the Cathedral; A Reflection of the Glory of the Gothic and the Middle Ages in the City by the Siene* (New York: Longmans Green, 1948). There turned out to be surprisingly little of a nonpolemic character about museums, at least as far as their social role is concerned. Most of the discussion is pejorative and this seems reasonable if perhaps the greatest service of museums is to act as conservators and to protect the work of the past from judgments that may often retrospectively seem frivolous. However, if one wishes to see how museum experts see their own role, see Alvin Schwartz, *Museum: the Story of America's Treasure Houses* (New York: Dutton, 1967), and Herbert and Marjorie Katz, *Museums, U.S.A.: A History and Guide* (Garden City, N.Y.: Doubleday, 1965), and the articles in reprint of *Art in America* 59, no. 4, *Museums in Crisis*, ed. Brian O'Doherty (New York: Braziller, 1972). The classic discussion of culture remains in the first half of Alfred L. Kroeber, *Anthropology* (New York, 1948); Felix M. Keesing's *Cultural Anthropology: The Science of Custom* (New York, 1958), contains a lucid account of the relations of art and play to culture in chap. 14, "Art and Play." Franz Boas, *Primitive Art* (Oslo, 1927; reprinted ed., New York: Dover, 1955) remains the classic. Finally, anyone who has tried to write in this field owes a debt to Sir Kenneth Clark. The lectures reprinted in *Civilization, a Personal View* (London: British Broadcasting Co., 1969) combine expertise and beguiling charm.

# 2

## Art as a Socially Constrained Pursuit

WHEREVER there are people there is art, and where people are not, there is no art. In any society there are persons who try to create sights, sounds, forms, and realms of thought that are more than what can be derived from the sensory world without the operation of the human mind. Moreover, art is itself a peculiarly human function, a function that involves an urge to create things that serve purposes beyond material, social, and hedonic needs. Only religion, science, and art can be called peculiarly human. None is inherent in the phenomenal world itself, but all are meanings that can be placed upon it on a symbolic level, which is to say that they substitute the manipulation of symbols for the mechanical manipulation of raw experience. In this sense each gives meanings to experience. Animals other than man can do many things but they cannot do that. They can use objects as tools, improvise from things at hand, play fairly complex games for pleasure, hoard, and even be taught to use sign language and verbalize on a minimal level. However, the symbolizing activities involved in science, religion, and art remain strictly human.

The differences between science, religion, and art lie largely in the aspects of the world that has been chosen for emphasis. Science emphasizes a desire to create a conceptual system that gives experience intellectual consistency; religion remains a search for some basis to our ways of living that transcends brute force; art grows out of the need to create signs, sounds, and realms of perception that express more than the hedonistic and survival needs of the organism. Man demands more than just survival; he has a compulsion for creative elaboration. In truth, keeping alive minimally is the immemorial lot of the generality of men, and if survival alone were the issue there would be no need to do anything more. This holds even for food and shelter; like Jeeter Lester in *Tobacco Road* one can stave off hunger with raw turnips, but it seems that people are concerned with tastes and looks. In an absolute physical sense, clothing needs only to provide warmth and protection from abrasion for our furless bodies, but the desire to adorn oneself seems ubiquitous. Popular thinking associates cave dwelling with a crude way of life and this it may well be, but in southern Spain the people who dwell in caves put pretty white facades over the openings. In terms of milk production there is no point in adorning goats, but those same cave dwellers groom them and put ribbons in their hair. (In fact, the propensity to decorate live domestic animals seems to occur in folk societies all over the world. One needs only mention our own poodle keepers.) The incredible pains that go into the breeding of special lines of domestic animals are part of the same thing—objectives that can hardly be related to the utilitarian needs that animals serve. Siamese cats are friendly and amusing and no more useful than alley cats, but above all, they are beautiful. The human tendency to seek beauty and to try to perfect expression of it seems universal.

So far, I have discussed this propensity to adorn beyond the needs of utility only in terms of a visual world, but it holds true in the realm of sound as well. We speak of some people as "having an ear for the sound of language." Let us look at two versions of

---

2   The interest in perception. Equal talents, a common culture and different readings of it.

James Abbott McNeill Whistler, *Alma Stanley in "The Street Walker."* Whistler started his career as an artist after he left the United States Military Academy at West Point. He was a handsome, colorful man of two sides— one, a Bohemian wit and the other, a very scholarly craftsman and experimenter. This big pastel—it is 99¼ by 38½ inches—reflects another aspect of nineteenth-century culture—the attempt to reconcile exotic Oriental ways of perceiving things with Western preoccupations with the psychology of personality and the perception of light. Little is lost in the half-tone reproduction. The dress is black and the woman wears a stark pancake makeup that recalls Japanese theater masks. Nineteenth-century people thought of pancake makeup as the mark of a harlot. That in itself would have said nothing to people a century earlier, and now, almost a century later, one has to explain what it meant. (Its date is 1893.) The drawing also reflects Whistler's careful study of Rembrandt's etchings and treatment of chiaroscuro.

Courtesy, Museum of Fine Arts, Boston. Charles Henry Hayden Fund.

the first stanza of George Meredith's "Love in the Valley," those of 1851 and 1883. The 1851 version goes

Under yonder beech-tree standing on the green sward,
    Couch'd with her arms behind her little head,
Her knees folded up, and her tresses on her bosom,
    Lies my young love sleeping in the shade.
Had I the heart to slide one arm beneath her!
    Press her dreaming lips as her waist I folded slow,
Waking on the instant she could not but embrace me—
    Ah! would she hold me, and never let me go?

He reworked the poem in 1883. This stanza became:

Under yonder beech-tree single on the green-sward,
    Couched with her arms behind her golden head,
Knees and tresses fold to slip and ripple idly,
    Lies my young love sleeping in the shade.
Had I the heart to slide an arm beneath her,
    Press her parting lips as her waist I gather slow,
Waking in amazement she could not but embrace me.
    Then would she hold me and never let me go?

If one analyzes the sense of what has been said on a line-for-line basis, there is little difference between the two versions. One can say that when one attempts to visualize "Her knees folded up, and her tresses on her bosom" trouble begins, and "knees and tresses fold to slip and ripple idly," does not give us quite the image of a person who is curled up to keep warm. The rest of the poem also shows that Meredith must have become more concerned with the actual visual images his language invoked as he grew older. It is also possible to show that the second version is more refined in its purely technical aspects of versification (as a scholar and a poet have done in my presence). But there has to be more than adept versification, for if only that were to be considered, Mark Twain's rendition of a mortgage contract into verse would have to be considered a major work of poetry, and Algernon Charles Swinburne's "Atalanta in Calydon" would be a fair contender for being considered the greatest poem of the nineteenth century. We do sense that the second version of the stanza is better, although it is hard to name what it is that everyone would be able to agree to. Clive Bell would have said it had "significant form," others would call it "music," others "beauty," others still "excitement." Whatever this quality is seems a question of aesthetics well beyond the scope of this essay. This much, however, we can say with reasonable cer-

**3**  Equal talents, a common culture, and different readings of it: a psychological portrait. Thomas Eakins, *Walt Whitman*.

Eakins's interests were largely scientific, and he was a recognized authority on the muscles and motion of the human figure. His capacity for minute observations can be seen in his portrayals of the psychological aspects of his subjects. It was not that he could not paint slick surfaces—the pink satin gown in his well-known *Concert Singer* shows that he could—but demonstrating that ability never became an end in itself. Instead, he looked into the souls of his sitters. That kind of probing and concern with emotional subtlety are aspects of nineteenth-century Western culture that gave birth to the psychoanalytic imagination and rise to penetrating novels.

Unlike Sargent and Whistler, Eakins was not a sociable man. His sitters did not always like what he showed and they were known to burn, reject, and refuse to pay him for his portraits.

This picture is tiny—5¼ by 5¼ inches.

Courtesy, Museum of Fine Arts, Boston. Helen and Alice Colburn Fund.

tainty: some expressions have a quality that brings this response, some people can catch it in the work of others, some can put it into their own work (and some cannot), but it always involves something more than utility.

We know that the first phase in the development of any culture object is as a tool, the utilitarian object that serves an ad hoc purpose. There follows a phase where the object may be an expression and extension of the person on a physical level. A good hammer extends its user mechanically, as do many other devices that are designed to amplify a person physically. It is made with a careful appreciation of the human body as a machine. The advantage, for example, of a carefully made sports bicycle over a clumsy sweat-shop product is that the former can be adjusted to anyone from a spry, albeit slowed-down, octogenarian to a man in his twenties and it will amplify each one physically in a way that makes its use pleasurable rather than burdensome. However, we can go beyond such simple cases. With technical proficiency there is always also kinesthetic involvement. A good potter lives with his wheel like a good rider with a horse. The forms he creates are the results of painstaking physical exercises, where delicacy and precision are developed in the use of all musculature from the largest systems down to the finger tips. A pencil or brush or pen is never held by professionals to draw in the way it is held to write. (The seeming exception lies in East Asian calligraphy, which is itself an art form.) A pencil, for instance, is pivoted by the fore and index fingers over the print of the thumb. If one is standing, this position makes it possible to involve the whole body—first the torso, then the shoulder, then the forearm, and, finally, the fingers over the thumb.[1]

None of these motions and positions in which one works takes place outside the context of culturally determined forms and habits. They are taught and learned. Similarly, the amount of space in which one has to work is pretty much a matter that is socially determined, and affects art forms.

Let us discuss a few cases where cultural forms of motion, position, and space distribution affect the work of the artist. An obvious one can be noted readily—the way of drawing that reached its apogee in the nineteenth century with its emphasis upon the artist as a free spirit. It is consistent with a whole cultural configuration that could make the poet Shelley envy the gorgeous freedom of the lark and celebrate the west wind. It is Puccini's image of bohemians

---

[1] The wrist does not enter in this—it is rigid with respect to a possibility of rotation and the hand is rotated by the forearm. If one sits, the largest mobile structure is the torso.

living for art and love in their garrets (*La Bohème*, 1896), or of Tosca who sang "Vissi d'arte, vissi d'amore" (I live for Art, I live for Love) before she gave Scarpia his due (1900). It is also consistent with Rosa Bonheur's *Horse Fair*—that tumbling stampede of wild horses that seems about to trample down the viewer (it is over sixteen feet long). In a more controlled way, it is seen in the way that drapery was treated in Baroque art and, later, in the best academic French and Italian painting of the nineteenth century. Still later it can be noted in the drawings of Degas, Renoir, and Picasso, and in Cézanne's *Bathers*. If one analyzes what is involved in these seemingly disparate things, it is the expansion of self beyond the point where the bonds that are supposed to contain it break. In fact in some Baroque work it did just that. We see it in ridiculous painted *putti* in Austrian churches who fly over the edges of ornate painted margins, and we see it in an elegant, refined form in work of Bernini in St. Peter's in Rome where ecstatic saints burst out of severe, restrained, classical architectural frameworks. The form of Mozart's motet, *Exsultate, Jubilate* (K. 165), translates the same tendency into musical terms. The first parts are carefully controlled. The coloratura sings in a measured, paced manner, keeping passion back. Then with the Alleluia, she lets go.

These forms are unlikely to be produced again under modern conditions. In the case of my examples from the visual arts, a huge amount of space is necessary to move around and show things. Saint Peter's Basilica, for example, is so vast one is caught unexpectedly by its size on a first visit, and I, for one, had to return several times to get used to it. The dome is 430 feet high (132.5 m.); the nave is about 630 feet long (194 m.), not including the portico; the height of the nave is 150 feet (46.20 m.); the transept is 446 feet (137.5 m). It is quite possible in such a place to keep oversized statues whose poses catch moments of wild motion. To produce huge canvases requires huge studios. Moreover, the very techniques of draftsmanship suppose that one has considerable room to move around, flail one's arms, and step back to see. Big places are required to show such things—large galleries, churches, and salons. The musical expression requires big orchestras and choruses, powerful, expansive vocal soloists, and the powerful organs that came to the peak of their development by the middle of the nineteenth century. Not yet mentioned is that most obvious case where the need for spatial expansion is great: the Elizabethan theater. Scholars have reconstructed the business of these plays and the character of the theaters. The Elizabethan playhouse provided a good-sized apron that went well out into the center of the theater. It gave a place where the poor player could indeed strut and fret his hour upon the stage. Proper expression of the language itself needs space for the actor to amplify himself physically. One should be aware that we have taken here a pretty grand time span of nearly four centuries—Shakespeare was born in 1564 and Meredith died in 1909. The ethos of European culture changed greatly, perhaps even profoundly, over that period; its ethos shows in its art and history, not in the motives of twentieth-century Western man.

Let us consider another case: the monkish art of illuminated books. It seems no accident that the draftsmanship in these books really is not very much, and that their appeal lies in the rich intense colors and textures of the pages themselves. If the kind of drawing that was revived in the Renaissance had an expansive exuberance that could only be achieved if one had made love to another person, this can hardly be said for what one sees in the work of the immediately earlier period.

The first thing that strikes us about this art is its contained, involuted character. Medieval manuscripts were fussed over. The art they show is small in scale—even when the books into which they are bound are rather large by postprinting press standards, as they often are. However, the lettering and drawing show a technique that uses almost no large muscles, but rather, for the most part, constrained movements from the fingers. Even when the illumination reaches very high levels of artistic sensibility it becomes apparent that those monks simply did not draw the way people drew later (or, for that matter, somewhat earlier). Even *The Book of Kells* (eighth century), that monkish splendor, shows no lines that could not be managed by the wrist and forearm. (The use of quills even limits the use of the fingers, because the quill has to be drawn over the surface with a very light touch—a limitation that even a user of modern wide-nib calligraphy pens will recognize. The quill also precludes motion from the grosser musculature of the shoulder.) The small compass of this art seems to be consistent with the jewellike effects that characterize so much of it. It is an art form that requires no greater ambience than a cell.

The constricted space of the cell and the attendant physical isolation constrains large mechanical expansion of the body. But variables other than such spatial limitations entered into the formation of this art. Foremost was the Christian attitude toward the human body as an instant provocation to sin. Virtually all pre-Renaissance Christian art manifests the Pauline shame of the human body, and this is of a piece with confinement to a cell. Rarely indeed do the drawings in these manuscripts ever show a delight in the body that

**4**  Equal talents, a common culture: another reading of it, by a man known mainly as a society portraitist. John Singer Sargent, *Rehearsal of the Pasdeloup Orchestra at the Cirque d'Hiver.*

Sargent became rich and famous doing society portraits, but in his letters he repeatedly warned young artists that the academic painting of his day was bad and he said that he considered himself an Impressionist. There indeed is a fair amount of his work that shows the same interest with the problems of perception that we think of with Whistler, Eakins, and the painters commonly associated with Impressionism. Psychological subtlety, however, seemed to interest him little—so little, in fact, that when he painted the murals in Harvard's Widener Library he gave a whole regiment of soldiers exactly the same set expressionless face.

Courtesy, Museum of Fine Arts, Boston. Charles Henry Hayden Fund.

results from an appreciation of its feel, textures, and mechanical structure. A famous teacher of drawing from life of the early part of the twentieth century, George B. Bridgman, called one of his anatomy texts for artists *The Human Machine*, and another, *Constructive Anatomy*. Both of them show—I think considerably better than the work of many people of the same period who are to be taken seriously as major artists—the extent to which the body must be studied systematically if it is to be drawn well. Of course, if one goes to the working sketches of major artists there is no question that such matters did interest them greatly. Anatomy was a central subject in training artists from perhaps 1450 to the Second World War.

The art of the Middle Ages shows a different feeling about the body. The spirit that could allow Agnolo Bronzino (1503–1572) to paint *Admiral Andrea Doria in the Guise of Neptune* (Venturi No. 61), a picture which showed the admiral stark naked, was not to be found in the cells of monks. Even in the late middle ages, artists continued this pervasive lack of interest in the human body. The Limbourg brothers (fl. ca. 1415) and Jean Colombe of Bourges (fl. ca. 1489) in *Les Très Riches Heures du Duc de Berry* show few nudes, some swimming boys, the figures in the pages marked "Eden," "Heaven," "Hell," and "Purgatory," one of the thieves with Christ, some washerwomen with their skirts around their waists, and a peasant couple seated in front of a fire warming their genitals, but no person of any position is pictured except fully clothed. Moreover, the drawing of human figures is not really very good at all if we consider a convincing, accurate portrayal of the way the human body is constructed and moves an aspect of good drawing. What is interesting is that many other things created in the same period show extremely good draftsmanship. In cases where the castles that are pictured still survive we know that they are accurately drawn; a garden within a castle wall is so carefully done that there is little trouble in recognizing what things were; we can tell that the plane trees were pollarded in exactly the same way that is still done in southern Europe; and so it goes—and this was already in the late fifteenth century. It was even truer earlier. Roger Hinks tells us in his now-standard *Carolingian Art* that the best of this art was shown in its small-scale work—its ivories and manuscripts. Little of its larger work in the form of frescoes has survived and practically none of it has much more than antiquarian interest. There are a few sculptures of the Carolingian period and works that are identifiable with the later Gothic period that show that as the style evolved people began to develop the skill to express emotional states in articulate forms that could be communicated, but it is still very clear that abstract, bookish, cell-bound ideas dominated and that the body was taken to be of little consequence.

It is fair to ask whether the great Gothic churches fit under this rubric of a bookish constraint. They are, after all, often huge. First of all let us dispel any idea that the Gothic style was a popular manifestation. It was not. It no more represented popular taste than the work of Louis Sullivan, Frank Lloyd Wright, and Frank Furness represented popular taste in the early twentieth century. The medieval bishops who built these great churches were no more concerned with the tastes of the lower orders of society than the Guggenheims were when they put up their museum in New York seven hundred years later. The medieval architects were satisfying what were basically upper-class tastes derived from involuted, scholarly sources. The kind of scholarship they indulged in emphasized formal containment and constraint and a fidelity to formal, rational intellectual systems that existed apart from the world of sense.

Such indeed is what is found on seeking the rules by which these churches were built. In George Lesser's *Gothic Cathedrals and Sacred Geometry*, we find that these edifices were planned, if not always built, according to very precise geometric relationships which could become incredibly complex and which were constained and involuted. In this planning there is affinity in spirit to the fussy cosmic conceptions of the Ptolemaic astronomy with its endless hypothesizing of epicycles that remain within larger circles of movement. There is little reference in either the medieval planning or Ptolemaic astronomy to the phenomenal; both are nurtured by scholars in their cells. They "smell of the lamp." In the same vein, Otto von Simson notes that many of these rules emanated from the monks at Chartres who insisted that the planning take into account numerological elements based upon a garbled medieval fragment of translation of Plato's *Timaeus*. In contrast, the main distillation of Renaissance rules for design comes down to us from Palladio's treatise on architecture which was, in turn, based upon the first-century *Ten Books On Architecture* of Vitruvius, which was itself as much a general treatise in engineering as architecture. It was very strongly concerned with the problems of how to do things in ways fitting the practical needs of man, and was little concerned with the expression of the formal, mystical elements that intrigued medieval church builders. Even the engineering of these churches similarly emphasized a constrained formal system in which there were only a few structurally random elements.[2] Even they are products of monastic involution.

Another case of the interaction of spatial arrangements and art forms lies in Japanese drawing and calligraphy. Recent Western practice attempts to separate living and working arrangements sharply. This is almost entirely a consequence of the factory system of production. The Japanese do not thus delineate if they can help it. Much of this has been very simply a matter of ratios of usable land to population. Over a very long period of time the Japanese have had to adjust themselves to living under crowded conditions. These conditions came about in part because of the physical danger that existed in Japan's preindustrial period when the need for protection made living in relatively large towns and villages a necessity for all but the very wealthy who could build castles.[3] By living tidily in their small quarters and contenting themselves with little furniture people gained some escape from congestion. Moreover, the dampness and the scarcity of fuel meant that possessions had to be kept in waterproof chests when they were not in use. The severe, bare beauty of the Japanese house evolved quite naturally in such a context. There was little room for furniture so people ate, slept, and carried on most of their daily activities on the floor, a practice that made tracking in dirt especially repugnant. The characteristic pose for sitting came to be one in which the lower leg was flat on the floor with the toes pointed backward and the weight of the body resting on the heels—a position that limits each person to a defined space. This affected drawing and its complement, calligraphy. Most drawing was done with a round pointed brush with its longer hairs on the outer perimeter. The ink came in a pressed dry stick which was rubbed against the end of a slot in a fine abrasive stone where it was mixed with water. The brush was used full with ink and pressed straight down. Nuances of line were achieved by varying the downward pressure on the brush. The effect this created was one where a line that suggested a wet liquid became characteristic. The calligraphy is a definite art form in itself and is considered just as important as the drawing of objects. These effects simply could not be attained if one drew on an upright sheet because there would be streaks running from the full brush where the thick drops of ink were placed

---

[2] It has been contended that from a purely engineering standpoint these churches were perhaps the most sophisticated structures ever built.
[3] Castle building, if one is to accept Edwin Reischauer's authority, began only in the sixteenth century under Portuguese influence.

upon the paper. The drawing of objects as well as the calligraphy showed the same character.[4]

Let us be cautious. I have quite deliberately confined myself to the effects of spatial and living arrangements upon art forms. I have avoided any discussion of the effects of culture upon aesthetic systems. There is little doubt that Taoist and Zen aesthetics with their emphases upon an empathic contemplation and identification with the essentials of the phenomena of the visual world fostered the need to provide a plain, undistracting ambience. Before considering this at all, we must take into account the development of those special conventions of performance, symbolism, and execution that we term technique. This too, unexpectedly, turns out to emerge from the way people live and the way society is organized. It is with this relationship that the next section will concern itself.

## BACKGROUND NOTE

Before writing this chapter there seemed some reason to consider the nature of action that might be an end in itself, "play"; but the literature was meager that treated the so-called play-impulse as an autonomous source of motivation. Pareto, in his great general treatise on sociology, *The Mind and Society* (New York: Harcourt Brace, 1935) spoke of a residue of an instinct for combinations. Looking to the literature specific to the subject itself, one finds that it is neither the joy nor the propensity to play itself that occupied American researchers but the possibility for utilitarian, commercial, or educational exploitation. Perhaps much of this results from a puritanical idea that life has a purpose beyond any joy of living itself. The way play is treated here is better understood by Europeans. Play as a source of creativity can be found in Roger Caillois's *Man, Play, and Games*, translated from the French by Meyer Barash (New York: Free Press, 1961); Erik Homberger Erikson, *Toys and Reason: Stages in the Ritualization of Experience* (New York: Norton, 1977); and Johan Huizinga, *Homo Ludens: A Study of the Play Element in Culture* (Boston: Beacon, 1955). One cannot fail to mention in literature the attempts to isolate the peculiarly artistic in the works of Ernst H. J. Gombrich, especially in *Art, Perception, and Reality*, with Julian Hochberg and Max Black (Baltimore: The Johns Hopkins Press, 1972) and *The Story of Art* (London: Phaidon, 1966) and in his two works on Renaissance art, *Norm and Form in the Art of the Renaissance* (London: Phaidon, 1961) and *Symbolic Images: Studies in the Art of the Renaissance* (London: Phaidon, 1972). For works on the nature of art without distracting rules, see Roger Fry, *Vision and Design* (London, n.d.), Clive Bell, *Since Cézanne* (London: Chatto and Windus, 1922), and *Civilization, an Essay* (London: Chatto and Windus, 1920) and *Art* (London: Chatto and Windus, 1920) and Roger Fry,

[4] The Chinese, from whom the Japanese derived their notions of painting, were insistent upon training in calligraphy as a prerequisite for training in drawing. Neither the Chinese nor the Japanese make any sharp difference between drawing and calligraphy.

*Transformations: Critical and Speculative Essays on Art* (London: Chatto and Windus, 1926).

To see the effects of spatial constraint upon an art form as it shows in illuminated manuscripts there is no better place to look than the manuscripts themselves. First-class facsimiles are common. Among many there is *Les Très Riches Heures du Duc de Berry Calendar by Pol de Limbourg and Jean Colombe, Fifteenth Century.* Text by Edmond Pognon, trans. David Macrae (Chantilly, France: Crescent Books, n.d.) and *The Book of Kells Reproductions from the Manuscript in Trinity College, Dublin with a Study of the Manuscript by Francoise Henry* (New York: Knopf, 1974). Sabina Mitchell gives a general discussion in her *Medieval Manuscript Painting* (New York: Viking, 1967) and David Diringer's *The Illuminated Book, Its History and Production* (New York: Philosophical Library, 1958) is also of value. The involuted spirit of Gothic architecture is shown in Otto von Simson's *Gothic Churches* and George Lesser's *Gothic Cathedrals and Sacred Geometry* (New York: Pantheon, 1965), Robert Gordon Anderson's *The City and Cathedral, a Reflection of the Glory of the Gothic and the Middle Ages at their High Tide in the City by the Seine* (New York: Longmans Green, 1948) and Henry Adams, *Mont St. Michel and Chartres.* Any standard text on Baroque art will confirm the comments on the spatial expansion demanded by this style. My own favorite is Germain Bazin, *The Baroque Principles, Modes, Themes,* trans. Pat Wardropper (Greenwich, Conn.: New York Graphics Society, 1968).

# 3

## Technique, Significant Experience, Abstraction

IN addition to the emergence of interactions between spatial variables and the actual extent to which these limit art as the physical, kinesthetic expression of the person, there is also the emergence of technique and conventions of form. As proficiency of expression increases, the power to extend the person becomes easier; in fact, as in the case of any other physical skill, even autonomic. The development of the power to express the intellectual and emotional states without constant ad hoc calculation we term technique. It may well be that what I am about to say makes me a brash, intruding fool rushing in where my betters fear to tread, but I think this must be said: if art can be expressed without having the techniques become structured into the autonomic nervous system itself, it is virtually the only human activity where this is possible. There is a good argument for the rote learning of skill. It is, in the long run, efficient in the development of self-expression. Once one learns to do something so well so that it is no longer necessary to think about doing it, one has arrived at precisely the moment where one can think of objectives and ignore technique. It does not really matter whether the activity is classified as artistic. This can hold true in virtually any field of endeavor. The good craftsman, the good artist, the good athlete, the good surgeon, and anyone else who has learned to do anything well have reached the point where they can virtually will their expression for their bodies to follow, and what they express only lacks precision insofar as their conceptions lack precision.

A question may arise about literary forms. Here a similar type of discipline emerges on a level of verbal facility. The good writer develops an ear and gradually develops the ability to avoid the logical and stylistic traps to which the classical rhetoricians have given terms. (I for one do not know them, but I suspect that if I did know them well enough to avoid them I would not have to indulge in the constant ineffectual trial and error that dogs me every time I put my thoughts to paper.) Technique develops and gradually the process of intellectual and artistic expression is not bedeviled by the constant necessity of stopping to think about means. This does not entail kinesthetic habituation and its extension and refinement through tool-using, but the same autonomic habituation of technique is involved.

However, as technique for expression improves, conventions of expression become established. The art of cultures other than those of the observer always seems to have a mannered character. What actually, I think, lies beyond such feelings is that we become accustomed to familiar conventions of expression. It is easy here to give an example. The use of strong contrasts of light and shadow to achieve form was virtually absent from far Eastern art until Western influences were absorbed in the nineteenth century, and examples are still found only minimally in Chinese art. Structure is achieved by a control of line. In the famous seventeenth-century manual of painting, *Chieh Tzu Yuan Hua Chuan (The Mustard Seed Garden Manual of Painting)* translated and published with Mai-mai Sze's *The Tao of Painting*, each page presents an illustration of brushwork. Structure is studied always through line. There are almost no cases among the examples where structure is portrayed architectonically through the juxtaposition of planes and the use of shade to create form. Perspective seems to be achieved through atmospheric effects which are accomplished by making the ink more or less dilute as subjects are closer or farther from the surface plane of the picture or drawing. As in Western artistic conventions, size is also used, but rarely do Chinese and Japanese painting and drawing depend upon a discernible convergence of lines upon a focal point.[1] One does not find such atmospheric creation of perspective in the West until we reach the Barbizon School and the Impressionists, and we have ample evidence that they studied examples of Japanese and Chinese art that became available in Europe in the eighteenth and nineteenth centuries. The lack of concern with geometric elements is even more apparent in a good deal of Far Eastern portraiture which almost lacks architectonic ele-

[1] The use of geometric perspective is a result of Western influences.

ments completely and is usually little more than line drawing with colored-on decorative elements. A few nineteenth-century portrait painters in the West did paint and draw so that the light was directly in front of the subject (e.g., Ingres), an emphasis that forces a concern with line, but it remains a minor element in most work. Among earlier painters, Sandro Botticelli seems to have encased his forms with lines, but when his pictures are examined closely the lines can never be found. What we are discussing here—the Chinese and Japanese work—seems to have a character that is embedded in a matrix that is dreamy and exotic, a mannered fantasy if you will. However, is it entirely that? What is the basis of the fantasy?

These precise visual effects can be found on some mornings in rural New England if one knows when to look for them. If one rises just before sunrise on a warm spring morning, the same visual reality becomes apparent as form develops in the waxing light. One gets a similar feeling of being in an Oriental visual world on a sunny morning after a snowstorm when the crystalline character of the new snow has not yet been destroyed by any melting, and light is still highly diffused. Such moments have the same "unreal" character that one sees in much Chinese and Japanese work.

It was only in the nineteenth century that attempts were made in Western art to capture such evanescent effects. With Cimabue (1240–1302) and Giotto (1276–1337), the art of painting in the West developed an architectonic character that was to continue to dominate until it began to break up in Impressionism and even for a time became lost in Cubism and Abstract Expressionism in the early and middle twentieth century.[2] Structure is not created through line; it is created through the building up of forms that when analyzed can be shown to be mechanically sound, blocklike structures. In fact, one of the most commonly used texts on art appreciation of the 1930s and '40s, Helen Gardner's *Understanding the Arts*, did take a fair number of pictures and reduce them to essentially block forms. Perspective in early European work was generally achieved by geometric means. Some of this may, perhaps, be attributed to the fact that the brilliance of light in much of Italy does not provide a very good environment to study the effects of atmospheric variables on distance perception. However, this is not really a sufficient explanation. Sunny Italy turns out to be an

[2] The question of whether Cubism was simply a fraud is irrelevant. One can argue that any following of an artistic formulary—even the most egregiously academic—is a fraud whenever it is an attempt to gain recognition without intellectual effort.

Italy of Neapolitan canzone rather than an omnipresent fact. It is only sunny south of Rome, along the littoral on the West, and southward along the Adriatic side. Moreover, when we consider later Italian Renaissance painting and northern European painting, we see basic architectonic structure was realized through chiaroscuro as well, and geometric perspective was, by and large, retained. There remained implicit in Western visual arts a rational geometric structure. One needs only look to some of the great examples of virtuosity among the minor Baroque painters to see how highly developed this became. In one of the largest Baroque churches of Rome, San Ignazio Loyola, Fr. Andrea Pozzo (1642–1709) painted a barrel-vaulted ceiling perhaps 75 feet wide and 200 feet long entitled *The Entrance of San Ignazio into Paradise.* In its iconography and technique, it is typically Baroque, and other works of his contemporaries have certainly interested critics and scholars much more (and if this were a critical essay one could give good reasons). The church itself is overshadowed by more famous monuments of the Roman past in the neighborhood—the Pantheon, the Gesu, Santa Maria sopra Minerva, the Palazzo Venezia, and many others. One may question considering Fr. Pozzo's ceiling as a major artistic feat, but there is no doubt that it is an astonishing intellectual one. When one stands at a brass plate set in the floor, one discovers that from this point the columns and pilasters of the nave appear to continue into the picture. There is a false dome interior painted at the crossing of the nave and the transept that fooled me completely until I had seen it a number of times. If one is looking for examples of this sort, one could give a seemingly endless list spread through Europe. Such performances are really a reductio ad absurdum of a portion of the Western tradition in the arts that emphasizes the structural, the architectural, and the geometric.

In many other cases, the function of the technique is to portray certain kinds of motion. I think this is particularly true in much of Indian sculpture. The thing to catch there is the endless cosmic dance. The world is seen as in a constant Heraclitan flux in which, as B.A.G. Fuller wrote: "All particular, concrete objects, of whatsoever kind, come into and pass out of being. Generation after generation of them appear, hesitate a moment between existence and non-existence, and are gone. The seemingly all too solid earth of which they are made crumbles, liquefies and vanishes before our eyes. There is no let-up in the process of generation and dissolution, no stability, nothing for hand or foot to lay hold of."[3] One's

[3] B.A.G. Fuller, *A History of Philosophy* (New York: Henry Holt and Co., 1938), 1:73.

first impression of this is that it refers to a very mannered art form. One feels that the reality that it expresses is ideational and it involves no imagery that really corresponds to the phenomenal world.[4] The figures do not seem to portray real human figures. However, from time to time, Indian dance companies have performed for Western audiences, and at these performances one begins to see that this perceptual world has an objective counterpart. (It is hard to miss the structure of the human body in much of Western dance. Seldom is there ever much attempt made to conceal its structure, and this is especially true of modern dance. We know that the dancers have beautifully developed athletic bodies, and pauses which show it are frequent. And I refer to the female members of the company too, for they demonstrate that women can have beautifully developed musculature and still look enchantingly like women.) In Indian dance, continuous motion is sought. The dancers are trained to bend their joints in such a way that they appear to have a continuous undulation. The physiques of the performers are largely hidden by lush and often billowy costumes that seem to overwhelm the "fragile" people whom they cover. How does this connect with what I am discussing here? As one begins to relate the style of painting and sculpture that is recognized as Indian—covering better than two millennia—one realizes that it does capture this type of perceptual world of constant movement of a continuous sort, what F.S.C. Northrop called "the undifferentiated aesthetic continuum." In Indian art the emphasis upon structure that so dominates Western art has no real importance. Indian art does indeed capture a perceptual reality, but not one that Westerners are trained to select.

Specialists in the history of art could multiply these examples indefinitely, and I do not even believe that primitive and abstract art forms are exceptions, but rather that they simply abandon the familiar forms of objects as a matrix for the expression (and acceptability) of art. It was not insensitivity, I believe, that led to our reluctance to accept primitive art at the turn of the twentieth century. (It was that the reality, which moderns and psychoanalysis both sought, was that of the dream, le rêve, which defies rational structure.) In each of the cases mentioned here we see where in different cultures different aspects of reality are selected for emphasis and for different reasons. We all hear and see and feel the same things, but the significant forms that we abstract from the world

---

[4] I hesitate to use the terms "rational" and "projective" that were in vogue in the 1950s under the influence of Kardiner's *Psychological Frontiers of Society*, because they showed that Kardiner really ignored common epistemological usage. He should have used "empirical" where he used the term "rational" and "rational" when he used the term "projective."

of perception are patterned by underlying assumptions derived from different traditions.

Perhaps here it is appropriate to mention that the portrayal of reality is always selective. It is quite easy to make a mask from a living or dead face, but the result does not turn out to be very convincing as portraiture. It usually turns out to be utterly monstrous. Few moles and blackheads have character, and most wrinkles turn out to be "meaningless." Even in photography, one does not try to catch everything and, indeed, the trick is to know how to make the camera select "significant form" from the clutter of our perceptions. In a similar vein, one can make almost any situation appear ridiculous (or bizarre) by telling exactly what happened. Bergson, in fact, contended that comedy was no more than the detailed portrayal of reality. It has been said that the sociologist Erving Goffman looks upon life as bad slapstick. It is hard to tell from his writings whether, indeed, he regards everyday life as bad slapstick or a grave game of self-protection. They are not, in fact, incompatible, for, as Plato has Socrates say, "the genius of comedy was the same with that of tragedy, and . . . the true artist in tragedy was an artist in comedy also" (*Symposium* 225). However, Goffman's minute description of the world around him certainly does give rise to both impressions. Reading *Relations in Public* gave me a disturbing sense of déjà vu until I realized that in a metaphorical sense I had been there hundreds of times: he was describing the people on the north side of Market Street between Ninth and Thirteenth Streets in Philadelphia when I was growing up many years ago or, equally well, the people on Washington Street in

---

**5**   The social determination of perception: a society portrait, Egyptian style. *Colossal Statue of Mycerinus*, Old Kingdom, ca. 3000 B.C.

It is perhaps startling to call this statue a society portrait, but it is not incorrect. The rendering of the figure has been dictated by the social position of the sitter rather than by the artist's own perception of his character. (It would not have mattered in any case what the sculptor thought.) Unlike the royal statues from the New Kingdom, this one shows an identifiable person; the treatment of musculature shows that the sculptor knew anatomy. But in the present context it is important to note how such elements were distorted by what was required of a sculptor portraying a king. The shoulders are huge; the legs too are powerful, and so are the hands. They are all meant to express the power that could cause one of the great pyramids to be built. (At 365½ feet along its base Mycerinus's is the least of the three, but it is still no mean tomb.) The face is serene; it is the face of the great, just, and powerful god-king. He lives above and beyond mortal limitations; his power is the power of the society itself.

Courtesy, Museum of Fine Arts, Boston, Harvard/MFA Expedition.

Boston in the vicinity of Jordan Marsh's and Filene's stores when I was in my twenties.

The portrayal of life that comes from such attempts is often chaotic. It is like a photograph in which everything is equally in focus. It lacks depth; it is confusing; it is uninteresting. But what is most damaging is to say that it lacks meaning. At its most benign, it is tedious, and at its worst, it is "a tale told by an idiot, full of sound and fury, signifying nothing." There has to be a selection of what fits into the system of meaning from this chaotic mass of perceptual data. Let us consider some examples.

Before World War I, an anonymous wit said "Gloucester [New Jersey] has a racetrack, forty saloons, and two policemen." If one thinks about this within the system of meanings and the common experiences and associations of most Americans, it tells as much as one needs to know about Gloucester. No one needs to say that there were gamblers, *filles du pavé*, panders, fortunetellers, and the rest of the personae of the floating world of a rip-roaring working-class resort.

Mention is made of this anonymous quip because it catches something essential to all art: the evocation of common systems of meanings and experience. Here are two more examples that deal with a common human preoccupation—perhaps a universal one: the mystery of death. The first is a poem by Emily Dickinson:

> Drowning is not so pitiful
> As the attempt to rise.
> Three times, 'tis said, a sinking man
> Comes up to face the skies,
> And then declines forever
> To that abhorred abode
>
> Where hope and he part company,—
> For he is grasped of God.
> The Maker's cordial visage,
> However good to see,
> Is shunned, we must admit it,
> Like an adversity.

The second is perhaps the most famous Shakespearean soliloquy:

> To be, or not to be—that is the question:
> Whether 'tis nobler in the mind to suffer
> The slings and arrows of outrageous fortune,
> Or to take arms against a sea of troubles,
> And by opposing end them. To die—to sleep—

No more; and by a sleep to say we end
The heartache, and the thousand natural shocks
That flesh is heir to. 'Tis a consummation
Devoutly to be wished. To die—to sleep.
To sleep—perchance to dream: ay, there's the rub!
For in that sleep of death what dreams may come
When we have shuffled off this mortal coil,
Must give us pause. There's the respect
That makes calamity of so long life.
For who would bear the whips and scorns of time,
The oppressor's wrong, the proud man's contumely,
The pangs of despised love, the law's delay,
The insolence of office, and the spurns
That patient merit of the unworthy takes,
When he himself might his quietus make
With a bare bodkin? Who would these fardels bear,
To grunt and sweat under a weary life,
But that the dread of something after death—
The undiscovered country, from whose bourn
No traveller returns—puzzles the will,
And makes us rather bear those ills we have
Than fly to others that we know not of?
Thus conscience does make cowards of us all,
And thus the native hue of resolution
Is sicklied o'er with the pale cast of thought,
And enterprises of great pith and moment
With this regard their currents turn awry
And lose the name of action.—

One may ask why both of these speak to us? Aside from any technical aspect of the use of the language, it is essentially because they come to grips with a fear that is inherent in Western thinking—the day of reckoning—*dies irae*. Acceptance of the idea of total annihilation of the person seems to require a massive, distasteful intellectual effort. Of ancient peoples whose thought comes down to us, only the Jews seem to have had no strong belief in an afterlife for even the very good. The Gentiles believed in one, and Plato created a complex eschatology as well as a philosophic proof based upon a doctrine of the immortality of the soul. The Egyptians took elaborate, bizarre, and economically ruinous measures to assure that the souls of the powerful would be comfortable and survive the perils of the next world. Indian religious beliefs come to terms with the dreadful prospect of utter annihilation of personality by a doctrine of reincarnation whose form is tied to the merit of the individual in this life and his ability to free himself from metaphysical error. In the systems that came out of India, however, personality is an excrescence that disappears with philosophic and ethical perfection. However, Western belief provides no possibility of escape; death in the West means, sooner or later, a confrontation with judgment. It is no accident that Michelangelo painted all the figures in *The Last Judgment* naked and even showed the Christ Himself naked.[5] There was probably no other way for him to conceive of it—a naked confrontation before a naked God who stands to mete judgment in His terrible glory. Of the sights that the Buddha of history saw—disease, old age, and death—it is the last that gives the most trouble. One can come to terms with disease and old age and learn to live contentedly with both, because we have the experiences of others to provide us with examples of how one may cope with them. Belief may prepare one for confrontation with death, but experience cannot. What gives these passages their force is that they lay bare fears that nothing we experience can mitigate. Moreover, the statements are cogent and do not suffer from the distractions of extraneous speculation. Perhaps we have come to what is essential for an artist in dealing with the tragic: a confrontation with those agonies that people deal with that remain intransigently resistant to collective attempts to deal with them. This is a particularly apparent aspect of a good play. I am told by colleagues in the field of English Renaissance literature that it is simply not accurate to consider Shakespeare *primus inter pares*. Shakespeare was, in fact, as far beyond his contemporaries as Eugene O'Neill was a generation ago; as perhaps Edward Albee is today. Each of them abstracts from the unorganized data of experience the universally significant problems. What is more, they all create an ambience that sharpens our perceptions of them and formulates their meaning clearly to us. Less obviously, the same holds for visual arts and music as well. They also abstract the crucial, perhaps even inescapable, aspects of common experience. The artist is always a creature of society if he achieves recognition—he must have something to say that has a nexus to common experience, but paradoxically, in that he illuminates experience from angles that amplify common understandings, he transcends normal collective definitions. Such amplifications hold for the visual arts too. It is a commonplace piece of advice to people learning to draw and paint that one should not go beyond the backyard for subjects—there are plenty right there. In driving through the back

[5] The draperies were painted on later by Daniele da Volterra.

roads of western Massachusetts and Quebec I developed a fascination for the strange beauty of those jumbles of old barns where people seem (in an economy of cheap lumber) to have built more and more outbuildings rather than look ruthlessly at their possessions and winnow them. The pier in Rockport, Massachusetts, is said to be the most painted spot in America, but if one seeks to amplify experience such places tend to sidetrack one with the picturesque. Sometimes the experiences that are amplified by art are not the perceptions of sights and sounds, but attempts to illuminate and amplify experience that is essentially subjective and to bring it into the realm of perception. This, if we are to believe Herbert Read, is what much modern painting is about. It is particularly true of what are almost its most bizarre manifestations—Surrealism and the Suprematism of Klee and the Bauhaus group. The experience of World War I had brought to the Western consciousness the Gothic substratum of decay, lust, and brutality. The unconscious id of Freudian psychology turned out to be closer to the surface than even Freud himself thought. The Surrealists under the aegis of their chief theoretician, André Breton, brought this collective unconscious to the surface and translated it into perceptual terms. I think it is not fortuitous that the work of men like Arp, Miró, Kandinsky and Duchamp, and, later, the Abstract Expressionists, continues to hold our attention in a way that the chimpanzee's finger painting cannot. We see meanings to their works that speak to us even when we approach them without a concomitant and often distracting verbal apparatus. Later the idea of the fundamental autonomy of machines was to become an omnipresent fact; it ranges now from the fury that comes with trying to fight a computer that is wrong to the terrifying implications of Jean Piaget's *Structuralism*. Perhaps ultimately the difference between the work of artists who continue to hold attention and involuted private fantasies is that the former illuminates panhuman experience and the latter does not. But an exemplary caveat is in order: Hieronymous Bosch's work seemed no more than diseased fantasy before Freud made us by-pass the censors of our stinking collective unconsciousness.

Perhaps I should interpose a warning by Benedetto Croce from that wonder among books, *Aesthetic*. Art, he pointed out, does not exist separately from its expression. Croce saw ideas and their expression as utterly inseparable. There cannot be mute, inglorious Miltons. What makes Milton a great poet—and not just an obscure, misogynist Puritan censor—was that he wrote great poetry; one may reject the message, but the "music" remains. It may be questionable that *Paradise Lost* succeeded in justifying the ways of God to man any better than several score of tiresome Protestant theological tracts, but it not only presented a way of understanding the seeming immorality of history, but did it with style.

However, one begins to enter another realm. There is inevitably a tendency of the artist to produce an accentuation of emotional and intellectual states. I mention the intellectual as well as the emotional because many art forms do indeed emphasize what are essentially intellectual states to the exclusion of emotional content. Much of music that is "caviar to the general" has its appeal on a purely intellectual level. One may mention particularly a great deal of the nonreligious music of Bach. What do *The Well-Tempered Clavichord, The Goldberg Variations, The Art of the Fugue*, and similar works have in common? They are essentially explorations of intellectualized, formal relationships. They develop and have their principal appeal within that human activity we term music-making. There is no real expectation that they be generally understood by any but a small part of the laity any more than explorations in the more creative aspects of mathematics are expected to be generally understood by everyone. There are examples of this within the visual arts. Much of modern dance requires such special knowledge of its technical and aesthetic objectives. I have already mentioned the work of the Bauhaus; the works of Maurits Escher and René Magritte assume the character of structuralistic logical exercises that generate their own development once started. Earlier work in painting, architecture, and sculpture showed the concern with rational formal structure, which is the essence of the classical tradition, even in the portrayal of the human figure. It is the body as a perfect machine and not as the medium for the expression of polymorphous passion that interests the classicist. Perhaps the best example after ancient times is the *School of Athens* and other decorations by Raphael in the Vatican. In the 1920s and '30s fashionable criticism downgraded Raphael, and I am loathe to examine such judgments (because I think them silly). However, when one looks at Raphael's works in terms of their being essentially intellectual attempts to portray order they become a series of remarkable performances. Order as a dominant value in Renaissance culture is hard to escape. It provides a rubric under which may be put both the demand for elegant precision that Palladio made upon architecture and the portrayal of the human body as a beautiful machine.

The emphasis upon emotional states—or affective orientations if one wishes to use the terminology of the Verstehensoziologie as it was developed by Parsons—is a more obvious matter. However, it is not an emphasis that leads to the bathos of *Smiling Through, Just Plain Bill, Ma Perkins,* or even Charles Dickens's *A Christmas Carol.*[6] It is rather an emphasis that leads to a clarification and apprehension of the nature of the emotional states of common experience. "Soap" neither illuminates nor refines our perception of any aspect of experience, but provides only homilies that exemplify a known message. Frequently, the truth of the message is dubious. We know from nonfictional sources, for example, that *The Pickwick Papers* tells us more about the actual quality of life in nineteenth-century London than the tale of how Mr. Scrooge, who acted sensibly to survive in a mercantile society, was made to act irrationally. Mr. Pickwick's misadventures are plausible emergents of the interactions of the ambient cultural, psychological, and social systems. These range from being punched in the face by a cabbie who has mistaken him for a police informer when he was observed taking down the cabbie's facetious answers about the horse's age, to being committed to debtor's prison for defaulting a libel awarded his widowed landlady in a breach-of-promise suit after she mistook a circuitous question about the cost of keeping a manservant for a proposal of marriage. ("Do you think it's a much greater expense to keep two people, than to keep one?" chapter 12.) The bookish innocent Mr. Pickwick, loose in the world and suffering, becomes a symbol for what happens to innocent goodness. His manservant, Sam Weller, who couldn't have gone straight if he tried, manages quite well. What is actually occurring is not the moral universe of popular theology, but the ineluctable development of circumstances. At first glance—when it is not yet apparent that neither Sunday School platitudes nor Marxist homiletics portray anything but themselves—*The Pickwick Papers* and *Ah! Wilderness* seem on the face only to be kindly farces, but later one realizes that they show a world that is about as good as life can be for most people.[7] However, at this point a caveat must be introduced. *Smilin' Through, Ma Perkins,* and *A Christmas Carol* do have a reality, do indeed illuminate experience for those who think in their terms. It depends entirely upon what one considers to be the core of reality. If one sees society as a structuralistic system whose rules are gener-

[6] The last could be read as a tragedy of a man of probity being suborned by his inferiors. I find it difficult to apprehend the possibility that the man who could write *A Tale of Two Cities* and the comic masterpieces that were put together to make *The Pickwick Papers* could have taken *A Christmas Carol* seriously, but the record shows he did.

[7] Each, in fact, portrays worlds that were better than either O'Neill or Dickens experienced for some of their lives.

ated by the interactions of its variables, these are indeed bilge. The data of sociology, the new "dismal science," show that life is just not the way they show it to be. However, if one considers social reality to be what I am dismissing as platitudes, then the world of Erving Goffman and *The Pickwick Papers* represents a dissolution of order that is to be fought whatever the psychological cost. (In fact, Goffman sees the farce as the attempt to create order.)[8] Since the perception of reality always is given order by the observer, it depends entirely on which segment of the phenomenal one wishes the artist to put in order. We are forced to ask the question of how well any art expresses universal concerns. To return to our earlier ruminations upon death, the passages from *Hamlet* and Emily Dickinson epitomize our fears and emotions about death from which the consolations of neither religion nor philosophy ever fully free us. Emily Dickinson's drowning man feared to see his maker but when Ma Perkins died, she went straight to Paradise and took her place in the Mother's Day parade of Robert Nathan's fantasy.

This leads us to consider another level. As artists seek our common problems, events, emotions, and intellectual states, the next stage is perhaps inevitable—the evolution of a common set of cues and symbols to evoke such states. This is a stage at which conventionalization takes place. The symbols become so conventionalized as to be entirely abstract in very much the same way that alphabets can become so far removed from the original pictographic forms that the connections are only made apparent through the work of experts working backward through all the transitional forms. Conventionalization of form takes place in both folk and studio art forms.[9] If one considers briefly here various modes of expression, this may be pointed out easily. Almost everywhere that dance is cultivated as an art, conventions of representation arise in varying degrees. This can range from a Western modern dance company that has its special forms that are understood only by a particular coterie of fanciers through to the extraordinarily complex set of widely understood conventionalized motions and gestures that are found in southeast Asian dance traditions. What should be noted here is that such gesturing can be completely incomprehensible (if not actually boring) to the person who is outside the culture, but to the observers who are privy to the system of symbols it can be intellectually and emotionally meaningful simply because they have

[8] Goffman himself never calls the interactions of the personae of his vignettes "farce."

[9] The difference between folk and studio art forms is not considered in the present essay. The difference is ultimately sociological rather than aesthetic.

been taught that such conventions are supposed to invoke particular states of sentiment.

The same symbolization appears in design motifs that appear in architecture, textiles, and pottery. In many instances one appreciates the objects for what one senses to be their beauty, but it is only in the context of a symbolic system that emotional and intellectual values are given to them by the viewer.

With musical forms the same uses of conventions appear to have operated. Perhaps to the modern reader the strictures Plato places in the education of the guardians against certain modes of music seem strange (*The Republic* 399–401), but become understandable if considered in terms of conventions within which the proscribed modes were supposed to invoke certain emotional states. Even in the case of musical forms that have evolved in the Western musical traditions there are these same learned responses. One, for example, responds to much church music not because of its inherent formal structure but because those who are within certain symbolic systems are accustomed to responding—and believe they should respond—in a certain way. To the urbanized observer gospel hymns may be little more than the visceral complaints of tired evangelical Protestantism, but to the person who has grown up within their imagery and symbols, they may be deeply moving. A similar type of learned response takes place in a good deal of mass-appeal music. Teenagers of a few years back wore large aggressive lapel buttons which proclaimed defiantly, "I like Elvis." Their perceived enemies lay in a number of camps which were often not even on speaking terms with each other. The foes included those who liked Victor Herbert and Sigmund Romberg, those who liked Puccini and Donizetti and Verdi, those who liked "good" jazz and "good" rock forms and knew something about both, almost every other coterie that regarded itself as having cultured tastes, and, perhaps largest of all, those who just wanted quiet.[10] But if one looks upon the art

---

[10] There seems to be no doubt that Presley had a promising, perhaps even brilliant, start as a musician. He began by creating a music that combined rock forms with the folk music of the American South, both black and white. His performance of it was both proficient and creative according to a knowledgeable colleague, Professor Randall Stokes. However his promoters seem to have selected for issue only recordings that they thought would be salable and this seemed to have been entirely what had already caught on. Early in his career he fell into repetition to satisfy such demands. The music itself stopped commanding interest or respect and its enemies became more and more numerous. At the time of writing this note (1981) most of the recordings he made remain unissued. We do not yet have any open basis for judging whether or not he had an unpublicized line of development—perhaps less salable than what we know. The recording companies have not yet said.

of Elvis Presley as that of a person with an understanding of the unrequited longings of adolescence and of the alienation that sub-adults can be persuaded they feel, his music is a remarkable tour de force.

Finally, in these examples one may mention conventions of acting. The emphasis upon acting in this century has been upon the naturalistic performer. We have little taste for the "dazzling" formal dialogue of Oscar Wilde or George Bernard Shaw. Mannered performance is viewed as bad; it is no accident that "The Method" emphasized empathy rather than learned technique. We have come to take naturalistic acting so much for granted that we are very likely to forget that we find it to be the exception rather than the rule when crosscultural comparisons are made. In every other culture area where a theatrical tradition has developed, the viewer learns a complex series of conventions that convey the emotional and intellectual message of the actor. He knows what emotions and themes the conventional forms of the acting are supposed to convey. A parallel can be found in the acting of the French and Italian classical theater. I found a performance of Molière's *Le Bourgeois Gentilhomme* excruciatingly boring. However, many others in the audience who had been through a French curriculum knew when to laugh and why they were laughing. The actors were highly accomplished, but I just didn't know what was funny.

One can sum this up simply enough. No one is born knowing what the books, the pictures, and the plays are and why they are good, but some are told why they are good and what they are supposed to respond to. Appreciation is learned. To an uncouth fanatic like Savonarola, all of the glories of the secular Renaissance of quattrocento Florence were vanities and abominations, anathema to truth faith. Savonarola was a profoundly ignorant man, he was alien and hostile to new currents and too inhibited by his prejudices to learn anything new. Appreciation depends upon the extent to which one is able to respond to the cues from the particular culture in which the work of the artist is embedded. It does not exist in vacuo.

## BACKGROUND NOTE

The "how-to-do-it" literature about the techniques of Western visual art is at worst simple minded and at best high-level "workbooks." The ingenuity to which the theory of perspective was developed is shown in Andrea Pozzo's *Rules and Examples of Perspective Proper for Painters and Architects* (New York: Blom, 1971) [*Prospettiva de Pittori e Architetto d'Andrea Pozzo Nella Stampa di Antonio de'Rossi, 1717–1723*]. Helen Gardner's *Understanding the*

*Arts* (New York: Harcourt and Brace, 1932) lays out the "architectonic aesthetic" lucidly.

This may be contrasted with Mai-mai Tze's *The Tao of Painting* (New York: Bollingen, 1956) which accompanies and contains her translation and facsimile of *The Mustard Seed Garden Manual of Painting* [Chieh Tzu Yuan Hua Chuan], Osvald Siren's *Chinese Painting: Leading Masters and Principles*, 7 vols. (New York: Ronald, 1956), and his *The Chinese on the Art of Painting: Translations and Comments* (New York: Schocken, 1963). For more on Eastern work, see Sastri K. Ramaswami, *Indian Aesthetics; Music and Dance* (Tirupati: Sri Venkateswara University, 1966), and Russell M. Hughes, *The Gesture Language of Hindu Dance* (New York: Blom, 1964). Perhaps Erving Goffman's own books best give a picture of the dead-pan slapstick that an exact portrayal of everyday life gives. It is set out in *The Presentation of Self in Everyday Life* (Garden City, N.Y.: Doubleday, 1959) and *Relations in Public; Microstudies of the Public Order* (New York: Basic Books, 1971).

# 4

## The Playing Out of Artistic Styles

THE preceding section dealt with the development of conventional systems of expression understood mainly by particular audiences. It must be emphasized that the professional contexts are so isolated as to be virtually autonomous with respect to other parts of the social system, and it is in such isolation that the conventions of expression that are called style develop. Such development can become so hermetic that it has no possible course except toward involuted manipulations. The process leads to a recurrent phenomenon: classical traditions and the forms that they engender to express themselves go stale. For example, there is little question that Franz Joseph Haydn almost played out the form of the classical symphony and went nearly as far as one could go within its rules for development by the time of his death in 1809. It was not a matter that no composer could write classical symphonies after him, for as late as 1916 the youthful Sergei Prokofiev wrote *Symphonie Classique* op. 25 as an homage to Haydn, and many lesser figures continued to write them through the nineteenth century, but once the great man had put his talents to bringing the form to its fullest development it held little interest for composers who were on the limits of creative consciousness. By 1820 this type of symphony that could be performed by small amateur orchestras was not to be written much more. Composers whose works are still in the active symphonic repertory found both the form and the then current orchestral forces inadequate for what they wanted to express. Beethoven only wrote two before he cut completely loose from the form in his Third Symphony and Schu-

bert did four, of which only the second is still commonly performed. Within the classical concerto form, Beethoven's Third
Piano Concerto op. 37 was the last written by a major composer
that is still performed. (Even here his fancy carried him so far that
it was unplayable on most of the pianos of his time as they often
did not have the highest octave of present day instruments.) At
some point artists find significant things to express that can no
longer be dealt with easily under the rubrics of the academically
trained, or their instruments and techniques. After Richard Wagner
heard an early performance of Beethoven's Ninth Symphony, he
wrote to a friend that it was apparent that the conductor did not
know what the score was about. (Many years later he performed
it to his own satisfaction.) Wagner himself had trouble getting his
own music performed properly until the mad King Ludwig II of
Bavaria gave him an orchestra and theater of his own at Bayreuth
in 1861. Three-quarters of a century later Igor Stravinsky was to
encounter similar trouble with the three big orchestral works, *Firebird*, *Petrushka*, and *The Rite of Spring*. Each of them grated on the
ears of both the performers and the audiences who were still
wallowing in the perfumed sonorities of nineteenth-century romanticism. In chamber music performance is perhaps less of a
problem. Finding solo performers who can empathize with the
composer is not generally insuperable, and finding four or five individuals who can play together well is easy compared to mounting
a major orchestral work that calls for new techniques, new understandings, and perhaps even new instruments.[1] In other arts the
same problem of conceptualization running ahead of techniques
occurs. In sculpture the problems of getting artisans who will do
what they are told and who understand one's intentions can be considerable as soon as work is off the beaten track. The history of
architecture has many records of first-rate men who were like
Michelangelo at least in regarding builders as adversaries. Not only
do the creative artists have trouble with these ancillary functionaries (and one must include among them publishers, museum curators, gallery owners, and other impresarios), but with their publics
as well. However, these difficulties seem to point to one fact: a system of expression that we term a "style" loses the interest of the
important artists precisely because it is stale and does not permit
expression of meaning and emotional states that have become important. One may fairly ask why. Here I think one must go to a
realm of analysis that relates to the societal ambience rather than

[1] The number of woodwinds greatly increased in the nineteenth century as
composers began to write music that required greater subtleties of tone.

the work itself. A form has vitality as long as it can express common meanings that remain vital to the society as well as the inner world of artists.

So far, this discussion really begs the question. It does not explain anything to say that when a form is stale major artists lose interest in it because all the possibilities for variation within it have been exploited and it is inadequate as a medium of expression of new visions. There is also a cultural level upon which this phenomenon can be discussed: that the form fails to express important meanings that have appeared in the society. An example lies in the decline of sculpture in the ancient gentile world. Perhaps some readers would prefer a discussion of academic painting and sculpture in nineteenth-century Europe. That may well be, but in the last forty years there have been so many burials, followed by incantations and resurrections, that I am loath to talk about the last century. (A guess is that some of what has been brought back into vogue never really was very bad at all, but simply could not be easily dealt with under the critical verbiage of the moments when they were censured.)[2] Since it is not only beyond my competence to sort this out, but extraneous to the purposes of this essay, it seems well to take an earlier period. First one may say confidently that no matter what point in time we take as the apogee of Greco-Roman art, critics agree that sculpture declined in quality in the later ancient world, especially in its portrayal of the human figure, and that first-quality original work is scarce with relation to the actual expansion of Hellenic culture in land and influence.

The first sculptures of the human figure in this tradition appear in work that comes from the pre-Attic cultures of Crete and the mainland. Almost nothing that survives is of any size, but enough indeed survives to show that very high levels of skill were attained quite early, at least on small-scale work. However, by the sixth century B.C. enough big pieces of interest survive to show that the human figure could be portrayed with vigor and force. Moreover the figures have personality; they are not symbolic representations; they are identifiably Greek and Italian faces of a type that we still see today on the European Mediterranean littoral. As we approach the fifth century, the figures become anatomically accurate. It is apparent that people had become quite aware of the body as a beautiful machine[3] and tried hard to show that aspect of it. When

---

[2] In some revivals I must confess to being an unregenerate child of 1920. Much of what has been revived does not "send" me anywhere, e.g., nineteenth-century academic painting.

[3] We know, of course, that the ancients were egregiously wrong when they came to consider questions of neurological and physiological function. (Need one go

we reach the sculptures of the Parthenon there is a grace and excitement to them that is utterly impossible to escape. This brings us to 447–438 B.C. The way the body is portrayed makes it clear that sculptors thought of it the way Plato and Aristotle seem to have thought of personality; it was a contained, gemlike structure in which education brought out the facets of what was already there—a realization of potential, to which nothing could be added. These portrayals are quite unlike in quality what had been developed in the Near East in previous millennia where the portrayal of the human form reflected the oriental absolutism that loomed so large in Hegel's *The Philosophy of History*. The pre-Greek oriental civilizations were hierarchical sacred societies culminating in a god-king or a divinely ordained steward of a sacred order. The principal personages are shown in a larger scale than others, and this sizing reflects the difference in importance in a world order. Common people and slaves are shown small and undifferentiated. Conventions of portrayal became rigidly established and individuality is lacking or minimal. (An exception is to be found in some of the sculptures from the Old Kingdom in Egypt which had considerable individual force, but in the high imperial period in the first two millennia before Christ the portrayals usually had so little individuality that one needed only to change the accompanying royal cartouches to change whom figures portrayed.) Hegel's *The Philosophy of History* may be as much of a phantasmagoria as its detractors have made it out to be in its particulars. However, when Hegel stated the Geist of the ancient Orient to be that it "knew that only one was free," he came close to the key fact about those civilizations. The Gentile cultures were, however, very different and (to quote Hegel again) "some were free" and the art reflected this fact. At its apogee the human form is apotheosized and the divine form is humanized. This continued into the Alexandrian period. The Venus of Milo (ca. 300 B.C.) and the Nike of Samothrace (306 B.C.), as well as lesser pieces like the Medici Venus and the Apollo Belvedere, still show this overriding preoccupation with the contained, beautiful body. This held for portraiture too. At its best

---

any further than saying that Aristotle considered the principal function of the brain to be the cooling of the body and said that it acted as a still when one had produced too many humors from drinking too much? When they rose from the stomach and reached the brain they were condensed to phlegm and drained out of the nose?) This was pretty typical of ancient understandings of such matters. However, where a phenomenon could be understood in mechanical terms, rather than through processes that had to be conceptualized in chemical terms, the ancients did quite well. Their bad physiology is not surprising if one considers that the two founders of modern chemistry, Lavoisier and Avogadro, were not born until 1743 and 1776.

there was the same deifying character, but even the Roman sculptures that come around the turn of the Christian era still show a
respect for personality. It was not an accident that Egyptian sculpture shows only a minority of portraits of identifiable people. In
a brief period of naturalism in Egyptian art under Ikhnaton
(1357 B.C.) sculptors showed a capability in handling personality
that resulted in the famous portrait head of Ikhnaton's wife, Nefre-
tete. Many odd pieces from the much earlier Old Kingdom also
suggest that they had the skill to portray the human form natural-
istically and to convey individual personality when they wished to
(e.g., the figure of Mycerinus ca. 2500 B.C. in the Boston Museum
of Fine Arts). Their culture by and large did not place value upon
personality in the same terms as Greek and republican Roman cultures did. However, to return to classical sculpture, discordant elements began to appear in the first century of the Christian era.
First, there was endless copying of earlier work of a high quality
but not always in a manner that was sympathetic. Bronzes were
copied in marble and marbles were copied in bronze. (Hence the
awkward tree trunks attached to legs. This often, but not always,
indicates a marble copy of a bronze.) Scale was ignored—even the
old rule that a piece of art work should be neither slightly smaller
nor slightly larger than life-size was ignored—and, worst of all,
large pieces were reduced in size.[4] Sometimes, indeed often, the
copying was just plain clumsy. Fashionable taste may still have
placed great value upon earlier work, but the impetus to create
first-class original work within these aesthetic canons was lost. The
great museum of antiquities in Naples has several rooms of big intact sculptures that were mined from Pompeii and Herculaneum
where they had been buried with the eruption of Vesuvius in
A.D. 79. Curious things begin to happen with much of this work.
First of all there is no loss of a knowledge of anatomy—the muscles
are still all there so to speak—but what is lost is a certain sympathetic, graceful understanding of the way the body worked. The
sculptures are often huge and cluttered with a loss of relative scale
from one element in the work to another. There is a big clumsy
piece known as the Farnese Bull[5] showing Dirce being tied to a
bull by the sons of Antiope. The scale is so inept that it is difficult
to escape the impression that the puny bull was more in need of

[4] Despite a long period of study as a sculptor I still do not understand why violating such rules of scale causes trouble, but I find the results are disturbing. It
may be that I was taught to think so.
[5] The work of the brothers Apollonios and Tauriscus of Tralles (Rhodes fl. ca.
second century B.C.).

protection than Dirce. Another shows a confused scene of what looks like gladiators fighting—they are big clumsy things. One finds a similar dreary procession in Rome in the Museo Vaticano and in the National Museum built into the Baths of Diocletian. Occasionally one finds isolated splendid originals such as those by Apollonios the Athenian, the seated bronze pugilist dug up by Mommsen in the nineteenth century, now in the National Museum in Rome, and the Belvedere torso in the Vatican. John Canaday has, however, described the pugilist as "a muscle man who was half brute" and has said that if his "body symbolizes anything it may be the eventual defeat of the human spirit through the buffeting of forces beyond its comprehension." By and large, however, what seems good imitates older Greek styles.

This repetitious period lasted for perhaps two centuries into the Christian era. Deterioration in quality became even greater in public monuments after the death of Caesar Augustus in A.D. 14 and was virtually complete within a century. Hadrian's column (circa A.D. 135) and the Arch of Titus (circa A.D. 90) show a process almost complete and by the time of the Arch of Constantine the figures are puny, clumsy, and crowded (A.D. 325). There are odd pieces of high-quality work such as the equestrian statue of Marcus Antoninus (Aurelius) from about A.D. 120 that is now on the Campidoglio, but the sense of a real concern with a contained, apotheosized person, the God in man, is not in any of this work. When we regard it as good it is for a different reason.[6]

Why did a style that portrayed the human body so sympathetically undergo this deterioration? It should, of course, be clear that I have only selected here one line of development—ancient sculpture of the Greco-Roman world—and have ignored everything else of the same period. An art historian may point out that as this style was dying superb Byzantine forms were evolving, but they were tied to Christian belief and hagiography. The precise point is that this Christian culture never could be articulated to the ethos of classical stylistic forms. Intellectuals as well as artists during the Italian Renaissance recognized a pagan culture that was different from Christian culture even though they saw it as coequal rather than anathema, unlike their earlier forebears. In the great Ducal Palace in Urbino there are two studies with intricately inlaid woodwork, masterpieces of the cabinetmakers' craft. In one there is only Christian imagery and in the other only pagan imagery. One

---

[6] Late Roman portraits remain highly proficient attempts to record faces, but one must ask whom these faces show—propertied people.

is dedicated to the muses of the Christian world, the other to the ancient world. Christianity, as many before me have noted, arose in opposition to the mainstreams of culture of the ancient world, both Gentile and Oriental. It has in fact been argued by H. Richard Niebuhr in *Christ and Culture* that there remains a mode of thinking about the Gospels and Pauline exegeses that emphasizes this separation from the possibility of secular life. The central fact of this thinking about man is that he not only is unperfectible in the flesh, but degraded in it. God does not enter into the world to enjoy its pleasures, but as a brief Incarnation to reveal both what God has intended man to be like and what will spare man from an eventual show of his wrath. An artistic tradition that places the fleshly human body as its central concern is ill adapted to express a thinking that sees the flesh as shameful and transitory.

However, such "decline and fall of the Roman Empire" reasoning about the growth in the later ancient world in terms of a Christian mentality that could not be articulated to Gentile pagan culture and institutions considers only a small part of the cultural changes that took place. Much attention has been given to the fact that the Romans proselytized the artistic and intellectual culture of the Gentile world, but curiously little, in popular thinking at least, has been given to the extent to which this world itself became orientalized in the process, although this is well known even to dilettantes. Probably the crucial reasons lie in political adaptations to demographic factors. Imperial rulers sooner or later consider their subject people as citizens, particularly when they need a soldiery. Legal distinctions can still be made among individuals, but they are made upon the basis of servitude, caste, class, and estate, and not on the basis of race or ethnicity. I cannot think of a single case of a settled encompassing empire that did not universalize citizenship if it lasted at all. It is not relevant here to go into the dynamics of the process. Once the political decision is made it has a demographic consequence, which is that people begin to move about freely. With the now-free movement the whilom subjects, now citizens, carry their culture with them. They, in turn, actually begin to diffuse their culture into the politically dominant one. The Greco-Roman world became orientalized in the sense that Gentile culture was buffeted by an uncounted number of Oriental cultures and cults which placed a minimal value upon personality. Perhaps the central difference lay in what started this discussion—only one was free. The individual was disvalued. Slaves became a larger and larger portion of the population. Slavery was omnipresent not only as a domestic institution (as it had been through classical Greece and republican Rome), but also as a large-scale public institution serving the needs of the state for large-scale public works. This latter aspect, of course, had been dominant in the ancient Near East. Moreover, the Roman world was big and technical exigencies of bigness always result in a disvaluing of personality. The Oriental cultures had encompassed big societies and their institutions allowed for little individual expression. The decisive concession to such forces came when Constantine the Great moved the Imperial capital to Byzantium because even by A.D. 325 republican institutions were still strong enough in Rome to be a nuisance to the complete absolutism that he sought. Juvenal's complaint of 150 years before had come to pass—"The Tigris and Euphrates [had] backed their waters into the Tiber" (l. 60, Satire 2).

There are many other cases where art forms have deteriorated when the artists could no longer express the principal system of meanings underlying the society in which they lived. A similar analysis, for instance, can be made about Gothic architecture as it is shown in the great churches. There was really never any deterioration of the Gothic style from a technical standpoint, but after the virtual stop of work on the great duomo in Milan in the fifteenth century, no more churches of any unassailable artistic consequence were to be built purely in this style. A great number of finely built edifices were to be put up late in the nineteenth and in the early twentieth centuries in this style in the United States and Canada, and Viollet-le-Duc (1814–1879) was to do substantial restorations and rebuildings in France, but however refined this work was with respect to craftsmanship, one senses that the iron and cable bridges better express nineteenth-century culture. Little has been said for the Cathedral Church of Saint John the Divine in New York City other than that it is longer even if not bigger than Saint Peter's in Rome, but one is hard put to find much else to say for it. It stands still unfinished and it seems likely to remain so, more because point rather than money is lacking for its completion.[7] That now dowdy old girl, the Brooklyn Bridge, better expresses the best of the industrial ethos. While Saint John's remains an unfinished sanctuary, the graceful elegance of the George Washington and Verrazano Narrows bridges testifies that the Roeblings were more with it than the Episcopal bishops. The neo-Gothic churches were for sober citizens who wanted to be properly buried

---

[7] The Protestant Episcopal bishops of New York go hot and cold on this subject. As of 1970 the bishop did not think it should be finished as long as the surrounding community remained in decay; as of 1981 his successor felt it should be finished to proclaim the permanence of faith.

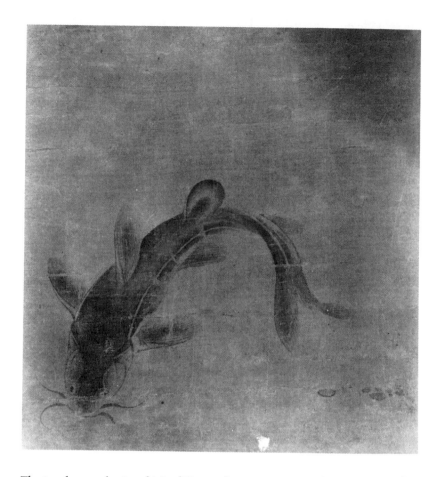

The toughness of a taught tradition and nature as a transient moving order.
6   *Catfish*, fragment of an early Sung painting, attributed to Lai-an.
7   *Fish*, Laian (?), Early Ming.

It is relatively easy to find examples of fish in motion in Chinese paintings; fish in still life, *nature mort*, are much harder to locate. Posed compositions of pots, flowers, and eatables, which form a separate genre of painting in Western art from the seventeenth century to the present, are relatively rare. William Merritt Chase's fish (fig. 11) are taken from the order of live, transient things. Drawings made by Weng Ch'ing-fang (1900–1958) show that the Chinese are still interested in drawing convincing fish in motion. The time between these two pictures is a good 300 years. The similar treatment can be explained in part in terms of carefully taught conventions, but not entirely; that explanation fails to tell why artists remained interested in painting fish in their live state rather than ready to be cooked. The fish are a powerful, mobile aspect of nature; they elude being caught; they are part of a perpetual flux.

Courtesy, Fogg Art Museum, Harvard University, Gift of D. W. Ross and courtesy, Museum of Fine Arts, Boston. Bigelow Collection.

in blue serge suits, the bridges were for people who wanted to get quickly from one place to another.

What succeeded the Gothic style was substantially less sophisticated from an engineering standpoint. The Renaissance style went back to the basilica form in which the weight of the roof was carried by thick outer walls and a pair of inner walls that sometimes— in fact, usually—could be reduced to a pair of rows of columns. The roof was supported by spans of large beams that were sometimes disguised decoratively by coffering; otherwise arches and barrel vaults were used. In either case it was necessary for the walls to be very thick to bear the weight in the absence of the buttresses of the Gothic style which carried stresses away from the walls of the building and opened large areas for windows which could be filled with dazzling, luminous stained glass. The basilica was, in fact, a late Roman form in which the outer row of columns and inner solid wall of the temple had been transposed. There was no exercise of the ingenuity that made it possible for the great mason-architects of the medieval period to enclose large spaces with relatively light structures. Renaissance architects turned to thick walls made of brick or rubble aggregate faced with stucco or more expensive stone.

Why was the Gothic style abandoned by the best artists and educated laymen—to such an extent that Voltaire, writing in the eighteenth century, described the great Gothic churches as "barbare"? The answer may be found implicitly in Otto von Simson in his *Gothic Cathedrals*. He speaks of the medieval idea of mystical light and shows churches had to express an ideology that saw religion as something that transports man in a mystical union with the Deity. In contrast, the greatest of the Renaissance churches, in size and perhaps even artistically as well, Saint Peter's, has been criticized for its lack of religious feeling and has been called a church where it is impossible to pray.

The reason for the eclipse of the Gothic style seems to lie in the changes in the European ethos that made things significant to man that hardly interested people of the Middle Ages. Suddenly nature and the world came again to be important. The artist began to study the minute aspects of nature, concerns that medieval intellectuals found to be trivial, if not actually contemptible when placed beside glorious, beatific visions. Medieval intellectuals were obsessed with a prolix mystical hierarchy. It was labyrinthine, even disorderly, in detail. The rich texture of its world view was lost in the early fifteenth century, and the Renaissance was to bring back a world of coldly observed, rationally ordered detail. One thing that is striking about much of this new work is its precision and order, a particularly striking feature in architecture. It is true that Gothic churches were laid out square and true in most cases, but this never becomes the obtrusive fact that appears for the next two centuries in San Lorenzo in Florence, and the Palazzo Farnese and Bramante's Tempietto in Rome, in Santa Maria della Salute in Venice, and in buildings throughout Europe in Palladian styles. (And let us not forget that English wonder, Saint Paul's in London.)

Another thing came to be important: the idea of the perfectibility of man. To medieval thinking, man could not transcend earthly depravity and misery; he could only wait in fear and trembling. To this must be contrasted what Jakob Burckhardt called the idea of fame—*fama*. To achieve it man had to transcend the chronic fear and misery that the medieval man saw as the central fact of the human condition. The Renaissance man was above all skillful, handsome, intelligent, and unafraid of the future. He was a figure against the sky and stood out clearly as Raphael and Michelangelo were to see him. *Fama* was the ideal portrayed by Raphael in the School of Athens and by Michelangelo in the brooding figures of Lorenzo and Giuliano in the Medici tombs as well as in the idealized portrait of Julius II as Moses that is now in San Pietro in Vincoli in Rome. We know what each of these men actually looked like from other portrayals. Giuliano della Rovere (later Julius II) appears as a toothless old man with two sinister looking nephews mincing beside him in Titian's *Julius II and His Nephews*. The busts of the Medicis in the Bargello show misleadingly pleasant, bourgeois Italian faces; neither shows any hint of the brooding supermen of the tombs or the Moses. Renaissance artists sought inspiration from antique architecture and sculpture because it could express Renaissance ideology; the symbols and abstractions of Gothic art expressed only a subjective ideal world quite foreign to most of the concerns with the secular condition of man to which the best minds had now turned. However, in the simplest possible terms, by the end of the fourteenth century there were underlying intellectual and social changes which made Europe ripe for a new style. There had been adumbrations of this even in Dante (1265–1321). We must not forget that although Dante wrote *The Divine Comedy*, which we think of as containing an epitome of the medieval image of the cosmos, he also wrote the *De Monarchia* and the *Convivio*, which wrestled squarely with the problems of contention and disorder that beset his world because of an egregious inability to maintain stability in the face of internal social stresses. European man was ready for a new ideology and intellectual system and a new set of symbols.

But how does the ability, the techniques to effect these new meanings arise and how is it possible for the artist to achieve this? It comes through that isolating process that we may term the professionalization of art.

## BACKGROUND NOTE

The playing out of styles can be found in the histories of any art form. Any first-class textbook in art history reveals such tendencies. My own favorite remains Helen Gardner's *Art Through the Ages*, 6th ed. (New York: Harcourt Brace Jovanovich, 1975) rev. Horst de la Croix and Richard G. Tansey, even if perhaps a little too much was left out. Better still are specialized histories that focus on particular styles. In some of these cases a good scholarly "picture-book" tells the story. For the sculpture of the Gentile ancient world, one may look at Charles Picard, *La Sculpture Antique de Phidias à l' Ere Byzantine* (Paris: Laurens, 1926) and Georg Heinrich Karo, *Greek Personality in Archaic Sculpture* (Cambridge, Mass.: Harvard University Press, 1948). The background on the orientalization of Rome was first laid out in Edward Gibbon, *The Decline and Fall of the Roman Empire*, and more recently (and more manageably for the contemporary reader) in Mikhail Rostovtsev, *A History of the Ancient World* (Oxford: Clarendon Press, 1926), where there is considerable awareness of the orientalization of Gentile culture. The process is seen completed in Henri Pirenne, *Mohammed and Charlemagne* (New York: Barnes and Noble, 1951). There is an embarrassment of riches on the decline of the medieval world and Gothic art. The presentations closest to the viewpoint of the present study are Otto Georg von Simson, *The Gothic Cathedral; the Origins of Gothic Architecture and the Concept of Order* (New York: Pantheon, 1965), and George Lesser, *Gothic Cathedrals Sacred Geometry* (New York: Pantheon, 1965), Erwin Panofsky, *Gothic Architecture and Scholasticism* (New York: University Publishers, 1951) and John H. Harvey, *The Gothic World, A Survey of Architecture and Art* (London and New York: Batesford, 1950). The attempt to revive the Gothic style in the face of the intransigent fact of industrialism can be seen in Augustus W. N. Pugin's *Apology for the Revival of Christian Architecture in England* (London, 1882; reprint ed., London: Blackwell, 1969). Sir Kenneth Clark gives his own view in *The Gothic Revival: An Essay in the History of Taste* (New York: Holt, Rinehart and Winston, 1962). The story of why the Gothic ideology and its styles no longer expressed important meanings (even by the end of the Middle Ages) can be found in Barbara Tuchman, *A Distant Mirror: The Calamitous Fourteenth Century* (New York: Knopf, 1976), whose "high" culture is shown in Johan Huizinga's *The Waning of the Middle Ages: A Study of the Forms of Life, Thought, and Art in France and the Netherlands in the XIV and XV Centuries* (London: Allen and Unwin, 1970).

# 5

## The Professionalization of Art:

## Isolation and Technology

ART always becomes professionalized. This is true even in primitive societies, where the professionalization of anything is minimal. There are always some people who are artistically skillful in the sense of being able to practice learned artistic techniques, even when they are not recognized as occupations separate from the priest, the craftsman, and what would be termed the professional man in a society with an advanced division of labor. (Even in the single case of a high level society, Imperial China, where artists were usually primarily scholars, there was substantial technical practice involved.)[1] There are reams of Rousseau-like nonsense about the pristine simplicity of primitive art. I cannot think of a single instance where I have seen such art described as simple by academically recognized ethnographers, and close study usually shows it to be very complex. Much, for example, can be made of the spontaneity of Navaho sand paintings and chanting that goes with a three-day "sing" for healing purposes. The late Clyde Kluckhohn, however, described such an affair as "a feat of memory comparable to memorizing the whole Ring Cycle including the stage business and the details of the sets." In the case of settled, highly developed civilizations the trained character of the work of the artist is always apparent. It seems

[1] The man of "total culture" among the Chinese literati knew his classics verbatim, and his skills in calligraphy and drawing were developed to a point where they could convey a quality appropriate to whatever his texts sought to express.

primitive only because the techniques do not express subtleties we recognize.

A second generalization emerges where we have historical data about artists. Those who prove interesting to posterity very often are ahead of both their immediate clients and the wider public. It is best to start with an example. When the late Igor Stravinsky told the journalist Mike Wallace in a television interview that he had always known what people were going to want before they were aware of it themselves, he made a boast that many major artists could make about some of their work. (Sometimes, of course, it is difficult to tell when such claims are boasting and when they are complaining. Stravinsky did not seem to be doing either.) Turner painted a great number of almost abstract dawn scenes for his own satisfaction, which he never tried to sell. Cézanne, who had the advantage of being well-to-do, settled down quietly at Aix-en-Provence to become the greatest painter of the last hundred years (in the opinion of most critics). Whistler was also ahead of most of his contemporaries but did not settle down quietly. (He liked a fight so much that he sued Ruskin for slander. He collected a shilling and wore it as a watch fob. Although Whistler had been slandered it is not clear to me that he had been much damaged, even though he did have to go bankrupt to pay the court costs. His English property was inconsiderable, his capital—his talent and reputation—remained intact, and his move to Paris does not seem to have affected his fashionable life style.) Had public opinion affected their work, it is probable that they would have been lesser artists. Unfortunately, not every quiet, seeming nonentity is a Cézanne, nor is every colorful West Point dropout a Whistler; it is the work itself that has to speak to the future.

It seems wise before considering the isolation of the professionalization of art to dispose of an old canard quickly and with as little attention as it deserves: that great artist's art always is spurned in the world in which it is produced. The record shows that it is rarely spurned completely by other professionals, and is appreciated by at least a few laymen. Not a single artist of consequence from Giotto to Charles Ives lacked a coterie of connoisseurs among his fellows and laymen who thought that his work was good. This is not unexpected when analyzed, even in terms of the simplest textbook psychology. No one will continue, barring conditions of neurotic compulsion, in any activity that does not bring some response from others. There is another point to be considered. In some fields the production of great art requires big commissions and access to costly resources for execution. For example, nearly everything, perhaps all, that Michelangelo did as an architect survives and we know for that reason that he was an architect of considerable power. But nothing whatever of Leonardo da Vinci's work in this medium is extant other than what we see in his notebook sketches and we cannot even make an outside guess of what his powers in this field may have been from these, even though he understood the technical aspects of construction as well as anyone of his time.[2] However, we can quote a critical consensus that in one case one man is a great architect, in the other case we can only say that he probably would have been a good architect because he was good at everything else he tried—but this is a pretty weak assumption. Similarly Thomas Hart Benton had enough commissions as a muralist for us to judge that he had substantial powers in this direction; nothing can be said about Grant Wood on this matter because he died when still a young man (at 46) and never had a commission to do a mural as far as I have been able to determine. Earlier mention was made of Croce's dictum that art is expression; it is not intention or talent.

Earlier we asked how professionalization evolves and began with the fairly obvious point that frequently the work of an artist goes ahead of the taste of his clientele and often even sets its standards. A simple recurrent process appears to operate here: artists and craftsmen seem to engage in technical play for its own sake without reference to what is being done around them or what has been demonstrated to provide a living; moreover, familiarity brings a perception of new problems. As they learn their crafts they come to do things better than they would need to if they were only working for the overwhelming majority of their clients. The first chapter mentioned segmental autonomy as inherent in the very process of professionalization and a simple implication is that the most important audience[3] to the professional in any field is other professionals who speak not to the world at large but, for the most part, to other professionals. Just what variables determine the way professions develop in the arts?

The first determinants and limitations in the artistic output of any era lie in its technology. No art form can ever achieve things that do not lie within technological possibilities that are extant or easily obtainable. To start with as simple an example as possible let us take the carving of stone sculptures. Except for sandstone

[2] I am not considering the fortress at Milan, parts of which may be his, as an attempt to produce artistically significant work. The guesses about work at Romantin, France, seem farfetched to me.

[3] The term "reference group" is the term in social psychology.

and soapstone—which, by and large, do not have surfaces elegant
to the touch or eye—one cannot do large amounts of very refined
work unless a metallurgy has been developed to permit the production of tempered cutting tools sharp enough to cut and tough
enough to take impact. One exception is very ancient work in the
East where sculptures were produced by abrasion, but it is perhaps
all too easy to forget that when the quantity that survives is related
to the millennial time spans in which they were produced there is
not really much. Similarly one must develop enough skill in using
abrasives to make it possible to achieve finely polished surfaces
when wanted. Whatever the artistic merits of Michelangelo's Pietà
are—and it is not every man in his twenties who can turn out
work of this quality—there is one respect in which it is interesting
with regard to technique; its creator was experimenting with trying
to revive the ancient art of polishing marble. Marble, if properly
polished, allows light to penetrate below the surface. It is then reflected outward as it encounters the crystals of the stone, creating
an effect of luminosity, a technical feat whose achievement entailed
a minute knowledge of the character of the stone. The use of
marble that became the fashion among those who followed Michelangelo was possible only because he rediscovered this technique.

In music as well, the effect of technology is ubiquitous in creating possibilities for the development of the art forms. Let us look
at the evolution of the modern violin after the middle of the sixteenth century. The first great maker of the Cremona School was
Andrea Amati who was born before 1511 and died before 1580. His
first extant violin is dated 1564. His sons were Antonio (ca. 1540–?)
and Girolamo (1561–1630), the father of Nicolo or Nicola (1596–
1684), who taught Antonio Stradivarius. The last great maker in
the family was Nicolo's son, Girolamo (1649–1740). The Stradivari
(Stradivarius) family comes to notice as makers of violins with
Antonio (1644–1737), and his sons Francesco (1671–1743) and
Omobono (1679–1742). The Guarneri overlap both families.
(Pietro) Andrea (ca. 1626–1698), the first of note, was a pupil of
Nicolo Amati. His sons were Giuseppe Giovanni Battista (ca. 1666–
1739 or 40) and Pietro Giovanni (1695–1762). Giuseppe was the
father of Pietro (1695–1762). The greatest of this family was
(Bartolomeo) Giuseppe (del Jesu) (1698–1744), who was the grand-
son of Pietro Andrea. The time span itself is interesting. After
Andrea Amati and his sons worked out a substantially modern violin, the development and perfection of the instrument was achieved
before 1750. (We may dismiss the idea that no fine instruments

have since been made. Enough is known about the construction[4] of the old violins to have allowed major craftsmen to make good bowed string instruments since, but they are produced in such minute numbers that their prices are high. However, the development of all later string music depended upon the type of instrument perfected by the earlier makers.)

The most common bowed string instrument that preceded the violin was a viol. It is an instrument with a much mellower sound than a violin, but it is ill suited to fill a large hall and cannot carry the melody with the clear force that we expect from a good violin. The violin can not only provide mellowness when it is wanted; it also offers the possibility of carrying the melody strongly and presents a dynamic range that makes possible displays of virtuosity that would have been impossible for earlier performers. Such features gave composers an easy instrument to use for carrying the melody in combination with other instruments of the modern string sections which were perfected at the same time as the violin by the same craftsmen. The modern orchestra, with its overwhelming dependence on strings, became a distinct technical possibility. Bach and Handel, both of whom were born in 1685 and died within the 1750s (1750 and 1759), were in fact the last great composers to make any extensive use of harpsichords in symphonic music.[5] (Harpsichords were used as chamber instruments until the end of the eighteenth century.) By the last part of the eighteenth century the string-based symphonic form was quite well established and that could not have happened without the modern violin. Classicism gave way to romanticism in the nineteenth century and, along with big noisy orchestras that could fill large halls with sound, great ingenuity began to be exercised in creating woodwinds and brasses that could render subtleties of tone far beyond any previous possibilities. At the start of the nineteenth century orchestras became huge by earlier standards and were able to play richly toned complex pieces. Big opera houses and concert halls were built to accommodate them in the great capitals and in smaller places throughout Europe and the new world. The same big houses that were built for concert performances made it possible to stage ballet on a scale that would have been impossible in the smaller and often tiny theaters of the immediately earlier period. Operating in all of these cases was an interplay of art and technology—the develop-

---

[4] Lately the physics as well has been understood.
[5] The use of a harpsichord for continuo in recitativo in opera continued until well into the nineteenth century.

ment of the art demanded a more complex technology and the more complex technology made possible more complex art forms. (And I have not even dared to mention in this context the development of grand operas with complex staging and large casts that has continued almost unabated since Mozart.)

Let us consider briefly a form that is almost peculiarly American in its development: the skyscraper. Many very tall structures have been built without steel framing. Gothic churches with interiors that accommodate several floors along a lofty aisle are common, but their great height was achieved by a complex system of flying buttresses that made the land area these churches took up greater than the spaces they enclosed. The system allowed a great deal of light to enter but in terms of the space they needed, these churches were no more economical than the mortar-faced aggregate structures of the Romans and the Renaissance, which achieved their height with a tapering wall on a huge base. It was well into the nineteenth century before the problem of building a tall building that did not use large amounts of ground space was solved. Saint Peter's in Rome and Saint Paul's in London do indeed have domes that go to commanding heights but they are accomplished in both cases by the support of massive piers. The problem of building a light, tall, thin-based structure was simply not within the range of practical technology prior to the nineteenth century. Such a development was made possible at the end of the eighteenth century because of the manufacture of cheap architectural members of iron. Eugène Viollet-le-Duc in his *Entretiens sur l'Architecture* of 1863–1872 (Paris) devoted considerable space to the possibility of ornamental cast iron. It is no surprise that his antiquarian interests were reflected in the work it influenced. The buildings were at first simply fanciful productions of iron in which the ornamentation was cast integrally with the structural members, resulting in forms as diverse as the dome of the National Capitol in Washington (which is held down and together by gargantuan nuts and bolts) and graceful structures like the Crystal Palace (1865) in London and the now destroyed Horticultural Hall (1876) in Philadelphia. This form gained validity in 1889 when Alexandre Gustave Eiffel (1832–1923) built his tower for the Paris Exposition of 1879. A laboratory was placed in the lantern at its top, but the main reason for the building seems to have been whimsical and patriotic—to show that it could be done and that Frenchmen could do it. It is an open graceful affair that proves startlingly big when one actually gets under it—it is on a square of 336 feet and is 900 feet high. However, the possibility of putting in floors and walls existed from the very first.

It showed that a very tall building could be built of prefabricated iron beams. (John Roebling had already developed the good steel cables that long elevators require.)

It is not surprising that for a considerable time the Eiffel Tower remained as nothing more than an example to the world of the ingenuity of French engineering. Aesthetic considerations prevented a more utilitarian use being made of the skyscraper form in European cities which usually have skylines with identifiable landmarks that local sentiment cherishes. Building high-rise structures in these settings would have been very unpopular (and it still is).[6] The obvious place, however, to use this technique was in New York from the early part of this century onward. In the nineteenth century the real locus of power in the United States was New York City, so much so that Alexis de Tocqueville in *Democracy in America* spoke of "the capital in New York." The money that was raised there expanded the economy and it was there that the wheeling and dealing in economic and political power went on as a not-at-all-gentlemanly upper-class game. Unfortunately, it all took place in a space of Manhattan Island considerably smaller than a Middlesex village. (The entire Manhattan Island covers only twenty-two square miles.) Competition for space became so intense that it could only be expanded by building upward. At that time—the period before World War II—we had not yet developed the complex system for the communication of business data that made it far less important that all the upper executive personnel for any given enterprise work in one place. Economic incentives for intensive use of ground space were substantial. It was inevitable that the skyscraper form would be developed if the technology for it existed, and it did—in the books. At first architects simply elongated the decorative features of Gothic cathedrals, classical temples, and Renaissance palazzos (e.g., the old Times Building and the Woolworth Tower), but gradually it became apparent that the structures themselves required a new aesthetic, and beginning in the middle 1920s architects developed decorations for these structures that seemed more "natural" to their construction. By the 1960s and '70s this process was complete and the use of ornamental masonry had disappeared.[7]

[6] There was considerable opposition to building the Eiffel Tower itself for this reason.

[7] It may be possible to argue that the Immigration Act of 1924 stopped the entrance of skilled artisans, but the fact remains that masonry decoration and sculpture were used until World War II, despite the shortage of skilled men. What seems more likely is that the materials used and the styles rendered such embellishments discordant.

At that time a style reached its apogee that had been well started in such great works of forty years before as the Philadelphia Saving Fund Society Building, the Empire State Building, the Chrysler Building, the Chanin Building, and the Rockefeller Center complex. Even the masonry and brick facings that covered (without really hiding) the frames of these earlier structures had given way to vast expanses of glass. By that time the style had taken on an autonomy that was independent of functional needs, but if it served any subjective purpose at all it was to show that owners and architects alike were confronting, if not brash. However, the evolution of this style simply would not have been possible in the context of the technology that existed prior to the working out of the engineering problems entailed in steel-frame construction in the 1880s and '90s. Such examples of aesthetics following engineering can be multiplied endlessly and can even be documented in antiquity (one would need only to look into how the Romans learned about enclosing large interior spaces through the development of the arch and barrel vault).

There is a consequence to the development of technique on a professionalized level. The artist and craftsman become interested in technique for its own sake and so become interested in the formal aspects of art without reference to a lay clientele's ability to understand it. The consequence of this is that a segment, perhaps a very large segment, of the oeuvre of any given period becomes utterly incomprehensible to the majority of laymen as well as to professionals who are out of the avant-garde of the creative arts. From Bach and Handel, to Bartók and Ives, and through to composers who arose after World War II such as Anhalt, Cage, and Piston, much music has been caviar to the general. In music too there was the ostensibly absolute exploitation of all the artistic possibilities within the context of the technology through which it is expressed.

Another example of the playing out of technique is the progressive complexity that the symphonic form developed after 1800. Beethoven, Berlioz, Schubert, Schumann, Brahms, and, later, Bruchner and Mahler introduced a complexity to this form that went beyond anything dreamed of in the eighteenth century. Wagner and Verdi (in his later operas) showed the same interest in developing the aesthetic and technical resources of the orchestra. By the first decades of this century Stravinsky was to carry it to an unbelievable level of complexity in his big three—*The Rite of Spring, Firebird,* and *Petrushka* (after which he wrote no more important pieces for big orchestras for over a quarter of a century).

The same process can be seen in painting. The attempt on the part of Turner to portray the light of the dying day had led him to a general interest in the problem of capturing the quality of light on canvas. At the time he was doing his best-known canvases he painted scores of scenes in the inchoate, evanescent light of daybreak for his own satisfaction. Later in the century Whistler showed a preoccupation with similar problems with his "Nocturnes." The work of Monet, Renoir, Sisley, Cassatt, and Henri continued the interest in light. Cézanne, who was greater than any of them, tried to hold the fort on architectonic form, and it was ultimately no accident that his influence led straight to Cubism. But Impressionism was the dominant tendency within modern art. The movement that it exemplified was to break up in the work of Jackson Pollock and other abstract expressionists in the second third of this century. These men went as far as they could go in freeing themselves from the conventions of "block-built" architectonic painting.

We sense that the utter breakdowns of form and structure in painting and in much of music as well are related. There is no doubt that the lush, richly colored, but often strident form that orchestral music assumed after the turn of the century came because "conservatory" classicism was played out technically and artistically. The visual arts show the same breakdown of form into a chaotic stridency of Abstract Expressionism on the one hand and the almost chaste images of Surrealism and Suprematism on the other—each in different ways was a breakdown of architectonically structured forms. The technical possibilities for variation had been exploited as far as possible. There may, however, be an explanation that is far more important than the playing out of form and aesthetic. It is this: the best art has always been "ghost written," not in the sense that it has been written by one person for another, but in the sense that each age has its own meanings, its own cues, and its own insistent things that have to be said. The best artists sensed things more deeply and earlier than the rest of us. The most interesting perhaps only differ from the mediocrities in that they see more and express their feelings with greater clarity. It is no accident that much modern art including our music reminds one of a cat fight. The phenomenological aspects of much of our daily lives often indeed suggest cat fights—growling confrontations, strident climacteric moments, and the nervous calms of Pyrrhic victories.

This "ghost writing" can be seen also in other forms and in other places and times. Perhaps the most obvious historical case lies in the novel. Solzhenitsyn was not the only Russian literary man to wonder what that strange collectivity known as the state did to the human spirit. Tolstoi and Turgenev saw it and perhaps Dostoevski's novels make everything that his contemporaries said superficial.[8] In central Europe Kafka saw the same callous mindlessness that forced him to write about certain things—about the insularity of power in *The Castle;* about the sense of being judged for who knows what in *The Trial;* about the crushing of a sensitive man by a hooliganish Umwelt in *Metamorphosis.* In America, Steinbeck, Dreiser, and a score of others told their own tales of degradation because the stories compelled themselves to be told. No writers of feeling could ignore what they saw about their era. In our own time novelists are still telling what the Second World War did in creating a world in which the Nazis may have been the victors. They have hardly started to talk about Indochina.

One must hasten to add, however, that the message that must be heard or seen is not necessarily one that arises from weariness, gloom, disillusionment, and degradation. Sometimes it has been a new perception of life that is essentially optimistic. When the great Impressionists got out into the sun from the burnt sienna and black shadows of the nineteenth-century studio they presented a joyous celebration of sunlight, the fresh greens of spring, and clean blue streams of the countryside; pretty women in colorful gowns and picture hats; young mothers with babies promenading along the boulevards; lively beer gardens and bistros. As Beethoven put it in the introduction to the chorale of his Ninth Symphony— "O Freunde, nicht diese Töne! Sondern lasst uns angenehmere anstimmen und freudenvollere" (Oh friends not these tones, but let us sound a note more pleasant and full of joy). And this is what they did—they went on to sing more joyous songs. Post-Napoleonic Europe looked as though it were only a matter of time before it would be the best of all possible worlds, and, indeed, everything did seem to be happening for the best—if one did not look too closely.

The art forms have arisen out of the necessity of the Zeitgeist and technique has evolved to express it in the cases I have considered here, but I should mention that even the skyscrapers that seem to be so much an emergence of economic factors are an assertion of personality and culture. It has been said that skyscrapers really do more to satisfy the vanity of architects and clients than to save ground space. Indeed, they have often been uneconomical, impractical, and unjustified by space needs. The nature of Western

[8] Tolstoi's dates were 1828–1910; Turgenev's, 1818–1883; Dostoevski's, 1821–1881.

ethos leads to a confrontation with nature, and that is precisely what the tall building represents. Compare this with the Japanese and Chinese aesthetic that tries to make structures emerge from the earth almost insensibly and insists that the Tao of the site be observed.

One more consideration must be mentioned. Technological advancements often precede art forms and their adoption by artists is not necessarily immediate. The grinding of pigments in oil and adding a drier to help the oil set seems to have been evolved fully by the twelfth century. Painting in oil was a particularly good technique where one wanted to make subtle, delicate changes after the pigment was on the canvas.[9] The technique was so little used that Giorgio Vasari thought that it had been invented by Jan van Eyck (1390–1440). What seems to have brought oil into use was that the effects artists wanted to portray were more easily obtained by using oil as a medium. They wanted to portray live men with shifting expressions rather than the personifications of religious abstractions that had characterized medieval and Byzantine painting. Painters and clients alike wanted the luminous, glazed effects that could not really be easily attained in tempera.[10] The techniques by which painters portray such effects is not germane to this discussion, which is meant to be mainly sociological; however, the reasons *why* Renaissance artists wanted such effects is. People began to want an art that conveyed nature with a sense of the liveness of things. It is true that it can be done with tempera, but it is easier with oil. Whether it can be done as well with tempera is a moot point, as few major artists have tried. Later, as painting moved into the breakup of discrete forms into abstract patches of color applied impasto[11] oil paints were still used because they were thick and had body enough to give rough surface textures.

Engineers have now given us a number of materials and devices that have not yet come into their own as artistic media. The first impulse in using a new medium is use of designs that were appropriate to older materials. Later designers who are artists seek out the Tao of the medium and with this effort the material comes into its own. The use of chromium-plated steel to make furniture comes

---

[9] Artists did not solve the problem of the oxidation of the oil until much later. Many so called "black madonnas" are a result of painting the flesh tones in oil, which darkened, and the draperies in tempera, which did not. Later, when entire pictures were painted in oil, everything darkened.

[10] "Glazing" is a term applied to a technique in painting whereby transparent layers of a darker pigment are applied over a lighter color—a process that will produce a luminous effect.

[11] "Impasto" is paint that is applied thickly with the surface left rough.

to mind here. The first attempts were patterned after wooden furniture and aroused no great enthusiasm; later a group of good designers began to produce furniture that seemed to them to be designed with the character of the material in mind and their work was deemed worthy of being taken seriously in critical terms. In a few cases the art has not yet come along to go with the technology. One can buy in "hi-fi" stores devices that project colored lights upon a screen or wall and the most involved forms are so-called color organs with keyboards. However, they still seem to labor under one major difficulty: the effects in light that will be projected are not consistent from one moment to another, or from one instrument to another, or even when using a single instrument.[12] So far, also, no person has produced effects interesting enough to receive much critical notice.

The Moog synthesizer presents another case where a complex technology exists. The music has so far been given little acclaim. The results are brutally consistent, but some other characteristics make the music uninteresting so far. A well-maintained pipe organ also gives consistent results and a harpsichord presents practically no possibility for accenting. In the latter cases, however, there are taught, disciplined traditions of performance that give the player a starting point from which to overcome the mechanical rigidity of the instrument. Rigid effects are overcome by subtle accelerations and delays in timing and speed. The synthesizer so far (1979) has no such canons of performance from which interpretations of the music itself can be built and there is little critical interest in how it is played and little separate music adapted to its character. For one reason or another artists have not yet shown interest in developing the consistent ways of using electronic media that would allow ways of playing them to be taught, but this may change soon.[13]

How canons of performance and technique arise that give such consistency is an aspect of the institutionalization of art forms through what the late Roscoe Pound called "the toughness of a

[12] Recent (1979) laser-based equipment does produce consistent images.
[13] There are some exceptions to these comments. There is the "cult" record *Switched-on Bach* (Walter Carlos performing on the Moog synthesizer, Columbia Record M 7194). It is worth noting here that Carlos did not try to make the synthesizer sound like any other instrument. Walter Carlos has written much music of his own for electronic instruments. Edgard Varèse (1883–1965) composed some work for electronic instruments and Karlheinz Stockhausen (b. 1928) composes for nothing else at this point (1979). There are other adumbrations of change. Young people who have never used acoustic instruments seem to be evolving ways to play electronic instruments in a musically interesting way. I give this to my reader from rather vague say-so.

taught tradition" and is a matter that seems to deserve a chapter in itself.

## BACKGROUND NOTE

Professionalism and its consequences through the occupational structure constitute a field of study in itself. In fact, the artist as loner is really essentially a nineteenth-century image, and has few parallels except perhaps in the scholar-calligrapher-painters in China and Japan. Historically, most art has been produced in studios with a definite hierarchy of management, marketing, and manufacture. Until the nineteenth century engineering and applied science were often not clearly separated from the work of the artist. Vitruvius's *Ten Books on Architecture* is mostly engineering. Leonardo boasted of his competence at designing fortifications, and Dürer wrote a treatise on the subject. The great master-masons who worked on the Gothic churches of the later Middle Ages served as both architects and engineers.

However, to consider specific areas: Franz Boas, *Primitive Art* (Oslo, 1927; reprint ed., New York: Dover, 1955), written before the apocalyptic disruptions of primitive societies brought on by the expansion of air travel after 1950, should dispel any notion that "primitive" art is untrained. The literature is extensive on the relationship of technology and art forms. For the violin there is Emile Leipp, *The Violin; History, Aesthetics, Manufacture and Acoustics* (Toronto: University of Toronto Press, 1969), and A. A. Buchmann, *An Encyclopedia of the Violin* (New York: DaCapo Press, 1966). Musician friends tell me that the seminal treatise on the modern orchestral coloring that depends on the "new instruments of the nineteenth century" is Hector Berlioz, *Treatise on Instrumentation: Enlarged and Revised by Richard Strauss including Berlioz' Essay on Conducting* (New York: Kalmus, 1949). There is also Louise Cuyler, *The Symphony* (New York: Harcourt Brace Jovanovich, 1973), and Felix Weingartner, *The Symphony Writers Since Beethoven* (New York: M. B. Dutton, 1971). The skyscraper form seems a whipping boy of modern architectural criticism. Harold Bush-Brown writes of *Beaux Arts to Bauhaus and Beyond: An Aesthetic Perspective* (New York: Watson-Guptil, 1976); there is also Reyner Banham, *Theory and Design in the First Machine Age* (New York: Praeger, 1960), and Carl W. Condit, *The Rise of the Skyscraper* (Chicago: University of Chicago Press, 1952). In painting and sculpture, the relations of technology to artistic form are obvious from any number of handbooks from Cennino Cennini (fl. 1390), *The Craftsmen's Handbook* (New York: Dover, 1933) to Ralph Mayer, *The Artist's Handbook of Materials and Techniques*, 3d ed. rev. (New York: Viking Press, 1970), and Max Dörner, *Materials of the Artist and Their Use in Painting, with Notes on the Techniques of the Masters*, trans. Eugen Neuhaus, rev. ed. (London: Rupert Hart-Davis, 1969). Andrea Pozzo's 1707 *Rules and Examples of Perspective Proper for Painters and Architects* (New York: Blom, 1971) is exemplary for showing how essentially technological and scientific knowledge can be used in art.

# 6

## The Professionalization of Art:

## The Taught Tradition

IT seems clear that artists are always held back from realizing their full creative potentials as well as the ultimate technical possibilities of their media of expression by a process that is precisely analogous in operation to the way that the "toughness of a taught tradition" hinders lawyers from responding to the world outside of courts and law schools. It is professionalism itself and it is natural to ask what does produce professionalism.

The first requirement is application. Max Weber wrote that without it one remains an amateur. The professional sets himself apart by being "with it," and this involves constant, intensive study. One perforce adds a point strongly to Weber. The professional has to accept the fact that he is often going to look at least odd, often like an outright nut, to laymen because the professional often reasons and works in ways that are not only pointless and incomprehensible to anyone but his fellows, but which often do violence to common sense. Nothing much can change such impressions unless it is striking practical success. Modern physics is a series of mathematical abstractions that are hopelessly beyond the understanding of the generality of us. The physicist, however, was taken out of the category of harmless, ineffectual savants when the atom bomb brought the seemingly invincible Japanese to heel in a few days. The consequences of the work of artists have never been felt with such speed. Whether analysis would show that what creative men do is hardly innocuous in the long run is quite another matter. Even creative work that is generally conceded to be bad and false can have profound effects if it obtains a large enough audience. The science-fiction writer Michael Crichton, who is also a physician, summed it up very neatly in a panel discussion of alterations of behavior by mechanical and surgical interventions in the psycho-neural system; he pointed out that what neurosurgeons could do to alter behavior was trivial compared to what occurred every time the television set was turned on. Extensive data gathered by clinical and social psychologists suggest that Crichton did not exaggerate, but there is rarely an apocalyptic moment to give force to the idea that what is written, read, seen, or performed has practical consequences. That it can be substantiated systematically simply remains part of the common knowledge of professionals. Application also entails isolation with others of like interest or by oneself. It is inevitable within this isolation that separate systems of meaning will become established and, along with them, a special vision of what is studied. This always creates opposition to the lay world. Many years ago I taught social anthropology. Little of it has stayed with me except the awareness that everything that is commonly assumed to be true about human nature is wrong. Once one knows what anthropologists teach us about human nature nearly all the everyday assumptions about it seem erroneous and daily life becomes a make-believe. The artist experiences the same predicament. He sharpens his perceptions more. For this reason he sees more than the rest of us and not only that, he sees with the special intensity that marks those who have been taught to perceive a segment of human experience in a specialized way. Like all such people he will be different in the eyes of the world. This is the consequence, indeed, the penalty, for application and it holds for the artist as well as the scholar.

The second point to be considered is that professional work is almost inevitably addressed to other professionals. There is more public inclination to accept this about some areas of professional endeavor than about others. A neurologist or physicist (or perhaps even a house electrician) is expected to be dealing with matters that are recondite to laymen. It is freely accepted to be the case. It would not be too hard to buy the saws necessary to do trephinations as a Saturday morning relaxation, but it might be difficult to get patients. However, it seems less accepted that much artistic endeavor is addressed to other artists. Most of us find it easy to understand that a physician whose only reference group is his patients is unlikely to be much of a physician. However, there seems to be an expectation that the work of the artist must amuse, be pretty, and be apprehended by everyone without training or effort on their part. Not only is much contemporary work of the artist incomprehensible to laymen, but so is a great deal of the work of the past. Sir Jacob Epstein considered that the best thing that Michelangelo ever did was his very late work—perhaps his last piece—the Randomini Pietà in Milano.[1] This has hardly been a subject of very much enthusiasm. When "in the room the women come and go talking of Michelangelo" their chatter does not usually include the Randomini Pietà. One can name scores of works whose merits are unclear to laymen but generally admired by professionals. As a person whose knowledge of the technical aspects of music is very limited, I can say that I do not know why I should (and do) like Bach's Suites for Unaccompanied 'Cello; the Hammerklavier Sonata no. 29 of Beethoven and his Quartette in E-flat Major op. 74, "The Harp." It is no surprise that I do not understand my preference; these are works that a layman is not expected to understand without effort because they were written for professionals and highly knowledgeable amateurs.

In visual arts the example of modern art stands strikingly from its very beginnings in Turner's dawn scenes and later in Whistler's nocturnes, both of which adumbrated tendencies that were not to be fully exploited for a century. Moreover, even popular "great art" appeals to professionals for largely technical reasons rather than for its "journalistic content." Norman Rockwell's works come off pretty badly because, despite their careful execution, his paintings have practically no technical interest to artists. There is nothing to them but their stories. However, the work of Grant Wood, an equally "realistic" painter, has a compelling technical interest. You can give a story to any of them. One can say *American Gothic* invokes the rugged self-respect and puritanism of this farm couple.[2] As one wit put it, his *Daughters of the American Revolution* is a good picture to bring out if you are trying to make trouble. His portrait of his mother—a solid old lady holding a potted sansevieria—invokes a picture of a tough guardian of the culture. However, what is technically interesting is that all of these pictures employ conventions of painting that had not been used since the early Renaissance. In *American Gothic*, for instance, there is virtually no chiaroscuro, surfaces are painted flat, the woman's pinafore has an unmodeled, all-over pattern (as it would have had in medieval painting), the man's overalls and the faces repeat the pitchfork theme, and, finally, trees are shown as geometric topiary

[1] He was working on it three days before his death.
[2] The models were his sister and his dentist.

forms in a way that had not been common in paintings for four hundred years at least. Leonardo's Mona Lisa probably invokes more speculation than any other picture ever painted. Most of this is nonsense about the meaning of her inscrutable smile and her piercing gaze.[3] The list of all the things that the smile has been thought to mean would be a massive compendium of fatuities. Anyone can catch such a gaze with a camera by posing someone three-quarters face and having the subject look directly into the camera. However, if one wants an indication of why this painting interests professionals, Guy Pène du Bois comments that he was utterly fascinated by the structure of the head and the skill with which it was drafted. Another sentimentally interesting picture comes to mind. Whistler called the picture for which his mother was the model *Arrangement in Gray and Black #1*. It is unlikely that as he painted he was thinking the beautiful thoughts about her that the picture has evoked in others. Whistler's mother was a sharp, well-educated, witty woman who seems to have had a fond, rousing, almost-brawling, unsentimental relationship with her son. What is interesting about the picture technically is the precision of its composition and that it is a study in gray and black—an exceedingly difficult thing to produce.

However, the contrast of the intention of the artist and the sentimental meanings given to his work is often at the root of his alienation from the laity. As professional artists work with (and for) each other they develop their own lingos, their own meanings, and their own signs, symbols, and techniques for expressing them. Gradually they develop formalized conventions of expression that are understood mainly by other professionals. The arts involved thus become structured and for this reason teachable.

It is clear that professionalization itself leads to teaching students a carefully structured subject matter in the context of a consensus as to what they must learn. The most obvious consequence is that schools arise in a stylistic as well as an organizational sense. These schools are not necessarily corporately constituted organizations with a panoply of administration and degrees; they can also be the ateliers of masters with students who come and go with very little organization except, perhaps, a pecking order. However, they are frequently organized into conservatories or art and craft schools, especially on elementary and intermediate levels of instruction.

---

[3] The actual history of the picture is well known: Leonardo eventually sold it to Francis I of France for 4,000 gold florins which works out to perhaps $60,000 in 1979 prices of gold. The subject's husband thought it took too long to paint and that Leonardo wanted too much for it.

What follows may perhaps seem a truism to a creative artist. The attempt to teach the arts in an organized way may operate to inhibit creativity, perhaps in many cases seriously. A common process produces this effect. Once one "schools" things it becomes almost impossible to treat each student as a separate person who should be dealt with ad hoc in order to develop optimally, especially if the school has sufficient reputation to attract more than a handful of students. Teachers feel it necessary to give what they are teaching a logical structure and out of the need for logical structure arises a curriculum. The very presence of a curriculum tends to place different values upon different kinds of talents and skills, and, indeed, often may actually suppress certain types of skills.

Let us take a simple example—the traditional beaux-arts curriculum in painting as it was carried on in the United States until the Second World War. Students were first set to do line drawings of casts of famous statues, or, in cities where there were a significant number of famous statues, the famous statues themselves, preferably marble ones. When able to transfer the outlines to paper with some accuracy they were allowed to shade the drawings in half tones using varying techniques for different effects. Later they went on to drawing portraits in very much the same fashion and, after that, nudes. Along the way they studied design, anatomy, and color. When they were considered ready to paint they were set to doing still life. (Still life was presumed to be simpler than other things one could paint, a very arguable assumption.) However, the fact that the still life was immobile was given much importance as a prop for the students. From there they went to painting portraits and nudes and landscapes.

I am not prepared to say whether or not anyone has ever produced an interesting painting as a consequence of this curriculum. It may be argued that the proponents of such curricula mistook accidents for essentials. Many of the great artists of the past drew from antique models because they were interested in studying them as works of art and not as elementary didactic exercises. Moreover, since photography was not practical until well into the nineteenth century,[4] copies and drawings were a way of recording what these works were like. Later much more copying went on for much the same reason. Perhaps if one looks into the matter closely most artists learn their *craft* in schools, but learn their *art* from nature and museums, in theaters and concert halls, and from other places where unstructured stimulation is present. Whether one learns more

4 Nicéphore Niepce's (d. 1833) first practical photographs were in 1827.

from nature or the work other artists do is a matter of some controversy, but it is worth noting that when Edgar Degas was asked where one learned to paint he replied "A la musée" and, indeed, he regarded it as an utter waste of time for a student to try to learn anything from nature. His position was extreme, but there is no question that artists find what other artists do and why they do it to be matters of continuing lively interest.

The first consequence of the tendency of professional schools to develop fixed ways of training the artist is that certain kinds of skills are underplayed and the range of expression is limited to those things that can be dealt with in the framework of the learned technique. When I was studying drawing forty years ago the ways of teaching were so bound by the beaux-arts system that little was done to turn out people who could produce a good, spontaneous drawing. My first inkling of any other possibility came as a youngster of thirteen when an off-beat teacher in a children's class at the Philadelphia Museum of Art tried to teach us drawing in the Chinese manner.[5] It was quite different from what was done in the art classes of that time. One learned by using a full brush directly and practicing the drawing of certain recurrent natural forms— exactly, in fact, the same forms of *The Mustard Seed Garden Manual of Painting*—until they could be turned out with "absolute accuracy" (e.g., bamboo, grasses, chrysanthemums, rocks, blossoms, and fruits such as pomegranates). The purpose of this was to give a proficiency that would make spontaneity possible.[6] One learned the Tao of each form and individual examples varied only accidently. Beaux-arts training, however, had absolutely no place for the development of this type of proficiency in a direct, rapid, empathic rendering of natural forms, although Monet and many other Impressionists showed one could portray direct apprehensions of color and light and still remain within the development of European painting. This is only one example of how professional schools inhibit the development of the skill necessary for particular creative ventures.

Two major influences, however, mitigate the inhibition of creativity by the educational system. The first is interaction among the students themselves. They talk to each other about their art, whether it be painting, sculpture, music, dance, or whatever. From this they arrive at peer consensuses about their specialities and (in

---

[5] This teacher was the late Cheves West Perky who had had a previous career in psychology and had produced a still famous series of papers on perception.
[6] A consequence of the prestige of this work was that it became a stultifying influence on the development of Chinese painting.

my own experience at least) the results are often pretty far from the ambient academic party line. The very isolation with knowledgeable fellow students seems to encourage new directions and new visions in art. The second influence lies in giving specialized individual attention to the most able students through the schools and its contacts. However, even the largest of such organizations service only a small percentage of all students—e.g., the Berkshire Festival School admits only 400 students a year, a number that is less than the separate enrollments of many well-known, high-level conservatories such as Juilliard, Curtis, and New England. However, such mitigations seem not to have altered the schools themselves much, but have merely served to foster an experimental peer culture in opposition to the curriculum culture set by the faculties. (Any curriculum, no matter how liberal, is in a final sense authoritarian in that it always makes assumptions as to what the students should know that may not be in accord with what they think they ought to know.) It is in such contexts that younger artists so often band together to form bands of brothers to confront the establishment with manifestos for a new and more timely art. It is fair to ask why the academics do so often hold their ground against this wild army (les Fauves).

The inhibiting effects of schools are aggravated by a "fat-cat" effect. The academic with a secure job can easily become a priest and a doctrinaire of orthodoxy of a field. At the very best these teachers remind the students that there is a body of knowledge that has been considered important by professionals, but at the very worst they spend much time in academic rituals that are little more than masses to affirm the validity of the status quo. They may spend much of their time ferreting out heresy because they sense that their own position and security depend upon maintaining one form of orthodoxy or another. The comfort and isolation and the assured income that a position within a school affords may make the teacher unresponsive to the forces that lie in the extra-academic ambience.

We are led almost inevitably to some simple realizations: if creative art (or art that is at least a vital response to the social and intellectual forces that distract the artist as well as new aesthetic and technical possibilities)—as distinct from repetitious academic exercises—is to be produced at all, it must come mainly from outside the context of the schools. It must come because the artist is insistently nagged either by a personal vision of new possibilities within his art itself, or by happenings in the world that demand a direct response. Art schools of various sorts may do an exceptional job in turning out technicians, but they may be the worst possible places to turn out creative artists. (A qualification should be made here. One must make a distinction between the teaching studio, where creative problems are explored as one learns, and curriculum-bound art schools. Martha Graham for example seems to have been far too much of an artist ever to allow her studio to become stodgy but the Bolshoi Ballet has lost some sensationally good performers who wanted to perform more than a largely nineteenth-century repertory.)

So far consideration of the inhibition of creativity has only been given with respect to an educational structure with its curriculum and fat-cat professors. There is yet another source of limiting factors. Organizations develop that are supposed to bring the work of the artist to the extraprofessional community. For the moment, at least, I will put aside sellers and impresarios and confine myself to established, corporate artistic organizations in which the money-making function is presumed to be subordinated to artistic purposes. Who controls these organizations?

In some instances—like the Juilliard School under William Schumann—they are managed by people who are, indeed, at the peak of their profession as practitioners. However, less fortunate types of cases are common. The first is that the people in power were once competent in their fields and lost interest because they were beguiled by promises of influence or affluence. (Here I must confess a belief: I do not think that any professional is ever kept from his field by administrative obligations for long. People do what satisfies them most. If these people were actually still interested in practicing their professions that is what they would be doing.) Another type of situation arises when people are brought in because they are considered to have some superior understanding of art that professionals are thought to lack, or because they are virtuosos in public relations (even if their relations with the artists may be chronically and irretrievably alienated). What is important here is that the reference group of such functionaries is not the artists but a lay public. The public may not, in fact, actually exist, but the important consequence to artists is that the managers believe it to exist.

Above such managers there may be other echelons of trustees, directors, or philanthropists who are presumed to be able to support the organization and bring in money. This is the rationale for giving them ultimate control of the organization. I have not been able to locate systematic data on whether or not they do indeed bring in significant support from their contacts with government, business, foundations, and rich friends and relations. There is no question that a few significant organizations are endowed by single individuals or families, creating a situation that always causes the organizations to express their taste and outlooks (although the tastes are often on very high levels). But aside from such Huntington Galleries, Getty Museums, and Curtis Institutes, this is a reliable source of funds only for highly prestigious organizations like the Boston Symphony, the Philadelphia Orchestra, the Metropolitan Museum of Art, the Detroit Symphony, and the like.[7] The economics of most organizations are those of the broad-based clientele at the box office and the inevitable compromises in artistic quality that catering to such audiences entail. One can expect only timid excursions into the avant-garde. There is little data on the sponsorship of experimental art and music. It seems mainly subsidized by colleges and universities that lack the rigid controls characteristic of professional schools of art and music. With the visual arts a special complication arises: not a single major museum has a practicing artist for its director, but rather one variety or another of art historian who may or may not be able to get along with artists as well as he gets along with his trustees. In all the instances that have been considered, essentially sociological factors are operating not only to create approved forms, narrow the range of skills of the artist, and define what directions creativity can take, but to define what the lay public will see and hear. Such strategic positions in determining institutional sponsorship are held by professional managers whose reference groups are not necessarily the artists themselves, and what they expose may not be what the artists consider interesting, important, or exciting. The artists in fact may be perpetually alienated from them.

### BACKGROUND NOTE

The topic of professionalism in general is well documented. It is hard to say just how the ideal of the gentleman-amateur became fixed. The "Renaissance man" stereotype really does not hold up. What may seem to be omnicompetence can simply turn out to be technical simplicity. It is easy to know many fields if there is not much to know about any of them. If any calling is pursued intensively, it is likely to go beyond lay understanding and require specialists if it is to be practiced in a way that satisfies specialists themselves. Artmaking seems, in fact, to be one of the first areas of human activity to experience specialization.

[7] Since writing this, a practice has arisen for museums to organize "eye-buster" shows that bring in huge sums in admissions—e.g., the Chinese Imperial Treasures, the Chardin show of 1979, the Vesuvius A.D. 79, the Treasures of Tut-ankh-amen, the great Picasso show of the Museum of Modern Art in 1980, and many more.

The world's oldest profession is not prostitution, but that of the artist, potter, sculptor, and, perhaps earliest of all, cave-painter. Wilbert Moore discusses the role of the specialist in the modern world in *The Professions: Roles and Rules* (New York: Russell Sage, 1970), as does Philip Elliott in *The Sociology of Professions* (London: Macmillan, 1972). Magali S. Larson also takes up this phenomenon of increasing professional differentiation in *The Rise of Professionalism: A Sociological Analysis* (Berkeley, Ca.: University of California Press, 1977). For art as a profession, we have Francis Kelly, *The Studio and the Artist* (New York: St. Martin's Press, 1975). Donald Holden, *Art Career Guide: A Guidance Handbook for Art Students, Teachers, Vocational Counselors and Job Hunters* (New York: Watson Guptil, 1973), gives some inkling of how complex professionalism has become just in the fields that require a training in only the visual arts. Maurice Rheims in *La Vie d'Artiste* (Paris: Grosset, n.d.) gives a French view of artistic isolation. Roger Shattuck, *The Banquet Years*, rev. ed. (New York: Vintage, 1968), gives an entertaining, sensitive picture of the isolation of the avant-garde in Paris in the decades before World War I.

Art schools are discussed in Nikolaus Pevsner, *Academies of Art, Past and Present* (Cambridge: The University Press, 1940). I have not yet located a sociological study of schools of music. The annual *National Association of Schools of Music Handbook* gives minimal information on curricula. Writers, if they are trained at all in any professional sense, are trained in colleges and universities. The traditional images and function of art museums as sanctuaries, temples of haut bourgeois taste, as a source of "brownie points" in social-climbing in their control, and as havens of upper-class sinecures, have been under fire for some time. Nathaniel Burt, *Palaces for the People, a Social History of American Art Museums* (Boston: Little, Brown, 1977), Karl E. Meyer, *The Art Museum: Power, Money and Ethics, A Twentieth Century Fund Report* (New York: Morrow, 1979), and the interviews in Douglas Schwalbe and Janet Baker-Carr, eds., *Conflict in the Arts, The Relocation of Authority* (Cambridge, Mass.: Arts Administration Research Institute, 1977), give synoptic views of this area.

# 7

## Critics, Merchants,
## Consumers, Bureaucrats

THE villains so far have been professional artists turned professor or dean, directors of artistic organizations, who may or may not themselves be professional artists, trustees, and curators. Beyond these, however, lie four more publics who hem in artists and who try to define what are to be considered acceptable options for them. These are critics, merchants and impresarios, consumers and bureaucrats, public officials and policemen.

Most of the last we can dispatch quickly, unshriven and unsung. When policemen turn arbiter they bring to their role the tastes of people who have the usual education of policemen. Other bureaucrats often do little better because they respond to the dictates of the powerful and the articulate, neither of whom are necessarily very sympathetic to the daemons of the artists that compel them to respond to their own interests and to external forces that turn their attention to things that may be embarrassing to the powerful. Pleasing one's betters results in twentieth-century Russian Socialist Realist painters doing work that looks like nineteenth-century Italian academic painting. Troubling one's betters has almost bizarre consequences—consider the self-imposed exiles of some superb Russian dancers, some of whom chose new careers abroad because even material comfort and security in their homeland could not mitigate the boredom of being allowed to perform only twenty-eight ballets, and the spectacle of George Meany and Alexander

Solzhenitsyn in the same bed. However, we in the West cannot be patronizing. England used to have its Lord Chancellor, and the United States had the Watch and Ward Society of Boston, the Hays Office, the Society for the Suppression of Vice of New York, and a good deal more. The United States Supreme Court in Paris *vs.* Slayton (1972) added the police, not only of New York, Boston, and Chicago, but of every hamlet as well.[1] However, one must be fair: civil intervention has a side that unintentionally contributes to the liberty of the creative artist through impersonal support. A great deal of experimental art was helped along because the National Endowment for the Humanities and other such organizations released money on a purely formal legal basis to support artistic ventures until they became self-supporting. Because the present essay is a preface to the sociology of art and not a manual of grantsmanship, there is no point in going into the effects of this type of support and how it is obtained. Its principal advantage is that its impersonality results in a "benign neglect" of the recipients. By and large, the awarding organizations take the opinions of professional committees, and they rarely follow and evaluate what has been done in any consistent way. The very looseness of the system allows the artists freedoms that they lack where there are actively meddlesome police and ministries of culture.

Critics and criticism have to be considered separately from a system of sponsorship. Criticism exists on a number of intellectual levels. First of all there is a type of criticism that is an unthought-out direct response—the "I know what I like," and usually tells more about the critic than the work in question. The intentions of the artist are unimportant here. If the critic himself is interesting what he has to say will be interesting (e.g., Bernard Shaw on music). Criticism, like art itself, is expression and can never really transcend what the critic has within him to express. It thus often ends up as something that may oppose or agree with what the artist has expressed, but does not necessarily illuminate its significance. If such critics have more than a minimal clientele it is only because significant numbers of people can be led to respond in the same way. Their popularity or influence rests mainly on the extent to which they say what is in accord with the collective consciousness. But the artist's creativity lies precisely in his transcendence of the collective consciousness, and so this type of criticism has significance only in that it defines the range of the creative venture to respond

[1] The United States Supreme Court held that what was to be considered pornography was to be determined by local standards.

to the common tastes of an untrained laity, which is to say that it provides no inducement to understand the ways in which the creative venture amplifies our understanding of life itself.

The second type of criticism pretends to be scholarly. It attempts to see synoptically what has been done and to compare the work of an artist with that of his forerunners and contemporaries. Such solidly based scholarship should place critics beyond the transient whim of the society in which they live—indeed this is the traditional defense of the ivory tower. What often happens, however, is that the critics themselves do not control access to their public and, for this reason, not all kinds of criticism that pretend to historical validity are equally heard. Access to the public is controlled by rich, influential newspapers, art magazines, schools of art and conservatories, and book publishers. What they allow the lay and professional public to have access to is in large measure governed by their own tastes and what they believe to be the clientele for the criticism. (The clientele may have little objective existence.)

A more serious difficulty also serves to create confusion for the critics. Sometimes the intransigent perversity of the public to expert opinion as well as their own researches lead them to re-evaluate what is thought to be good. Anyone, for example, who suggested in the 1930s that Stan Laurel and Oliver Hardy were major artists would probably have been taken for a crackpot or accused of facetiousness. However, when compared with the unspeakably boring phantasmagoria of current (1980) TV series it is easy to see them as superb comic artists. Moreover, like *The Pickwick Papers*, they present a world that is inescapably true to the quality of life. Nearly all of us do have days of cumulative small frustrations that make us want to cry like Stan Laurel. Metaphorically speaking, we all try to get pianos up long outside staircases only to discover we could have driven the truck around to the back of the house. One suspects that it would not be difficult to convince any present-day film critic of the artistic importance of Laurel and Hardy, and of the reality of their presentation of the problems of daily life.

However, this constant re-evaluation of the past often gives the critics trouble in seeing how art is an expression of the inner dynamics of the society. This is the point at which the critical venture usually comes to be concerned with relevance, the attempt to relate art to what were the main concerns of the society in which the work was produced with special attention to its ideological content. Because the artists themselves are usually not asked, the standards of judging whether or not the artist has conveyed anything beautiful, exciting, or important often remain external impositions that do not necessarily value what the artists themselves feel is interesting or worthy of response.

The last role makes the critic into an ideologist, either for or against what has been recently called the establishment. There probably is no easier way to provide a fertile context in which to encourage an art that is utterly alien to the artist as a person who amplifies and clarifies common experience and creates new ranges of experience. Under an authoritarian regime the critic becomes censor. It is not surprising that the more pompous and authoritarian the regimes and ideologies for which the critic has become censor, the more constraining and pompous this art becomes. Much of officially approved present-day Soviet art is skillfully executed, but it is wondrously dull academic work that no first-rank artist in the West has done since the 1880s.[2] It is a truism that one cannot get a "Russian" novel published in present-day Russia. What little we have seen that comes out of the People's Republic of China does not appear to be markedly exciting, to say the least. It is obvious that the message about what is art has been given loud and clear. If the results do not strike responsive chords in persons steeped in Western bourgeois and traditional Chinese cultures in the same way that much work from previous periods of Chinese art do, that proves that the artists should be out in the countryside being re-educated by the peasants. Mussolini did no better than Chairman Mao as an arbiter. In various parts of Rome he had put up unbelievably clumsy marble statues that reeked of locker rooms and bull homosexuality unmitigated by any hints of tender, humane feelings. The art of Hitler's Germany was a good deal like this too. However, let me give a caution here: most of us cannot respond sympathetically to these arts because we are marching to different drummers; when we know what their cues are supposed to call forth we are repelled in much the same way that some of us are repelled by body-builders, weight lifters, and Japanese wrestlers. They may very well invoke positive responses from persons who are operating within their systems of meanings. If the essence of masculinity is ugly bull homosexuality the Foro Italico statues in Rome are great art.

Despite what anyone may think, it seems certain that the artist within the liberal bourgeois societies has been a good deal freer of the critic as ideological censor, except with respect to explicit por-

---

[2] People like Andrew Wyeth, Grant Wood, Augustus John, and other important artists who have kept to recognizable objects in "everyday" experience gain the attention of the artistically knowledgeable community for technical reasons that transcend the editorial content of their work and are, in technical terms, far from the muddy tones of nineteenth-century academism.

trayals of pornography. (In the last decade control has eased, but this is still a risky business in the United States and many more places.) There are various reasons why the artist enjoys his freedom. The first is purely economic. The most common and most powerful sanctions in our society against those who keep out of what is defined as the cultural mainstream are economic. Artists can choose poverty, the alms of their friends and relatives, or perhaps working for a living at something completely irrelevant to their artistic life. Charles Ives discovered early that America was not going to support a music of dissonances interspersed with off-key patriotic and hymn tunes, and instead made his living as an insurance company executive; E. E. Cummings was a department-store employee while Edgar Guest rode in Cadillacs; T. S. Eliot was an editor (although I think that he could quite easily have found a place in American academic life if he had not chosen to live in England). But for each of these there are probably twenty score who spend at least their youth on the left banks of the world's cities. Both Ives and the bohemian nonentity were free as artists because their art was economically irrelevant.

Being obscure has other advantages. Much of the freedom that artists enjoy may be unexpected rewards for disorganization and the use of symbolisms that are so recherché that only the initiate can understand them at all. Let us consider them in order. As long as any group remains unorganized and lacking in wealth or power it can threaten no one, and for this reason it can be ignored. Moreover it can become proletarian in very much the way that the sociologist Max Weber defined the term: "those who are in the society but not of it," and share neither its rewards nor its inducements. Except for organizations like the American Federation of Musicians, ASCAP, the Screen Writers' Guild, and Actors' Equity whose activities are, by and large, articulated to the entertainment industry, artists qua artists remain a largely inchoate congeries with little or no organization to maintain or improve their status vis à vis other economic groups. Indeed, if we say we can only call a group "social" if it is a collectivity in which a knowledge of the elements is insufficient to a knowledge of the whole, there is some question as to whether one can call artists, except for musicians and actors, social groups at all. The proletarian isolation of the artist allows him only rare encounters with the ultimate loci of power in a capitalistic society that lie not so much in people as in an intricate matrix of property relations that is invisible to the tyro.[3] This iso-

---

[3] Vide the unbelievable naiveté of the image of power relations behind the ransom, bank robbery, political kidnapping, airplane-hijacking syndrome. If such gestures change the system at all it is to replace a pose of liberal tolerance with active oppression.

lation from the mainstream of rewards, esteem, and power frees the artist to "have fun." Moreover, to the extent that his imagery and symbolism are so private, so involuted, and so recherché that it only communicates with a few initiates,[4] he is unlikely to disturb power relations in the society. It leads to being left alone by authorities. Roger Shattuck's discussion of art from 1890 to 1915 in *The Banquet Years* shows clearly how being isolated and incommunicable allows artistic freedom. Except for occasional arrests during some rowdy affair, his bohemians were left alone and even the most talented of them were rarely more than figures of fun, never threats to the bourgeois community.

Still, even if the artist is free of the stultifying authoritarian ideology of the censor-critics' totalitarian societies, he may not be entirely free of an ideology that assigns him to a limbo of irrelevance where there are few of the constant orienting cues that keep people in the other segments of society tied to some central set of standards. It becomes easy to drift into the private and involuted worlds of avant-garde, Dada, Surrealism, and nameless activities such as moving a whitewashed pile of scrap lumber from one place to another in a gallery. It may really be no wonder that Abstract Expressionism achieved such a high level of popularity among artists. It really put the artist in a very comfortable place vis à vis bourgeois society—absolutely out of it. This is not to say artists are ever really out of it. In fact, when one studies what they were trying to do, as distinct from what they communicated to the public, one sees that they were usually more aware of what would prove important than the rest of us.

It does not seem surprising then that in the last twenty years a number of now not-so-young artists have rejected assignment to private limbos and have turned to the shocker, a form exemplified by Pop Art. It is, after all, perfectly fair to ask whether indeed we do live in a world of the pearly evanescent colors of morning and the lazy summer afternoons of Post-Impressionism or one of Campbell's soup cans, parking meters, gun barrels, and the like. A few of us contrive to escape this world by taking the back roads. One can achieve a serenity by denying or withdrawing from certain streams of life. Those of us whose professions bring us in contact with educated young people often see blatant attempts to withdraw into the simple life. But when we look at the well-made boots, the real wool plaid shirts, and the whipcord hiking pants that encase these beautiful young bodies we know that this withdrawing is really very dependent upon some anonymous toilers in the dark Satanic

[4] Herbert Gans's contention that studio art has little or no effect on the everyday relations of the bulk of the population seems largely incontrovertible.

mills, and can only be toyed with now because previously there were the right shots in the infant fanny at the right time and the right dentists. Look at what people are like when these things are absent. Good clothing and straight backs and teeth come very dear indeed. We don't know how many of us escape permanently. Sooner or later one is on the freeways at 8:30 A.M., or parks a car in a shopping center lot, which is so vast that one can end up nowhere near the shops, and notices the ubiquitous beer-can rings. And so the young artist revolts from irrelevancy in very much the same way that Reginald Marsh and William Glackens threw their lot with the Ashcan School in the early part of this century. They too rebelled against establishment art that then made many genuinely talented men like John Singer Sargent and Anders Zorn into society flunkies for much of their careers.

But the critic in his most egregiously unpleasant role is little more than the mouthpiece and agent of the establishment; at best he tries to relate the work of the artist to the inner ethos of the society and what he sees as its truths. This leads to a few brief comments about the critics' relations to two more groups of villains: the merchants or impresarios and the consumers of art. With the artist they make an uneasy eternal triangle. The consumers of art—the theatergoer, the collector, the reader, the concertgoer, and the like— look constantly for cues about what they should want and appreciate. For this they depend largely upon the pronouncements of critics and, on the more exalted levels of society and education, upon the scholarly critics. (In some cases—like Bernard Berenson and Erwin Panofsky—they were indeed scholarly by the most exacting standards.) Similarly the entrepreneurs look to the critics for guidance as to what to expect the clientele to want.

It should lead to a situation where the critic is arbiter, but it does not always work in such a pat way. All sorts of particularistic factors intervene. The first is that not all artists have equal access to evaluation by critics. Critics in fact do not go to all galleries, theaters, and concert halls. They only go to some theaters, galleries, and concert halls, and they do not read all books of all publishers, either. This gives rise to a complex jockeying by the merchants for the attention of the critics. It entails a world of promotion and parties for which the artist himself must often find the money. Moreover, personal friendships arise that affect the notice that is given either to a particular artist or to the artists that are sponsored by a particular entrepreneur. Add to this that impresarios, merchants, and publishers often develop independent prestige that makes both critics and publics look upon what they sponsor with strong interest. Cases are numerous: Ambrose Vollard's sponsorship of the Post-Impressionists early in this century; the Castelli Gallery in New York in the 1970s, the performing artists under Sol Hurok's management, and the plays that the Theatre Guild sponsored. Another complication that arises in these interactions is that occasionally some artists begin to be able to set the taste after they get major critical notice. They thus gain an importance that is greatly disproportionate to their numbers because they can then create the tastes of their clients; every major artist from the early Renaissance down to the present has done so. These people sometimes simply went ahead despite the opinions of hostile critics and they got away with it (e.g., Thomas Hart Benton, Whistler, Rousseau, Picasso, Turner, Stravinsky, Wagner). While such cases are exceptional, they are, one must emphasize, of great importance in the formation of the tastes of their generations, both among other artists and among the laity.

Nevertheless, the overwhelming majority of artists do not escape this matrix. They are still dependent upon galleries, critics, and impresarios whose reference groups tend to be their clientele rather than the artists themselves. Earlier I implied strongly that one cannot become an important artist without commissions. It goes farther. Without the recognition that comes with a market no artist is likely to continue long, but for one condition—the recognition of other artists. If both a living and peer recognition are absent it simply does violence to the most elementary rules of learning theory to expect persistence. I cannot think of a single case where an artist of note was not recognized at least by other artists in his lifetime. The record shows, for instance, that there were a good number of people who thought that Blake's work was good. Henri Rousseau was a center of sometimes not entirely innocent fun to other artists, but as Shattuck shows in *The Banquet Years* many good ones respected his work. Picasso, in fact, bought some of Rousseau's pictures when he was almost broke himself. Even Paul Gauguin and Vincent van Gogh—the loners par excellence—had some appreciation for each other's work and were well regarded within Post-Impressionist circles. (Their colleagues lost patience with their personal behavior, not their work.)

There is no doubt that while our system of recognition has brought to the forefront many artists whose talents seemed questionable later and afforded little recognition to a number of good ones, it has never made a permanent reputation for a poor artist. When the supportive system collapses so does the reputation. However, the lack of support probably can also kill a talent. Technical proficiency cannot be maintained without practice. The performer who does not have work soon gets rusty simply because he has no inducement to practice for any kind of deadline; the painter whose paintings are neither selling nor recognized as good at least by other painters also soon loses the inducement to keep his art in practice and takes to the cafés of Bohemia or insurance offices. It is a moot point by the nature of the case whether the talents that withered from disuse were ever much to start with. Technical proficiency during one's youth is not enough because permanent reputations are not built on youthful facility—which is very common—but on the ability to evoke emotive and intellectual responses. This for many comes only after endless refinement of eye and ear, which develops a perception of one's ambience. Barring the development of some testing instrument that would make it possible to decide during youth which proficient performers would become exciting artists, one is unable to make even an educated guess. Perhaps the painter Joseph Stefanelli put his finger on it when he called the seemingly dazzling youngsters we both knew twenty-five years previously, "precocious kids" who were not really artists. He seemed to mean they could do anything they tried competently, but lacked the special qualities that make for an exciting artist. Data show he has a point; very few make it.[5]

With this I turn to the fundamental patterns that underlie the matrix in which art is produced and disseminated—the culture.

### BACKGROUND NOTE

The literature on censorship is extensive and for the most part centers on obscenity issues and only to a lesser degree upon political and economic issues. Historically, it shades off insensibly to the control of heresy. Paul Blanshard's *The Right to Read: The Battle Against Censorship* (Boston: Beacon, 1955) was

[5] The record for making it in art is not nearly as bad as professional athletics (2,500 in 1980), but it is bad enough. Estimates of the number of art students in New York City alone run from 10,000 to 50,000 depending on what one calls art, who one places under the rubric of art student, and what one calls an art school. In some cases this is easy because the schools themselves make the judgment (e.g., the Stella Elkins Tyler School at Temple University is said to kick out much of its freshman class at mid-year), but many equally prestigious schools never force the issue. However Bowker's *Who's Who in American Art* (1978) lists about 10,000 names. I counted 120 entries on the first ten pages of text. Eight were not artists at all, but auxiliary functionaries (i.e., dealers, critics, etc.); of the remaining 110 or so only 69 had no source of income apparent from their entries other than sales of their work. This leaves around 6,500 nationally since the 69 is just about 65 percent of the sample of 110. Whether this is a good sample may be questioned on a purely statistical basis, although since my ten pages only included "A" initials this would at least give us a patronymic initial common to every Western nation. Whatever the validity of my sample, it certainly appears reasonable to say that many more are called than chosen.

a respected book. There have been numerous books since: Harry Clor, *Obscenity and Public Morality: Censorship in a Liberal Society* (Chicago: University of Chicago Press, 1969); Robert W. Haney, *Comstockery in America: Patterns of Censorship and Control* (Boston: Beacon, 1960); Morris L. Ernst and Alan U. Schwartz, *Censorship: The Search for the Obscene* (New York: Macmillan, 1964); and, perhaps most relevant to the topics at hand, *Thought Control in the U.S.A. Complete Proceedings of the Conference on Thought Control Hollywood U.S.A. Council P.C.A. 1947*, ed. Harold J. Salemson, which considers not only the legal aspects, but specific topics of press, radio, literature, music, the arts, architecture, the film, and much more. English works are extensive since artistic censorship is of long standing in England. See, for example, Donald Thomas, *A Long Time Burning: The History of Literary Censorship in England* (London: Routledge and Kegan Paul, 1969).

Books about criticism are numerous. I cite here only works of people of major standing. In literary criticism there is George E. G. Saintsbury, *A History of Criticism and Literary Taste in Europe from the Earliest Texts to the Present Day* 2d ed. (Edinburgh: Blackwell, 1961); Cleanth Brooks and William K. Wimsatt, *Literary Criticism: A Short History* (New York: Borzoi, 1957); and Vernon Hall, *A Short History of Literary Criticism* (New York: New York University Press, 1963). Histories of special periods are numerous. In art criticism there is Lionello Venturi, *History of Art Criticism*, translated from the Italian by Charles Marriot (New York: Dutton, 1964); Frank P. Chambers, *A History of Taste; An Account of the Revolutions of Art Criticism and Theory in Europe* (New York: Columbia University Press, 1933); and, among many more, Solomon Fishman, *The Interpretations of Art Essays on the Art of Criticism of John Ruskin, Walter Pater, Clive Bell, Roger Fry and Herbert Read* (Berkeley: University of California Press, 1963).

The literature on patronage and markets is divided into at least two categories which reflect the shifts from personal munificence to impersonal bureaucratic support from industry and government through to art gallery marketing. There is Alvin Reiss, *Culture and Company* (New York: Twayne Publishers, 1972); Robert Wraight, *The Art Game Again*, new ed. (London: Frewin, 1974); John Russell Taylor, *The Art Dealers* (New York: Scribner's, 1969); and Steven W. Naifeh, *Culture-making: Money, Success and the New York Art World* (Princeton: Princeton University Press, 1967); and Faye Levine, *The Culture Barons: An Analysis of Power and Money in the Arts* (New York: Crowell, 1976). On corporate and business sponsorship of the arts see Nina Kaiden and Bartlett Hayes, ed., *Artist and Advocate: An Essay on Corporate Patronage* (New York: Renaissance Eds., 1967); the sheer complexity of this subject is apparent from *Private Foundations and Business Corporations Active in the Arts, Humanities, Education*, vol. 2 (Washington, D.C.: International Arts Letter, 1974). The most intensive account of the effects of government patronage is seen in Francis O'Connor, *Federal Support for the Visual Arts, the New Deal and Now; a Report on the New Deal and Projects in New York City and State with Recommendations for Present-day Federal Support for the Visual Arts to the National Endowment for the Arts* (Greenwich, Conn., 1969). The best synoptic account of private and public sponsorship remains Arnold Hauser, *The Social History of Art* (New York: Knopf, 1951).

# 8

Art and the Cultural System:

Nietzsche's *The Birth of Tragedy*

THERE is another function that is performed by the critic with respect to the artists; he is the agent of the culture—and insofar as the artist is a critic of himself, he too is such an agent of the culture. This is a role that is commonly assigned to teachers, clergymen, parents, peers, and other socializers. We must add scholars and, for the artist especially, critics. In their worst aspect all are what George Orwell called "duckspeakers"—people who can respond in an approved manner without the functioning of their higher nerve centers. Such functionaries, however, perform a more respectable role with respect to the creative artist; they serve to judge the extent to which his work is consistent with the ethical and epistemological substratum of the culture of the society.

It is readily apparent that critics do this for the neophyte. It is less apparent but just as certain that the mature artist is also subjected to their critical standards. Such standards serve to orient the artist to the culture, keep him within tolerable bounds of deviation from central norms, and define the collective consciousness that his art should express in the view of the scholar and critic. We may now ask what seems to affect the formation of this qualitative character of artistic output and what gives the work of any place and time a consistent ethos. Later we will consider why the artist so often rejects underlying critical canons.

What follows may be a little troublesome for readers who are not trained in classical sociology (or, for that matter, in any sociology at all). It is therefore appropriate to consider briefly older fields of interest in sociology.

In the third of a century since I began to teach, a sociology gradually has built up that has skirted what was formerly regarded as one of its central concepts—culture. A sociology that was presumed to transcend it has gradually evolved. Theoreticians borrowed a congeries of idols long since fallen into the dust in the shrines of epistemology (e.g., phenomenology). More recently we have seen a revival of what can only be called radical psychologism in ethnomethodology and in Erving Goffman's extended attempt to catalogue the behavioral, nonverbal manifestations of Pareto's residue for the integrity of personality. It is not necessary to consider here whether or not such attempts are "fads and foibles" as P. A. Sorokin called them. If one deals with psychologistic problems that confine themselves to how interaction generates itself, there is no doubt one can do it without any deep consideration of culture and culture itself may even conceal psychological forces. Aldous Huxley, I think, showed that he understood this when he suggested that the best preparation for writing a novel about Mayfair was to visit the Bantu and get a pair of Siamese cats. Some generalizations about interaction do transcend culture. Similarly, if one considers the data of sociology as a series of answers to ad hoc questions one can also probably avoid culture. Such research, in truth, should not be denigrated. The intuitive judgments of the experts have to be checked out by comparison, experiment, or events, if they are not to be any more than involuted illusions. Samuel Stouffer and his associates in their famous series *The American Soldier in World War II* sent one venerable turkey to the oven after another. They showed that a great deal that was believed by professionals but seemed bizarre to laymen was right and some of it, alas, was quite wrong. Stouffer and his associates did a remarkable job of separating one from the other. However, in little over a decade after Stouffer's death one was hard put to say what the fuss was about. Stouffer is as dead as anyone with his reputation can possibly be. He answered his own questions so well that there was nothing left to ask. It was precisely the strength of his work that laid it low. It was a very remarkable series of essays if one considers the central goal of sociological research to be the exploration of ad hoc problems, but it did only that and no more. The sociology was gone. As Russell Ackoff's *The Design of Social Research* shows, it is quite possible to be highly competent exploring ad hoc questions without knowing any sociology at all. However, the very success of Stouffer's group gave the interests that they exemplified a boost, at the expense of dealing with problems of values which, on the whole, were not illuminated by their methods. Robert Biersted perhaps put his finger on their limitations some years ago when he asked who reads Sorokin and replied that a great many people did, but they were not sociologists. Biersted saw Sorokin's work to be irritating to other sociologists because it dealt with problems that could not be subjected to the usual methods of the discipline, as is true of any concern with values. It is really no accident that the immediately older generation of sociologists who concerned themselves with problems of values, such as Robert Nisbet, Talcott Parsons, and Robert Merton, gave gracious bows to "empirical research" but remained consumers rather than producers of it in their own work.

However, no matter how hard one tries to evade it there is a final question one has to ask about the human condition: Is it indeed "a tale told by an idiot, full of sound and fury, signifying nothing?"

If one assumes that the core question of sociology as an intellectual—perhaps even as a moral—venture is why people organize societies at all, one cannot ignore cultures and the assumptions that give them form. The word "culture" has been used to mean three separate things. The first is the popular one of the human form of adaptation which is implicit in the classical definition of Tylor so dear to the elementary textbooks of a generation ago. In 1871 Tylor's definition was, "Culture is that complex whole which includes knowledge, belief, art, morals, law, custom, and any other capabilities and habits acquired by man as a member of society." As ethnographic work became more refined it gradually began to assume a second meaning of particular configurations of traits by which segments of societies as well as whole societies expressed their values and realized the functional requirements for going about their business. (One is hesitant indeed to say "their survival" because it is plain that much of history is a graveyard of societies whose cultures were not very good as instruments of survival if survival means the persistence of organization. Early in this century Pareto in *The Mind and Society*[1] compiled a massive, often inchoate, catalogue of lunacies which dwelt, perhaps too lengthily, upon the assumptions underlying "non logico-experimental" behavior. They showed little relation of custom to survival.)

Ruth Benedict concerned herself with a third meaning of the word in *Patterns of Culture*. There she defined culture as the deter-

[1] The Italian title is *Trattato di Sociologia Generale*. It does not translate to *The Mind and Society*.

minants of the eidos and ethos of social life with respect to their fundamental assumptions about the nature of life, of reality, and of epistemological systems.

This last meaning is the most relevant to my discussion because it has the greatest bearing upon how the artist expresses the inner qualitative character of the culture, the fundamental postulates upon which his perception of reality is based, and his modes of approach to action.

Many writers have approached the dynamics of culture in the last sense. The results are consistent at least in that there seems to be a consensus among them that underlying ethical and epistemological assumptions vary in regular ways with the qualitative aspects of culture. No attempt will be made to summarize much of this literature but I will focus instead upon works of four men which have been crucial to the understanding of the relation of art to what may be termed metacultural systems. The first is in Friedrich W. Nietzsche; the second is in the work of Pitirim A. Sorokin and Thorstein Veblen; the last is in F. S. C. Northrop's work.

So much attention has been given to the use made of Nietzsche's work in justifying Nazi ideology and to his strictures against Christian culture that it has beclouded his greatness as a classical scholar whose influence is still felt.[2] In fact, the complete bibliography given in Mügge's *Nietzsche* shows that up until 1871 he worked entirely as a Greek philologist publishing modest articles, none of them over forty pages long, in three specialized series in Germany. These studies of the spirit of Greek art led him to publish *The Birth of Tragedy* in 1872—a work that was said to have placed him far in the vanguard of critical and philological studies of ancient Greek literature and first indicated that he had a mind of seminal importance. Sociologists and anthropologists seem to derive their impressions of this work largely from the borrowing of two of its key terms by Ruth Benedict in *Patterns of Culture*. She picked up the terms Dionysian and Apollonian from it and nothing else. She did state a simple caution that the plays to which Nietzsche had applied these terms are found in societies that were considerably more complex than those of the primitive peoples whose cultures she was analyzing, but she nowhere mentioned that he introduced a third term to apply to the evolution of ancient Greek culture—the Socratic. Moreover, the definitions that she took from Nietzsche do considerable violence to the meaning he developed for these terms. The succinct definitions that she gave are indeed in the first few

[2] He died in 1900. I doubt that he would have liked Nazi Germany any more than he liked *Parsifal*.

paragraphs of *The Birth of Tragedy*, but she seems to have taken them too seriously. As Nietzsche's analysis of the evolution of Greek drama proceeds, it becomes apparent that he had been caught by his well-known fondness for short, well-turned aphorisms. Benedict writes:

> He discusses two diametrically opposed ways of arriving at the values of existence. The Dionysian pursues them through the "annihilation of the ordinary bounds and limits of existence"; he seeks to attain in his most valued moments escape from the boundaries imposed upon him by his five senses, to break through into another order of experience. The desire of the Dionysian, in personal experience or in ritual, is to press through it toward a certain psychological state, to achieve excess. The closest analogy to the emotions he seeks is drunkenness, and he values the illuminations of frenzy. With Blake, he believes "the path of excess leads to the palace of wisdom." The Apollonian distrusts all this, and has often little idea of the nature of such experiences. He finds means to outlaw them from his conscious life. He "knows but one law, measure in the Hellenic sense." He keeps the middle of the road, stays within the known map, does not meddle with disruptive psychological states. In Nietzsche's fine phrase, even in the exaltation of the dance he "remains what he is, and retains his civic name."[3]

Nietzsche himself says:

> Much will have been gained for esthetics once we have succeeded in apprehending directly—rather than merely *ascertaining*—that art owes its continuous evolution to the Apollonian-Dionysiac duality, even as the propagation of the species depends upon the duality of the sexes, their constant conflicts and periodic acts of reconciliation. I have borrowed my adjectives from the Greeks, who developed their mystical doctrines of art through plausible *embodiments,* not through purely conceptual means. It is by those two art-sponsoring deities, Apollo and Dionysos, that we are made to recognize the tremendous split, as regards both origins and objectives, between the plastic, Apollonian arts and the non-visual art of music inspired by Dionysos. The two creative tendencies developed alongside one another, usually in fierce opposition, each by its taunts forcing the other to more energetic production, both perpetuating in a discordant concord that agon which

[3] Ruth Benedict, *Patterns of Culture*, p. 72.

the term *art* but feebly denominates: until at last, by the thaumaturgy of an Hellenic act of will, the pair accepted the yoke of marriage and, in this condition, begot attic tragedy, which exhibits the salient features of both parents.

To reach a closer understanding of both these tendencies, let us begin by viewing them as the separate art realms of *dream* and *intoxication*, two physiological phenomena standing toward one another in much the same relationship as the Apollonian and Dionysiac. It was in a dream, according to Lucretius, that the marvelous gods and goddesses first presented themselves to the minds of men. That great sculptor, Phidias, beheld in a dream the entrancing bodies of more-than-human beings, and likewise, if anyone had asked the Greek poets about the mystery of poetic creation, they too would have referred him to dreams. . . .

The fair illusion of the dream sphere, in the production of which every man proves himself an accomplished artist, is a precondition not only of all plastic art, but even . . . of a wide range of poetry. Here we enjoy an immediate apprehension of form, all shapes speak to us directly, nothing seems indifferent or redundant. Despite the high intensity with which these dream realities exist for us, we still have a residual sensation that they are illusions; at least such has been my experience—and the frequency, not to say normality, of the experience is bourne out in many passages of the poets. Men of philosophical disposition are known for their constant premonition that our everyday reality, too, is an illusion, hiding another, totally different kind of reality.[4]

Nietzsche then proceeds with an analysis of the basis of Greek drama and poetry in these terms. It is generally considered a masterpiece of literary criticism and remains an exemplar of its genre. It is only some sixty pages later that Nietzsche introduces the fundamental problem of the introduction of order to art.

After a discussion of the seeming breakdown of a diametric clarity of these opposing forces in Euripides, Nietzsche wrote:

Euripides—and this may be the solution of our riddle—considered himself quite superior to the crowd as a whole; not, however, to two of his spectators. He would translate the crowd onto the stage, but insist, all the same, on revering the two members as the sole judges of his art; on following all

[4] *The Birth of Tragedy*, pp. 19–20.

their directions and admonitions, and on instilling in the very hearts of his dramatic characters those emotions, passions and recognitions which had heretofore seconded the stage action, like an invisible chorus, from the serried ranks of the amphitheatre. It was in deference to these judges that he gave his characters a new voice, too, and a new music. Their votes, and no others, determined for him the worth of his efforts. And whenever the public rejected his labors it was their encouragement, their faith in his final triumph, which sustained him. . . . Before giving a name to that other spectator . . . let us recollect how strangely we were affected by the chorus and by the tragic hero of a kind of tragedy which refused to conform to either our habits or our tradition—until, that is, we discovered that the discrepancy was closely bound up with the very origin and essence of Greek tragedy, as the expression of two interacting artistic impulses, the Apollonian and the Dionysiac. Euripides' basic intention now becomes as clear as day to us: it is to eliminate from tragedy the primitive and pervasive Dionysiac element, and to rebuild the drama on a foundation of non-Dionysiac art, custom and philosophy.

Euripides himself . . . propounded the question of the value and significance of this tendency . . . in a myth. Has the Dionysiac spirit any right at all to exist? Should it not, rather, be brutally uprooted from the Hellenic soil? Yes it should, the poet tells us, if only it were possible, but the god Dionysos is too powerful: even the most intelligent opponent . . . is unexpectedly enchanted by him, and in his enchantment runs headlong to destruction. . . . the cleverest individual cannot by his reasoning overturn an ancient popular tradition like the worship of Dionysos, and that it is the proper part of diplomacy in the face of miraculous powers to make at least a prudent show of sympathy. . . . Dionysos had already been driven from the tragic stage by a daemonic power speaking through Euripides. For in a certain sense Euripides was but a mask, while the divinity which spoke through him was neither Dionysos nor Apollo but a brand-new daemon called Socrates. Thenceforward the real antagonism was to be between the Dionysiac spirit and the Socratic, and tragedy was to perish in the conflict. . . .

Let us now look more closely at the Socratic tendency. . . . What . . . could Euripides have hoped to effect in founding his tragedy on purely un-Dionysiac elements? Once it was no longer begotten by music, in the mysterious Dionysiac twilight, what form could drama conceivably take? Only that of the dramatized epic, an Apollonian form which precluded tragic effect.[5]

Nietzsche then points out that Euripides, try as hard as he could, never succeeded in founding his drama on a cool Apollonian mood. He laid his plans, says Nietzsche, as Socratic thinker and carried it out as passionate actor. "It cannot possibly achieve the Apollonian effects of the epic, while on the other hand it has severed all connections with the Dionysiac mode; so that in order to have any impact at all it must seek out novel stimulants which are to be found neither in the Apollonian nor in the Dionysian realm. Those stimulants are, on the one hand, cold, paradoxical ideas put in the place of Apollonian contemplation, and on the other fiery emotions put in the place of Dionysiac transports." (Nietzsche then complains that this led to an inartistic naturalism in Euripides.) He then points out that Euripides was led to an "esthetic Socratism." Its supreme law, is that " 'whatever is to be beautiful must also be sensible'—a parallel to the Socratic notion that knowledge alone makes men virtuous." Following "this canon, Euripides examined every aspect of drama—diction, character, dramatic structure, choral music—and made them fit his specifications. What in Euripidean, as compared with Sophoclean, tragedy has been so frequently censured as poetic lack and retrogression is actually the straight result of the poet's incisive critical gifts. . . ."

Nietzsche proceeds to apply this ad hoc to Sophoclean tragedy, which is an analysis that seems plausible to me, but which may not appear so to a specialist. (I am told, however, that it has actually held up pretty well.) More important to the present discussion was that Nietzsche showed that criticism is essentially a process of trying to encase art in an apprehensible logical structure. It was, to use a term of Georges Gurvitch, noetic—it originated in the intellect. The critic tries to stop the Dionysian ecstasy and freeze the slow-flowing reverie of the dream. Nietzsche, however, held one process of great importance: the artist himself internalizes critical standards. Sometimes such internalization can lead to an utter effacement of expressions of the individuality of the artist himself. It is not only that one can see a deadly sameness in the life drawings of a class in a beaux-arts studio because the students have been taught to see the human body by rules that were set down long before they had been formulated for American students in Bridgman's textbooks, but one can also see similarities that come

[5] Ibid., pp. 74–77.

from following rules in the gracious French townhouses of New York and Paris and in the official "classical" architecture of Franklin Delano Roosevelt's Washington. These buildings represent a taste to which at least most of us over fifty are sympathetic, but the rules have so suppressed spontaneity that only a specialist or buff in architectural history is likely to know who designed them. Contrast this to the work of artists like Frank Lloyd Wright, Samuel Richardson, Edward Durrell Stone, Stanford White, and Michelangelo, work that is identifiable to fairly large numbers of people even if the architects themselves are not equally important. In the less identifiable work a set of academic critical standards has operated in the place of creativity. These standards involve rules and learned techniques. It is more than just the fact that we are habituated to the way of living to which they are fitted that makes them seem to work. It is an internal logic that conforms to the logical structures that in a final sense comprise the basis of Western thought itself, a common substratum that probably accounts for why almost any person of normal intelligence and coordination who is not inhibited by fixations can be taught almost anything fairly well within his physical capabilities including the crafts of the artist. It thus is no accident that such disparate persons as Freed Bales (an eminent small groups theorist), George Meany, Dwight Eisenhower, and Winston Churchill can turn out inoffensive, passable week-end paintings and why art schools and conservatories are filled with tens of thousands of technically capable young people who would not make it to lasting fame even if they could find a way into the market. Such rules are ubiquitous to "lesser" arts as well. There are manuals used to train interior decorators. All that the tyro needs is to want to be a decorator. He is told which colors enhance each other, which contrast, and which clash. The rules are all there for how much furniture should be in a room and for how big it should be with relation to the room. Similar rules exist for landscape architecture. There are rules for the width of paths, textures of foliage, the size of statues with relation to length of vistas, and the like. There is, as my high-school art teacher Earl J. Early used to say, a science in art, but he did not say that it leads to Scandinavian modern, Sloan interiors, motel bedrooms, and to the idea that arbor vitae should not be planted too close to a house. None of the results are offensive, but none are exciting either and almost anyone can get similar results because there are rules.

However, the professional training of the artist does two things.

First, it drills such standards in so rigorously that they are autonomic. Some systems of training go even farther than ours. In Japan the pupil is encouraged to reproduce the techniques of a master. The practice goes so far that in the classical drama the rights to play certain named classical roles are passed down from one generation of actors to the next. Originality is only allowed after craftmanship has developed. In the West such arrangements are not formalized, but the widespread practice of having protégés has the same effect of perpetuating the techniques and tastes of masters. Secondly, it requires a peripheral category of functionaries who must make it their business to assure that such rational standards are kept. Moreover they formulate them into exact rules and try to make them imperatives for artists, and attempt, often successfully, to penalize those who produce work that cannot be subsumed under their rules and rubrics.

There are, of course, the critics. But against such tendencies the Nietzschean Dionysian and Apollonian modes—of ecstasy and dreams—insistently manifest themselves. Neither dream nor ecstasy follows rational rules. Each goes on with a life of its own that seems not to be bound by any rules of structure or development. The artist as critic of himself and the critic alike attempt such projections of rationality upon the work of the artist. One fact, however, perhaps really differentiates the artist from the programmed automaton. It seems that where art becomes creative it is precisely because rules are broken and there is the shock of seeing the ecstatic state or the delicious world of the dream. It has been said that John Philip Sousa's marches are fine if you believe in a deterministic universe; the rules always lead you to know what to expect next. This may well be what condemns Sousa to perpetual nonentity. Contrast Sousa with Beethoven who seems to have followed his muse over one rocky path after another. Perhaps something similar dooms Corot to be a perpetual nonentity too. There is an old wisecrack about Corot that says that he painted 3,000 pictures of which 5,000 are in America. His rules were easy to follow and he was predictable. A good specific case lies in the vast Trevi Fountain. The rules say one should come upon it at the end of an avenue that provides a vista that befits its scale; it is in fact at the junction of four dingy streets. The effect shocks. The sculptors seem to have overfilled the tiny piazza. (In fact, if one counts the space of abutting streets it is only about one-quarter of it, but it seems like more.) Earlier Michelangelo had the same capacity to break out of such rational structures and some of the startling effects of the great staircase of the Laurentian Library in Florence result from its confinement by a space that is "too small" for it.[6] Leonardo tried to constrain himself with endless rules of nature whose very rationality makes them seem bizarre,[7] only to fail in the end. He remained creative in spite of himself. What appears to us is a dreamy reverie of faces and landscapes that we never find outside of the perceptual world that he created in his pictures. Such bursting of rational limits is probably ultimately the sine qua non that separates the creative artist from the craftsman. It is perhaps no accident that after the Bauhaus group published a new set of principles for art even their major formulators violated them—sometimes not too timidly.

Rules, however, are jealous gods. Critics do not deal easily with the embarrassment that arises when what they have denigrated as "wrong-headed" achieves success among both laymen and other artists. It is not a recent phenomenon that came with Impressionism. Wherever we know enough about the ambience of the very great artists of the past to comment on it at all, we seem to find such occurrences, whenever the resulting work is recognized, as good and as violating rules. Artists clash with the rules that the critics and the art schools and the conservatories set up. Such recognition is a troublesome problem that has to be dealt with by the critics. The easiest way to deal with such perversities is to try to show that the new work is actually good by recognized standards of criticism. The artists themselves exploit three possibilities when they know they are "breaking the rules." The first is not to care at all whether there are rules to be followed; the second is to contend that the work being produced is, in fact, truly orthodox; the third is to condemn the orthodox through manifestoes that state a new set of rules. All of these responses (or nonresponses) have occurred, especially in painting in the last century. These operations are only a process of symbolic manipulation. They really affect creative work little. (In fact both Herbert Read and Roger Shattuck, two of the most perceptive chroniclers of modern art of the last quarter century, repeatedly point out that there is a constant formation of art groups issuing manifestoes that tend to break up when the members themselves find it onerous to follow their own pronouncements.)

Still, behind such criticism one must look for an answer to the

---

[6] The Laurentian staircase is so large with relation to its space that it is impossible to photograph it in toto without distortion.

[7] Albrecht Dürer tried this too and even went so far as to correct the features of a self-portrait to make them conform to his rules.

questions that have been posed in order to make the assertion that the critic is an agent of the society. But in saying this one also says that he is an expositor of the culture as well. The culture must be considered upon two levels, the phenomenal, transitory eidos and the deeper underlying qualitative aspect—the ethos. The eideic aspect is variable in extreme, from place to place and from time to time, but there is more stability in the ethos.

What accounts for this stability? This question has to be considered upon two levels: the first is the underlying metaphysics and the second is the concepts of the nature of life. The present essay avoids trying to put the discussion on a psychological level. It is, above all, logically questionable to do so. Talking about ethnic consciousness[8] and the like ignores simple textbook psychology. The psychological *rules* that govern behavior and response to art as behavior are probably identical everywhere. This is an essay on the sociology of art, not the psychology of creativity or response. These matters are left where they belong—in psychology and psychoanalysis. We deal only with cultural meanings here.

## BACKGROUND NOTE

This chapter is based entirely upon Friedrich W. Nietzsche's *The Birth of Tragedy* (1879), translated by Francis Golffing (New York: Doubleday, Anchor, 1956). Edith Hamilton's *The Greek Way* (New York: Norton, 1930) is a sensitive account of the nature of ancient Greek culture that articulates to the Nietzschean categories. Ruth Benedict's *Patterns of Culture* (New York: Houghton, 1934) remains the classic, and despite my comments, an unexcelled attempt to apply the Dionysian-Apollonian dichotomy to a general theory of culture. As for works on the general nature of culture, I like the works of the older anthropologists best. These are A. L. Kroeber, *The Nature of Culture* (Chicago: University of Chicago Press, 1952), Bronislaw Malinowski, *The Scientific Theory of Culture* (Chapel Hill, N.C.: University of North Carolina Press, 1944), and Florian Znaniecki, *Culture Sciences: Their Origin and Development* (Urbana, Ill.: University of Illinois Press, 1952).

---

[8] Much of this should be put in the same category of scholarship as Houston Stewart Chamberlain's *The Foundations of the Nineteenth Century*. Chamberlain was an uncle of Neville Chamberlain and remains a leading theoretician of German, English, and American racist doctrines. The work was written in German and first published in 1899 and translated into English in 1910. It has gone through many translations and editions.

# 9

## Art and the Cultural System:
## The Social and Cultural Dynamics
## of P. A. Sorokin

NIETZSCHE'S greatest accomplishment in the study of culture was to describe the three tendencies underlying all art and the very human psyche itself, the excesses of dream and of ecstasy, and the presence of a rational critique that provides the restraints upon those excesses and makes form, perhaps even social life itself, possible. But he has told us nothing about the levels of meaning through which these fundamental psychic forces are expressed. The very appearances can often have radically different meanings irrespective of similarities in the psychic tendencies they express. Inevitably one must return to the cultural system through which such tendencies are filtered before they reach expression. A number of very important writers have dealt with culture in this way, Weber, Durkheim, Spengler, Brooks Adams, and Cassirer, to name a few. (I have not mentioned a single anthropologist because the present essay confines itself to art that has come out of societies that are literate and show highly developed occupational specialization.) We are not drifting in uncharted headwaters, but are in a well-surveyed territory in the literature of the classical sociology concerning complex societies.

The philosophers of the Enlightenment imagined idyllic jeunesses of the societies they knew where man apprehended his ambience unhampered by the sophistications of what ibn-Khaldun called "the things born of civilization." There were some off-key voices in the chorus of praise—men like Thomas Hobbes and David Hume—but by the end of the eighteenth century few intellectuals doubted that the civil condition would become incredibly good once everyone became enlightened and educated, and that by following the clear light of reason things would be the same everywhere. Most of the philosophes little doubted that all the varying manifestations of personality and society would finally express a common culture based upon reason. Only the two great archetypal sociologists, Montaigne (1533–1592) and Montesquieu (1689–1755), adumbrated a full understanding of the role of stubborn cultural differences that determined the qualities of human experience and achievement. Their works, however, were urbane, scholarly curiosities from the very start. By the middle of the nineteenth century what we now call classical sociology was dominated by Social Darwinism and Positivism. The exponents of each tendency took it as axiomatic that the world was getting better and better every day in every way. The Darwinists saw it as the benign mystical hand of evolution and the Positivists saw it as the progressive, incremental victory of science over error. When we look at their works a century later they seem only to be new varieties of metaphysical optimism and their foundations seem just as aery, and even in their own time one would have had to be a new Candide to take their promises seriously. Neither Comte nor Spencer ever gave any thought to what their "Progress" meant in terms of human feeling and, in a final sense, they promised no more than the divines who had already insisted that the purpose of human society was to glorify God. Marx—the best sociologist of the nineteenth century—was also ultimately optimistic and promised an eternity of rare days after Armageddon. The earlier writers did not expect things to get discernibly better from day to day and seem now not only to have been far better prognosticators of the actual course history took in the two centuries after the collapse of the *ancien régime*, but to have had a far better understanding of what the role of culture was in providing continuity to social life.

It is not easy to pick a good place to start, but there seem good reasons for not starting with what may have been the most striking development in everyday life in nineteenth century, the democratization of lavish consumption, waste, and destructiveness.

Purely materialistic explanations of the periodic manifestations of conspicuous waste had never taken into account the differences in the meanings underlying how material means are used. Does one build the great pyramids at Gizeh (tombs), Rockefeller Center

**8**  Ideational form and the Eastern emphasis upon the felt continuum. *Bodhisattva*, China, Wei Period, ca. 530, from the Pai-ma-ssu (White Horse Monastery) near Lo Yang (Honan).

The figure of the Bodhisattva contrasts strongly with the tension and power of Verrocchio's equestrian figure of the Condottièro Colleoni. This figure does not confront anything. It barely achieves its identity out of the stone; the face is serene, contented, aware of everything and nothing, and without passions to give it individuality. There is nothing either to arrest or overwhelm us. It is a moment in the endless flux. (See fig. 14.)

Courtesy, Museum of Fine Arts, Boston. Gift of Denman W. Ross in memory of Okakura Kakuzo.

(offices), or the royal park at Versailles (palaces)? Even the simplest comparisons by caste, class, and estate show often profound differences in the motives for conspicuous consumption. The expression of all such differences may be severely limited by a lack of wealth and the stages of development of technology, but what one may want to do can be very different indeed. The reasons for the differences in what the skills and talents of the artist express, the motives and meanings, continue to elude us if one takes display itself to be an end.

In the decades before 1930 it also became increasingly apparent to scholars that race was a poor way of explaining differences in artistic systems from one society to another insofar as they were an expression of the culture.[1] Racial differences as an explanation of cultural variability seem to be just as elusive today to tough-minded observers as they were a half century ago. Ashley Montague showed in *The Fallacy of Race* (1943) that such explanations were based upon extremely bad biology and P. A. Sorokin showed in *Contemporary Sociological Theories* (1928) that such explanations were often farcically contradictory. Geographical determinism met a similar fate at the hands of its detractors, as did all the other factor sociologies[2] of the nineteenth and twentieth centuries. When all such attempts were exhausted it became apparent that only society itself was left as a place to look for explanations of the cultural differences. The task seemed to be to answer a series of questions about how people see the role of culture itself. What differing social values do its varying manifestations express for them? What does it mean to them? What are the motive ideas and assumptions that account for its differences?

In the decades around 1900 a few major writers began to deal with such questions. For various reasons inclusive and convenient explanations eluded them. Sigmund Freud and Vilfredo Pareto missed out because their concerns with the irrational infrastructure of human activity led them away from paying any serious attention

1 Such nonsense continues in an uninterrupted torrent. Recently a great deal of comfort has been taken from studies of separated identical twins by advocates of innate differences. They have shown that identical twins will make strikingly similar choices when confronted with similar situations. I am not sure that we are able to conclude much more if two thirty-year-old males are found living a mile apart in the same city and two eighteen-year-old boys end up at the same state university campus. Moreover, there has been a quite inadmissible metastasis in the universe of discourse from individuals to races; not a whit has yet shown that the same similarities in choice will occur when race is the independent variable. Race remains a poor explanation for cultural variability.
2 The term "factor sociologies" was applied by Georges Gurvitch to attempts to consider the entire subject matter of sociology as reducible to some single factor, such as race, geography, or climate.

to whatever may have given consistency to total culture configurations. Max Weber was bogged down almost to his very last days with an abortive attempt to view modern Western society as an epiphenomenon of the Protestant ethic, a notion that was easily laid low by men who were not half the scholar that he was, although men like Kurt Samuellson and Richard Tawney were no tyros. Classical Marxists agreed that "the most heavenly ecstasies of religious fervor" had been drowned "in the icy water of egotistical calculation," but never gave much more than bourgeois comfort to the accretion of petty advantages as the end for all the "figgering." Émile Durkheim spoke of a collective consciousness that was a repository of science, religion, law, logic, and the aesthetic systems, but did not go much further than saying that when we spoke of such things we were talking about the very core of society itself. He never told us what values they expressed and why in a given context they showed a qualitative consistency. He knew such consistencies were present and tried to deal with them in *Primitive Classification*, but even there they eluded him.

Whilst the Marxists waited for the Holy Wrath and the others apotheosized their classes and their societies, the tycoons of capitalism paraded themselves before the world as exemplars of virtue. A broken Titan stood on the sidelines and spat at the splendid, barbaric procession. Thorstein Veblen, rawboned, poor, dressed in general store clothing, and always hungry in spirit and almost in body as well, asked who were these kings of glory and what they expressed. "Thorstein Veblen's America" was not his America at all; it was really the America of John D. Rockefeller and J. P. Morgan, Sr. It was an America where there were things to be grabbed and whatever could not be grabbed did not matter because it could not be grabbed. In 1899 *The Theory of the Leisure Class* was born, blushed unseen, and wasted its sweetness upon the desert air as did ten more books in the same vein that appeared at intervals until his death in 1929. Veblen called what he saw "conspicuous consumption" and saw American society as a contramorality play in which the meek would never inherit the earth and whose luminaries were men who could (and did) ride roughshod over anyone but each other. The seven deadly sins were prime virtues that produced a world that repelled Veblen by its blatant avarice and quest for sensation and its unashamed indulgence of megalomanic impulses What could not serve these desires was disvalued and, as one migh expect, its art became equated to opulent material display.

Veblen, however, never considered how the things people sought and valued expressed the existential postulates of the underlying

culture. One suspects that like the poor and unsuccessful everywhere he never really doubted the reality of the material world. The
full implications of Veblen's work were to lie unnoticed for a long
time. The ripe moment to ask what he saw expressed came just before World War II. It was apparent then that we had to start looking seriously at the values of Western society. Talcott Parsons began to wrestle with their role in *The Structure of Social Action*
(1937) and Ernst Cassirer was to develop the ideas that are set
forth in a short form in his *Essay on Man*.[3] Parsons, however, got
no more specific about what he was talking about than to agree
with Max Weber; and Cassirer, being a philosopher, kept to the
philosopher's task of ferreting out the common. It seems fair to say
that a coherent attempt to consider how ontological assumptions
determine the observable forms culture takes lay in what may well
be the most important work in sociology of the mid twentieth century, P. A. Sorokin's *Social and Cultural Dynamics*.[4] It was a study
to be reckoned with. Its size alone was intimidating—it ran to
around 3,000 pages; it was replete with diatribes; its author often
used words for what they meant to him; it often shows the hands
of poorly supervised graduate students. But despite all its faults
Sorokin's book did do rather well in relating the targets of Veblen's
jeremiads to the underlying ontology of our society and what he did
shows very close parallels.[5] Sorokin independently related what
Veblen saw to a dichotomy in our conceptions of the nature of culture and society based upon whether reality was seen to lie ultimately in the intellectual ideas about the world or in the content of
experience itself. In the first volume of *Social and Cultural Dynamics, Fluctuations in the Forms of Art*, Sorokin provided a key
to understanding the varying systems of meaning that underlie the
character that art assumes in particular cultural contexts. It was a
misfortune that Sorokin was himself egregiously sloppy in his scholarly techniques. The consequence of this was that much of the

---

[3] A popularization of *The Philosophy of the Symbolic Forms*.

[4] It is perhaps hard for me to look upon an important intellectual mentor of my
youth impartially, but I have yet to find anything that has dealt generally with
the ontological bases of cultural variabilities as well, except perhaps, F. S. C.
Northrop's, *The Meeting of East and West*, which is taken up in the chapters
that follow.

[5] I am fairly sure that Sorokin never read Veblen with any care, if at all. If he
had I do not think that he would have described Veblen's work as "diluted and
bled Marxism," as he did to me and many others. He was still following the
superficial denigration of it that remained current in American academic circles
until David Riesman did us the service of forcing us all to take a fair look at it
in *Thorstein Veblen's America*.

criticism of this work focused not upon its overall validity, but upon seemingly countless details.[6]

His hypothesis was simple enough and is probably well known to a substantial number of readers. Sorokin distinguished two "polar" attitudes toward the nature of reality as ultimately determining how man viewed his world, criticized and evaluated it, and organized his activities, and determined his artistic output. The consistency of culture to Sorokin did not arise from the mystic coordination of action as the functionalists had implied, but was a result of the view of the nature of reality that predominated from time to time. One of these was the ideational. In this, reality lay not in the world of experience but in ideas themselves. Man is always in Plato's cave, seeing through the senses only the fleeting shadows on the wall of a reality that remains forever inaccessible to direct experience. The other polar type he called sensate. In this mode reality does not lie in ideas that transcend the sensory world but in the senses themselves. Sensation is indeed the test of truth. In the ideational culture, the interest of man is directed inward. Reality is in the vision, the ecstasy, the exaltation of the spirit. It leads us ultimately to the Dantean empyrean and to Nirvana, the cessation of all desire. In the sensate culture, desire itself is the reality. The transient world of the senses has no meaning beyond such satisfactions. Life is exactly what it seems to be and that is all there is to reality. As Sorokin himself said on numerous occasions, the watchword was "carpe diem." The data, even as Sorokin saw them were not, alas, so clear cut. He admitted that neither the

[6] My own subsequent reading has made me ambivalent about these criticisms. There is no question whatever to me at least—and I knew him well—that his use of his sources was uncritical and that he set out special hooks for certain kinds of fish and he often did not consider what else the waters might yield. He gave specialists in the histories of everything about which he wrote many field days at his expense. Yet, paradoxically perhaps, the case for the entire study seems to improve when one reads special studies independently of his own work. Fifteen years after his death it appears, in fact, to be more plausible than during the controversies that may have been as much generated by his bad manners and his wild mode of expression as by what he was saying. Moreover, I know, from having assisted him as a graduate student, that he never really understood or had the patience to come to terms with the careful fittings of hypothesis, method, and data that characterize careful work. He wanted always to carve out things in mighty chunks. The real difficulty in this, I think, under which his Social and Cultural Dynamics labored, was that he did not understand these methodological questions at all. The result was that he often tried to prove more than anyone could handle, and his naiveté about such matters caused him to treat complex hypotheses as if they were self-evident truths. It seems no accident in the context of the way he worked that what should have been a hypothesis came out as a massive, outrageously padded, moralizing tract. I think that if he had waited for the data to come in it might have been happier for him, but waiting was not his calling.

ideational or sensate spirit was ever manifested without some elements of the other. (For art at least, this, I think, would necessarily be impossible. No art could really be purely ideational, for to be art at all it must be expressed and this means it must lend itself to sensory apprehension; on the other hand it seems equally impossible to have a purely sensate art because art without some ideas of organization would be without form and there may be a question as to whether it is art at all. Ultimately it may have been such difficulties that did in two dead modern movements—Suprematism with its cold squares and lines and Abstract Expressionism with its inchoate color.)[7] The manifestations of these basic orientations were not only necessarily impure, but some actually tried to express both of these outlooks. These last manifestations Sorokin called idealistic. Unable to let well enough alone he also introduced active and ascetic Ideationalism and, in the sensate culture, active, passive, and cynical mentalities (chap. 2). He seems to have had some very good times with such exegeses and one must admit they sometimes sound a little like Polonius showing off to Hamlet on the forms of drama. However, when such playing around with combinations of terms is put aside there remains a valid distinction that helps us classify and identify cultures with respect to their basic outlook. The implications of the distinction are shown in a list of contrasts given in the first volume.[8]

| First Culture [Ideational] | Second Culture [Sensate] |
|---|---|
| Dominance of | Dominance of |
| Rationalism, Mysticism | Empiricism |
| Idealism | Materialism |
| Eternalism | Temporalism |
| Indeterminism | Determinism |
| Realism | Nominalism |
| Sociological Universalism | Sociological Singularism |
| The Conception of Corporation or Juridical Personality as a Primary Reality | The Conception of Corporation or Juridical Personality as an Expedient Fiction |
| Ethics of Absolute Principles | Ethics of Happiness (Hedonism, Utilitarianism, Eudaemonism) |
| Few Discoveries in the Natural Sciences and Few Inventions | Many Discoveries and Inventions |

[7] Edward Lucie-Smith, a perceptive, sympathetic critic of modern art, was worried by precisely this point in the first and second chapters of *Late Modern: The Visual Arts Since 1945.*

[8] P. A. Sorokin, *Social and Cultural Dynamics,* vol 1, "Fluctuations in the Forms of Art," page 33. The odd capitalization is Sorokin's own.

| First Culture [Ideational] | Second Culture [Sensate] |
|---|---|
| Static Character of Social Life with a Slow Rate of Change | Dynamic Character of Social Life with a Rapid Rate of Change |
| Ideational Style of Painting "Scripture" as the Main Form of Literature | Visual Style of Painting (?) Secular Realism and Naturalism in Literature, with Sensualism and even Sexualism |
| Pure or Diluted Theocracy "Expiation" as the Basic Principle of Punishment and of Criminal Law | Pure or Diluted Secular Power "Adjustment," Re-education Mixed with Extermination of the "Unadjusted" and "Socially Dangerous" Persons. |

This gives, I think, some idea of the scope of the dynamics through its 2,912 pages. The text itself shows that Sorokin was pretty ignorant of many technical questions of epistemology, but this is another matter. The first volume (after 200 pages of vituperative prolegomena) deals with "Fluctuations in the Forms of Art." However, what became clear after the dust settled is that he always saw art in the matrix of a total culture and that to him the critical apparatus by which art is judged is ultimately an emergence of criteria that are based first upon the type of socio-cultural systems in which they occur and then ultimately upon the conceptions of how reality is defined. Sorokin saw even the content of epistemology itself as being changed along these lines.

What ensued was that Sorokin rushed in where experts feared to tread, but it is only his version of the spirit of art that concerns us here. He set himself up as judge and jury about where every

---

9  Rational architectonic form in Western painting. Francisco de Zubaran (1598–1664), *St. Francis.*

By the time of Giotto di Bondone (fl. 1300) architectonic form in painting was firmly established and 300 years later it was still going strong. Zubaran painted a solidly constructed figure, built up firmly from the floor. No anatomical inaccuracy is apparent and the "laws of drapery" have been carefully observed. But a new mode of painting that was less bound by such rational strictures seemed to be arising in Zubaran's lifetime. He was pushed out of courtly and fashionable favor by Bartolomé Estaban Murillo (1617–1682) who painted lush, flowing, ecstatic baroque forms. But it was not a permanent displacement; rational architectonic painting was too firmly rooted in Western patterns of thought to disappear for all time, as figure 10, a Matisse, shows.

Courtesy, Museum of Fine Arts, Boston. Purchased, Herbert James Pratt Fund.

artist—the greatest, the least, and all between—were to be put, and he set graduate students to support his contentions. They did this mainly, it seems, on the basis of pictorial content, a method that if followed consistently would place a Beato Angelico Madonna in the same category with a plaster Infant of Prague and Botticelli's *Birth of Venus* with a dirty post card. He knew that there were differences but really did not know how to respond when confronted with the implications of his methods. I knew Sorokin well enough to defend him from the charge of charlatanism that has been based upon this exercise. He was not acting dishonestly, he was simply egregiously naive about special methodologies in the social sciences and the agonies that proper historiographic technique exacts from historians. Such shortcomings left him with so little understanding of the monstrous complexity of art history and criticism that he never realized his off-the-top-of-the-head judgments could be questioned by experts (and was angry and hurt when they were). It is true that experts can reduce Sorokin's specific judgments to a heap of rubble, but special studies that employed a less rambunctious sort of scholarship show that Sorokin's dichotomy does provide a way to demonstrate how the artistic output of any society can be shown to have some consistency with both the elite and popular aspects of the ethos of its culture. Sorokin's distinction has held up surprisingly well as a key to understanding the dynamics of criticism from Aristotle to Vasari, Leonardo, Ruskin, Gombrich, Fry, Bell, Read, and Clark. When one puts aside the distraction of the editorial content, if any, of works of art and begins to look upon the formal, technical aspects of artistic output the case for his dichotomy becomes quite good. If you do not try to put a Primitive Italian background landscape and a Monet landscape together because they are both landscapes, it is fairly easy to see that Italian primitives regarded the idea of a landscape as a good deal more important than the transitory sensuous colors that were all a landscape was to the Impressionists. Similarly, when one does not try to put a Gothic church and a Baroque church under the same rubric (because both are religious edifices), but looks at the purely technical aspects of these structures from a standpoint of what they expressed, one can see that a concern with involuted, intellectualized content is central to the former and that facade, impression, and an attempt at breaking from the tension imposed by order is central to the latter. There is no point forty years later in reclassifying the work of the past in a way that might bring Sorokin into more favor. I think it sufficient to say that he sensed a relationship that could have been much more easily shown if he had kept to what the artists themselves were responding to in their intellectual milieus, rather than to what Sorokin himself was answering. I think he could have pulled himself out of such difficulties if he had not been so attached to the terms "sensate" and "ideational," which have gone into the limbo of hideous neologisms. I think that he would have conveyed a more easily understood pair of meanings if he had simply spoken of cultures in which intellectual content defines experience in contrast to cultures where experience was considered to define intellectual content. Whatever terms would have been better is now moot, but the influence of his students has been so great that the distinctions themselves are now inherent in the conceptual apparatus of modern criticism through their effects on the science of culture itself.

It now remains to ask if there is a deeper, more philosophical level that lies beyond Sorokin's dichotomy in the critical apparatuses that are brought to bear upon artistic output. *The Meeting of East and West* of F. S. C. Northrop may provide an answer to this question.

### BACKGROUND NOTE

The basic work for this section is P. A. Sorokin's *Social and Cultural Dynamics* (New York: Bedminster Press, 1937), vol. 1; *Fluctuations of Forms of Art*. He wrote a popular version entitled *Crisis of Our Age: The Social and Cultural Outlook* (New York, 1943). The literature critical of this work is extensive. Historians dwell on its bad historiography; American sociologists find its concerns are foreign to their training and sensitivities. Thorstein Veblen's *The Theory of the Leisure Class* still remains as good a book as anyone has ever written outlining the "barbarian" aspects of the nineteenth-century ethos. Ernst Cassirer's work is best introduced by his *Essay on Man* (New Haven, Conn.: Yale University Press, 1944) and is an unexcelled philosophical statement of the position that appears in sociology as symbolic interactionism. Those interested in non-Marxist economic interpretations of Western culture should see Oswald Spengler's *The Decline of the West* (New York: Knopf, 1945) and Brooks Adams, *The Law of Civilization and Decay* (New York: Vantage Books, 1943).

# 10

Art and the Cultural System:

F. S. C. Northrop's *The Meeting of East and West,*

Beginning, the Spirit of the West

I

N 1946 F. S. C. Northrop published what may well be the last work to appear in what has been called classical sociology, *The Meeting of East and West.* Northrop never called this book sociology, but sociology it is and as "classical sociology" it is among the grandest and finest to be found anywhere. It is easy to understand why. Few people in this century have been able to write with comparable knowledge and authority upon so many subjects—one thinks only of men like Max Weber, R. M. MacIver, and Arnold Toynbee, and they are part of a very small company in their understanding of the intensity of application that being an expert entails. The easy grades of the post-1950 collegiate scene and the concomitant lack of discipline in graduate education will probably preclude seeing many more people who can write books showing the same kind of authority. There may, of course, be a fallacy in my thinking about this work. I assume that Northrop's scholarship is always as fine as it is in those areas where I have had some training (which covers about half this work); I am unable to believe that it is not as consistently good throughout. Only parts of its analysis, however, are brought to bear in this study. *The Meeting of East and West* is an extremely complex book that not only considers two major world views and their aesthetic, ethical, and intellectual foundations, but several hybrid and derivative outlooks as well. Because the hope that led Northrop to write this book is irrelevant here, I may be emphasizing aspects of it that are more important to me than they were to him. He was trying to show that a synthesis of Eastern and Western cultures was possible and that it could be a basis of world peace. (A meeting of East and West indeed has taken place in the four decades since World War II. It has not, sadly, been upon the lofty levels he hoped but seems only to include the dreariest parts of each.) However, what is important here is that Northrop went beyond Sorokin's concern with the ontological aspects to a study of how differences in epistemological systems produce differing sets of underlying conceptions that give the common critical assumptions logical coherence and qualitative uniformity.

Northrop sees the central epistemological assumption of Western culture to be that everything in creation, including even human personality, is composed of discrete, separable parts from our universe—a view that Western scholars have questioned little until recently and which we find fully developed even in Plato and Aristotle. A metaphor that has been applied to this view of personality is that of the gemstone. No cutter, however skillful, can ever bring out what is not already there. This view has remained embedded in our thinking about personality for almost twenty-five centuries. It has an upper side and it has an underside—one exalted and romantic, the other grubby and mundane. It gives us the transcending hero of ancient, classical myths; the knight-errant of medieval fantasy who can only be vanquished by black magic; the prince who seeks fama of the Italian Renaissance; the tycoons of capitalism. The heroic level also includes many exemplars in whom courage is more apparent than wisdom—from brave, brawling, fleet-footed Achilles to Clark Kent, Superman. But it also has that other side that degrades the nonhero to Shylock who walks bent "low in a bondman's key with bated breath and whispering humbleness," or shows him as a scurvy knave who makes monkeys out of his fully certified betters—Sancho Panza, Figaro, Sam Weller, and, the best of them all, the Good Soldier Schweik and Leporello. Schweik did in the Austro-Hungarian empire by fighting its war; Leporello got the best of the morsels of food intended for Don Giovanni. (Both still live: Leporello now works in Atlantic City, New Jersey, where the going is good for a gentleman's procurer, and Schweik now is village selectman in Massachusetts. The others, as Leslie Fiedler has pointed out, are also still around.)

All, however, remain individualistic images. In this sense they have a qualitative consistency with the Jews' emphasis upon each man's confrontation with the Lord; with the figure of Saint Paul, the whilom perfectly observant Jew who concludes that he has no need to fear God; and even with Luther and the old reformers who were never sure that there was a mansion for each of them in their Father's house. None of these variations ever questioned that the core of personality had any existence beyond its discrete manifestations. This atomism did not stop, however, at the conception of personality alone, but extended to a certainty that the whole phenomenal world consisted of separable, self-contained entities.

Northrop traces this idea with great elegance through a number of chapters in *The Meeting of East and West*. His analysis is so concise and beautifully fitted that no précis or paraphrase can ever state it fairly. However, for the purpose of the present analysis, it is essential to try. According to Northrop, the philosophical epitome of the Western feeling about the nature of things was found in Locke's atomism and showed its most consistent social expression in what Northrop called "The Free Culture of the United States." Unlike Descartes who proposed a logic and methodology for science before the science itself was discovered, Locke proceeded from a seemingly experimentally verified Newtonian physics in

> which [when] mathematical reasoning [was] applied to its basic assumptions, and controlled experiment had confirmed, nature is to be conceived as a system of physical objects located in a public, infinitely extending, absolute space. It was to these objects guaranteed by Galilei's and Newton's physics that John Locke gave the name material substances. . . .
>
> In order to carry the theory through in detail and bring it into accord with the factual evidence, it was necessary to identify the material substances of the physics not merely with gross objects but also with unobservable exceedingly small particles termed atoms.[1]

There was never any doubt in the minds of Newton, Galilei, and, later, Einstein that what each of us perceives may be entirely private—the "mere appearances projected back upon the natural object by the observer." However, the private, "relative, apparent, sensible" time and space of each observer had nothing to do with "an absolute true and mathematical time" and space of the scientists. What became the dominant conception in the thinking of British and American empiricism was not such indefinable, analytic, a

---

[1] F. S. C. Northrop, *The Meeting of East and West*, p. 74.

priori concepts of science, but individually perceived atomized phenomena. In this sense, perhaps, Western scientific thinking is especially alien to the assumptions of American culture and the American temperament, both of which postulate immediate personal experience as the core of reality. This has made congenial a number of social fictions that suppose an equality of all possible interacting parties, such as contract as the basis of sociality and that oddest construct of all, the rugged individualist, who could be incarnated in avatars as different as Davy Crockett and John D. Rockefeller, Sr. When the atomistic mode of acting, thinking, and responding to the world affects the way we judge works of art it gives us an assumption that art and nature are separate orders of being, confronting each other. It removes the abstract structures that give perception order and coherence and goes to the emphasis upon atomized elements. At first—as early as the fifteenth century in Italy—it was man himself who was shown over and above nature, but these apotheosized creatures were still recognizably derived from the figures of living men. By the early twentieth century even the portrayal of man as the major focus of art interest was lost and the attempt to deal with atomized perceptions became the main preoccupations of both artists and critics. It is no accident at all that the two best-known abstractions of the first quarter of the twentieth century were Pablo Picasso's first *Les Trois Musiciens* and Marcel Duchamp's *Nude Descending a Staircase*. In both paintings the separate elements are out of the relationships that we normally see in our individual sensory worlds. Later Picasso was to go even further when he juxtaposed anatomical elements in ways that startled, surprised, and excited some (and confused and annoyed others) as we see in those many paintings where profile and full-faced eyes, ears, lips, and noses are combined only with the demands of design as the integrating elements of the picture.

We must, however, note one important feature of the development of nonobjective art in Europe. Europeans abandoned only the constraint that visual art needed to have an editorial content. Until very recently there was never any deviation from the Cartesian idea that design is the central fact of nature itself. There may seem to be an impassibly rough channel between Nicolas Poussin's mythological scenes, Paul Cézanne's apples and mountains, the Bauhaus's glass buildings, and Picasso's and Duchamp's paintings, but all of them emphasized structural, architectonic forms that are related to each other in accordance with an intellectually coherent, abstract, rational plan. The implicitly internalized standards of criti-

cism that European artists brought to their work remained Cartesian, and European critics continued to use these standards to judge
art.

The later indigenous American development was not, however,
Cartesian, but, as Northrop points out, atomistic and Lockean. For
this reason there was not the preoccupation with structured form
as a basis for art that was always central to European art. The
cutting loose from the constraints of structure took place considerably sooner in literary forms than it did in the visual arts. Sherwood
Anderson's *Winesburg, Ohio* (1919), Edgar Lee Master's *The
Spoon River Anthology* (1914), and John Dos Passos's *The 42d
Parallel* (1930) are atomized vignettes that achieve coherence by
quality rather than structure.[2] In music qualitatively similar tendencies were apparent. Charles Ives and Walter Piston seem tame
enough when compared to John Cage, but they all share the tendency to abandon a readily defined structure as a central characteristic of art. In the visual arts, especially painting, the emergence
of a new aesthetic was especially striking. The older American
painters and sculptors produced what was essentially European
work. At the American art schools the student was taught according to the basically European beaux-arts curricula and "if you were
any good" you were sent to European studios to study and to European museums to look at work that was part of European development alone, and of a Western European one at that.[3] It is not surprising that the resulting art was epiphenomenal to European work.
It really was not an implicit slander for the art histories to treat
the older American fine arts in hastily stated afterthoughts. In fact,
until the turn of the twentieth century there was good reason to
treat only our primitives as expressions of an indigenous peculiarly
American ethos. Architecture, ceramics, and furniture showed
somewhat more independence from European models, but the differences were more dictated by native materials and life styles than

[2] A contrast of these three books vis-à-vis structured form is interesting. Even
if one includes the slightly earlier appearances of parts of the first two in little
magazines the break-up of order took place in a very short time. There is still
a fairly apparent structure in *The Spoon River Anthology* and *Winesburg, Ohio*.
It is gone in *The 42d Parallel*.

[3] Until recently very little was known in the West about Chinese painting except
by specialists. The only significant Western collections were in London, Boston,
Philadelphia, Paris, Cleveland and Baltimore. Chinese scholars themselves knew
the history of their art far better than Westerners knew the history of theirs,
and had begun to study it expertly even in ancient times. They studied it so
well, in fact, that some reputations survived any examples of the artists' works
even in copies. The same Western ignorance obtains about much Japanese work.
We really only know the wood-block prints well.

any aesthetic developed in America. European aesthetics did not fit well with American egalitarianism. Not a single really big house by old-world standards was built in the United States until the 1880s even as the official residence of a public official. I can only once recall seeing the word "palace" used to refer to American domestic architecture. The word concerned some of the summer houses at Newport, Rhode Island, which were actually called "cottages" by their owners.[4] These and similar grandiose domestic fantasies did not last but were only actualized because of an ephemeral concatenation of big incomes, low taxes, and a large supply of immigrants who could be hired as servants. Even so, and perhaps most important of all, it would seem, as one wit put it, that "they were trying to be one with the Medicis." But none of this ever was of indigenous inspiration. Their architecture and furniture followed essentially European styles.[5]

When I first became interested in the study of art in the 1930s training was Cartesian in its inspiration, with an emphasis on order and design. The beaux-arts training of that period was replete with rules and laws. Numerous works were adduced that indeed did accord with the congeries of strictures that we found so tiresome. That large segments of work to which many had responded were out of accord with any of these rules seemed to have proved to the academicians that things had come to a low state indeed or that the works themselves would have been better if they had. The fact that the best work was often aberrant did not bother extra-academic artists at all. Indeed, it pleased them, because they saw the unsuitability of such rules to much of the best work of the past as well as to contemporary styles and technologies. It was apparent that older conventions belonged to their own times; it was fair to ask how much a classic pilaster can be elongated on the side of a skyscraper without looking like a taffy-pull in masonry. The most

---

[4] Evidence now seems incontrovertible that the super-rich did not move out of the big houses because they were broke, but because the houses are almost insurmountable nuisances to keep up, even with money. Moreover, the sign of having arrived today in an American context seems to be to have easy, perhaps even frenetic, spatial mobility—"jet setting"—and the overt control of strategic institutions in the economic and cultural spheres. It does not lie in keeping up huge domestic establishments. In addition, nearly all the big places in the United States were built between 1880 and 1920 and only a handful are big by old-world standards.

[5] Some earlier American furniture is now more appreciated than its European exemplars. American hardwoods such as maple and cherry were tough rather than brittle and for this reason permitted dramatic contrasts in the thickness of turnings and carvings. "Art" porcelains and bone china did not develop in America and were usually imported because deposits of pure kaolin were not found in North America until very late and only in limited deposits.

American architectural form had become the skyscraper. It was an indigenous development that was powerful, brash, and megalo-maniacal in its conception. The earliest skyscrapers were usually built without reference to any surrounding structures (as they still often are). It was not until Rockefeller Center was built in 1932 that we saw a coordinated complex of high-rise structures. The Chrysler Building and the Empire State Building—both products of the immediate predepression era—were built without any studied reference to the aesthetics of their sites and in surroundings that then were just as unprepossessing—if not crummy—as they are now. The much-studied Philadelphia Savings Fund Society Building (1934) replaced a group of decrepit corner structures. Abutting it on the south is a grassy, walled plot containing some graceful eighteenth-century buildings that belong to the Society of Friends, but as late as 1978 there remained to its west grimy four- and five-story buildings that housed typical, junky, inner-city, retail stores. The twin towers of the World Trade Center are perhaps the ultimate in confrontation. As confrontation became the objective there seemed to be considerably less consensus as to standards of performance. There were no longer any rules, either naive[6] or sophisticated[7] that could be used as touchstones of competence. The result was that there were not even simple-minded dicta by which performance could be judged and it became increasingly hard to judge. It is hard to escape difficulties in ranking results if one places no value upon subtle, complex, hard-to-learn techniques. If technique is ignored it is hard to differentiate an amateur rock concert from Igor Stravinsky's own reading of the *Rite of Spring*. (Both are, after all, rather noisy and involve a well-defined beat.) Edward Lucie-Smith has pointed out that with the tendency to ignore evidence of technical proficiency as a standard by which art could be judged, not only did artistic production become increasingly idiosyncratic, but by the 1960s the actual personalities of the artist often became the central focus of interest and the work itself assumed secondary importance. Lucie-Smith gives a number of examples in recent plastic arts involving bizarre personal behavior. He tells of Gilbert and George who

> with hands and faces gilded, stood on a plinth and mimed to a recording of the music-hall song "Underneath the Arches." The point, insofar as there was one, was the concern with the

[6] "The ultimate test of the ability to draw is a faithful rendering of the Venus of Milo."
[7] "If you can play the Hammerklavier Sonata you can play anything."

idea of style and stylishness. . . . the question of the division, or lack of it, between the creator and what he creates was brought up. Gilbert and George describe themselves as "living sculptures," and there is more than an implication that everything they do is to be looked upon as art.[8]

There was Jim Dine's staging of *The Car Crash* and of Stuart Brisley's "events," one of which, *And for Today—Nothing* (1972), involved lying "many hours, almost motionless in a bath full of water and animal entrails." To this one is allowed to add, I think, the "happening." Attempts to gain recognition for performance by the projection of colorful personality have not been confined to studio art. If anything, it has been an even stronger characteristic of forms addressed to mass audiences. Earlier the film industry used such devices to sustain products that serious critics considered artistically bad. One must say, to be fair, that Hollywood gave us a good many pictures where turning the attention of the audience from the picture to the off-the-set behavior of the players was not needed. *The African Queen* still interests audiences because one can look at it as anything from a rollicking good adventure story to a profound portrayal of the sexual arousal of a maiden lady who seems headed ineluctably to being an old prune, but for every African Queen there were many of "the worst movies we ever slept through."[9] This emphasis has been extreme with the emergence of the rock form from Elvis Presley onward. Often the music itself seems to convey little beyond banal adolescent longing to those of us whose tastes were formed in the context of a rationally structured prewar education. But the music itself does not seem as important to its aficionados as the carefully posed personalities of its performers.[10] Whenever we know anything about the contexts in which important artists worked it seems to include curiosity about their personalities, but as I read the records this has been a curiosity generated by their work. People were curious about them because the artists in question were thought to be good in their field. Michelangelo, Van Gogh, Gauguin, Leonardo, Alfred Jarry, and many others had personalities that diverged so far from the generality of men as to

[8] Edward Lucie-Smith, *Late Modern*, p. 271.
[9] It would have been hard to make its principals, Humphrey Bogart and Katherine Hepburn, good movie-magazine copy without lying. Both had Eastern seaboard professional backgrounds, elite educations, and both guarded their private lives so jealously that little was known about them.
[10] It became generally known after Elvis Presley's death from a surfeit of drugs that his actual personality was, to say the least, pretty maladjusted, and that the relatively innocent image of a callow adolescent sexuality obscured profound difficulties.

appear even by the most permissive rules, bizarre. What may be perhaps the oddest case of all, Robert Schumann was so disturbed that he was quite unable to understand that his perceptions of his own situation seemed delusive to others. But little of this showed in his work; it remained serene and romantic—often even sunny. However, there are the contrasting examples of J. S. Bach, Schubert and Haydn, and Ghirlandaio, Monet, Cézanne, and Renoir—all of whom displayed personalities and life styles that were more bourgeois than bohemian. Talking about people rather than things is no new temptation. However, the amount of sheer gossip about not-much-heard-of-since figures in Vasari's *Lives* leaves us to doubt that the shift in the object of criticism from the work to its creator is peculiar to the twentieth century, but Vasari (and even Cellini!) never expected anyone to equate the two. Moreover, artists themselves in the past have noticed that presenting a colorful facade does no harm at all in arousing curiosity about their work. It may be unfair to impute motives to action in such cases; both the personality and the work of the artist may show a march to a different drummer, but it is hard to shake off the suspicion that a colorful pose may have been affected to bring recognition to the work—even work that has held up.

Unfortunately for those who believe that taste is purely cyclical, the changes that have come about since the Second World War have *not* brought us back to a classicism that superimposes ornament upon structure, but have led instead to a renewed interest in structure that is now used to express confrontation. The most conspicuous manifestations came in op-art and super-realism, tendencies that cannot be considered seriatim because they overlap in time. We must begin by saying that much super-realism and op-art is

---

**10**   Rational architectonic form in painting. Henri Matisse (1869–1954), *Carmelina*.

Late in life when Zubaran stepped aside for Murillo as the central figure among painters in fashionable Spanish circles, it might have seemed that rational architectonic form was becoming passé. Post-Impressionist painting from Cézanne on tells us that it still had a long life ahead. In Matisse's *Carmelina* the planes are as definite as in Zubaran's *St. Francis* and the whole picture is a carefully blocked out construction. Perspective is geometric and an illusion of depth is achieved by a device used since the Renaissance, a succession of objects set in planes at increasing distances from the front of the picture. The tendency to think in terms of rational structure was too deeply rooted in Western consciousness to give way for good. It was to go much further; Matisse barely flirted with Cubism.

Courtesy, Museum of Fine Arts, Boston. Tomkins Collection, Arthur Gordon Tomkins Residuary Fund.

characterized by an expert control of old, indeed venerable, technique. But there seems to be something that was lacking in older art, a legerdemain in the manipulation of perception that has its roots in technical psychological studies that go far beyond the familiar rendering of distance through perspective and devices to correct perceptions to ideal images. In older work such illusionary devices were used to create a nexus between the created perceptual worlds of the artist and the perceptual world of the observers, but they have come to be used to confront the observer with the artists' world in a disturbing way. Confrontation seems also to be the dominant note in super-realist work. We are particularly startled by the sculpture. Some of it is plaster and Fiberglas casts of actual people which have been painted realistically and dressed in actual clothing and accessories: a uniformed museum guard; a beery workingman slouched in an easy chair; Duane Hanson's *Florida Shopper*, a bleached-blond, aging woman dressed like a twenty-year-old five-and-ten clerk. One finds similar tendencies in painters such as Robert Rauschenberg and Andy Warhol. It is, in fact, noteworthy that this work also confronts and jars even in the architectural context in which it is shown, often itself a calculatedly confrontational modern structure. Much of it is so alien to any of the usual ambiences in which everyday living is carried on that one is forced to think of it only as existing in vacuo. It is museum art by default of any other place to put it.

There has thus been implicit in any Western critical apparatus the twin themes of order and confrontation. Order, as Northrop points out, involves a reference to an abstract pattern to which the sensory world conforms only imperfectly at best. With Locke this attempt to impose order upon perception was viewed as trying to make understandable a world that was ultimately atomistic. It was an easy step for Americans to go from philosophic atomism to confrontation because of their special historic experience in settling into the new world. In Europe a habituation to neighbors and land had taken a relatively long time—well over ten thousand years of back-breaking toil. In the new world this was effected in less than two centuries in a process often both ruthless and brutal. Confrontation became our mode of action and eventually the mode of thought that went with it infused our art. It now remains to be seen how a profoundly different way of looking at reality and man's place in the natural order can determine the rationale of art.

## BACKGROUND NOTE

The basic work here is F. S. C. Northrop, *The Meeting of East and West. An Inquiry Concerning World Understanding* (New York: Macmillan, 1946); chap. 1, "The Contemporary World"; chap. 3, "The Free Culture of the United States"; chap. 4, "The Unique Elements in British Democracy"; and chap. 8, "The Meaning of Western Civilization."

For works that discuss the essentially confrontational character of Western art, see esp. Edward Lucie-Smith, *Late Modern: The Visual Arts since 1945*, 2d ed. (New York: Praeger, 1976) and Herbert Read, *A Concise History of Modern Painting*, 3d ed. with additional material by Caroline Tisdall and William Feaver (New York-Washington: Praeger, 1974).

# 11

Art and the Cultural System:

F. S. C. Northrop's *The Meeting of East and West*,

Conclusion, the Spirit of the East

THE Oriental world, as Northrop showed, conceives of order in terms that are quite different, indeed radically different, from those of the West. Order is never seen as lying in an abstract pattern. This was so foreign to the thinking of the Far Eastern world that none of its philosophical or theological systems can be stripped down to a technically logical[1] series of propositions. Even Brahmanical thinkers, whose speculations showed that they were highly adept in technically logical reasoning, usually resorted finally to the use of myth to illustrate truth even if, as Durkheim showed, what was seen as truth derived from the belief in the myth itself. Anyone who has tried to understand religion beyond the superficiality of seeing it as providing a theology for Baconian idols knows that there is at least some level in the religious consciousness where myth makes truth. For the Eastern intellectual the gut feelings that are personified in the myth are the essential aspect of truth, not its formal, logical structure. The historic Buddha himself was very adept in such matters, and in his final analysis of the paths to perfection showed that he thought feeling a better guide to action than logic and ratiocination.

The East, Northrop insists, sees reality to lie in feeling. The seem-

[1] The term "technically logical" refers to conformity with formal patterns that are in accord with the "laws concerning the valid rules of inference." It does not mean reasonable in any popular sense.

ing separateness of things and human individuality are regarded as consequences of continuing grave errors in conduct that arise out of philosophically erroneous attitudes. All other ostensibly discrete manifestations of nature and consciousness are similarly rooted in error. It is all illusion—*Maya*. There is no doubt that the desire for a rationally organized ideal order in Western thinking through Aristotle onward has made the development of abstract structures of rules a necessary intellectual comfort for us. In the high civilizations of the Orient—India, China, and Japan—the underlying conception of the nature of reality seems to have developed in so different a direction that Kipling's dictum that "East is East and West is West and never the twain shall meet" is true in a way he never thought. The startling difference from Western ways of viewing the world is that the dominant traditions of Oriental thinking never seem to have conceived of reality as manifested in atomistic entities that have an existence apart from the human mind. It saw individuality only as a result of philosophical misapprehension. It is now our task to point out how this essentially different way of viewing the world affects the ultimate critical apparatus by which the artist works and art is judged.

First of all I must give the reader the caution that what I will say here inevitably only skirts the subject. I have behind me only a dilettante's reading that has been made without a knowledge of the languages that a specialist would find appropriate. It does, however, extend over a period of more than thirty years and my first-hand mentors have been recognized scholars: Derk Bodde, Norman Brown, and Douglas Haring. When my curiosity led me to firsthand sources I have depended upon the great set *The Sacred Books of the East* edited by Max Müller. As anyone who has gone to such materials knows, resorting to the original texts does not help much. One has to go to secondary accounts to make much sense of them and often one sees that the secondary accounts make a kind of sense of them that is not apparent in the originals.[2] Such reading has sometimes left me highly suspicious even of scholars beside whom I remain a tyro, as in the case of Max Weber's studies of Indian and Chinese religions. The East is complex and varied in its local textures. It is divided by nationalistic grudges as stubborn as those of Europe and longer-standing feelings of identity have helped them root deeper. China and India, the seminal culture areas of the East, boast locally recorded histories at least as old as the gentile societies of the Mediterranean basin and a great deal older

---

[2] This sense may be a consequence of trying to reformulate these works within a rational framework that is understandable to Western readers.

than northern Europe, even if much of them is stated in ways that are exasperating to Westerners.[3] These records are often replete with supernatural elements that reflect an implicit assumption that exemplary repetitions strengthen a historiographic edifice. It often looks like very strange scholarship to anyone who has been taught in a tradition that assumes that human history proceeds according to some rationally comprehensive pattern whether it is divine law, natural law, conflicts arising from the scarcity of desiderata, or psychologistic explanations of drives for power, prestige, or sex. Our viewpoint tries to impute to the course of history a series of sociological laws whose applicability transcends individual experience. But as I get older—and read more—I am beset by persuasive intimations that it may be possible to read history as "a tale told by an idiot, full of sound and fury, signifying nothing." It may only be the world of Alfred Jarry's *Ubu Roi*, clumsy, bungling, meaningless. This view may be no more at odds with what passes through the flux of sensation, the world of transient, ever-evolving phenomena, than the selection of those impressions of the phenomenal world that can be subsumed under some scheme designed to bring order to our experience and ignoring what cannot be. In a sense any orderly reading of history may be, at best, the result of a fishing expedition that brings back only those morsels that go together in the stew. Inevitably, it seems, the historian is either a savant who tells the banker, the potentate, or the divine that he legitimately occupies his palace, or a petitioner who is pleading for a transcendental validity for his own idols and obsessions.

Suppose, however, that one proceeds from the idiot's tale assumption about the world of experience. Suppose one says that it is all *Maya*—illusion—or if we want to use the Japanese term for a portion of it, the "floating world" of transient sensations. We are then forced to ask what is permanent and stable if it is not the fact of perception itself. We are forced then to the Newtonian-Cartesian answer: it is only our own intellect that allows us to promulgate schemes for making the perceptual world sensible. We will never know, as Immanuel Kant showed in *The Critique of Pure Reason*, whether the sensible world is only the tip of a vast iceberg, or whether what we perceive is all there really is.

There is yet another question. How is our perception of the sensible world changed if we view reality not as ultimate monads as did Leibnitz, or atomistic entities as did Locke, or even hell-bent-for-leather forces which constantly collide with each other as did

---

[3] Indians show an insouciance about dates that is often irritating to Western scholars, but the record is there, nonetheless.

**11**   William Merritt Chase (1849–1916), *Still Life—Fish.*

Chase could have been added to Sargent, Whistler, and Eakins as another example of the museum's telling us how men of equal talent can select different aspects of the culture. As an academic technician he was second to no one. He was facile, so facile that he was "renowned for his figure studies, completed in three hours and executed entirely while standing before an assembled student body." He remains, however, best known for his studies of fish. He does not paint them in motion as Chinese artists did, but out on the table, waiting to be cooked. His model is the great eighteenth-century French still-life painter, Jean Baptiste Chardin (1699–1779). Chase certainly could have drawn a fish in motion if he had wanted to, but portraying fluid passing motion is an objective that is not easy to articulate when one looks at things from a point of view that demands precisely defined structures and rational relationships.

Courtesy, Museum of Fine Arts, Boston. Charles Henry Hayden Fund.

Hobbes, but as a continuum whose distinctions are purely illusive? As Northrop shows, such a difference gives us an image of the world that cannot be subsumed under any Western premises of observation. Our greatest difficulty arises in what Barbara Tuchman notes with reference to the civilization of fourteenth-century Europe: empathizing with the mentality behind what one finds. The ends for which any group organizes its activities depend upon the system of meanings current in the social milieu and upon the particular collective representations derived from the generalizations that emerge from the way that living in social groups is carried on, as Durkheim tried to show in *The Elementary Forms of Religious Life*. This is a way of saying that day-to-day living is carried on in the context of going concerns that only make sense in terms of their own implicit assumptions. It is certainly no new observation that when one is confronted with an ambience that seems to imply markedly different assumptions about the nature of the world some of us react almost catatonically until we re-enter a world that operates according to familiar premises. There is ample evidence that the ability to empathize itself can be really disastrous to the integrity of personality. It can be very destructive of certainty about

---

**12**   The Eastern aesthetic of empathy, the Tao of seats. George Nakashima (1903—), *Settee.*

Nakashima is an American who attended M.I.T. and various European and American art schools. He learned old-country methods of woodworking from a Japanese carpenter while interned during World War II. The settee shows how Taoist aesthetics can influence the way objects are made. The settee is a basically Western piece of furniture; the Japanese themselves would have had little use for a chair of any sort in their houses prior to the intrusion of Western influences. Here a Western object's character is transformed when subjected to an aesthetic that insists upon the articulation of human activity to the natural order. He seems to have made no attempt to give the plank any shape other than that of the forked tree trunk from which it was cut. The surface is not machine dressed, for that would have produced ridges against the grain. It is planed by hand with very long strokes that sometimes run the whole length of the board. This technique produces a surface that never goes against the character of the wood, and is satiny in appearance and pleasant to touch. The spokes, back, and legs are also hand shaped. He used no nails or screws. It is mechanically sound and so strong that visitors, uncharacteristically, are allowed to use it. There are none of the inherent physical stresses that one finds in so much of the museum's superb Western furniture. It is comfortable and fits well with the Tao of the human body as well as with the rest of the natural order.

Courtesy, Museum of Fine Arts, Boston. Commissioned by a grant from the National Endowment for the Arts and a matching grant from the Deborah M. Noonan Memorial Foundation.

one's own values. It is doubtful that anyone can ever really go native. The expatriates I encountered in Rome many years ago had not really become Romans. They had come to suspect not only the primacy of the idols of their own tribes, but of any other tribe as well, and this is what "culture shock" perhaps really is. It may be the difficulty of empathy that so often makes outsiders seem unpredictable, even shifty. The drummers to whom they march drum out a beat that is cueless to the untrained foreign ear. The difficulty is always there. The difference can be as narrow as a Bostonian viewing Philadelphia or a New Yorker viewing Chicago; it can be as wide as an American trying to place Oriental cultures in a sensible pattern. It is the last that is germane here.

Northrop masterfully lays out the view of reality that makes empathizing with the East so difficult in the ninth and tenth chapters of *The Meeting of East and West*, "The Traditional Culture of the Orient" and "The Meaning of Eastern Civilization." The first point in Northrop's analysis is that where Western knowledge tends to emphasize the interplay of abstraction and experience Eastern knowledge gives primacy to its felt, intuitive, aesthetic aspects. The component in the nature of things that is emphasized is that which "immediate experience and continuous contemplation can convey." Relating experience to a logically constructed abstract structure is neither a part of this process, nor, for that matter, essential to it. It is not appropriate to this essay to be concerned with problems that are appropriate to metalinguistics. However, logic, the visible keystone of Western science since Aristotle,[4] has never been as important in Eastern thinking as it is to us and indeed the language of China itself virtually precluded logic. Proof has been seen to lie not in conformity to formal rules, but in constant reassertion. Much of the tiresome repetition that one so often finds in Eastern sacred texts may be dictated by a desire to reaffirm the transcendental validity of what is being asserted when a logical infrastructure is absent.[5] What is true is what is perceived and felt, logical ways of reasoning always remain peripheral and supportive in Eastern thinking. The Chinese only approached developing a logic in response to an attempt to introduce Indian religious thinking. It was in the context of a short-lived, ancient school.[6] If one pays no atten-

[4] It should not be forgotten that both of Aristotle's Analytics codified a way of reasoning that had been long established in Greece.
[5] The multiplication of miracles in the Holy Bible, especially in the New Testament, suggests that this may happen whenever beliefs do not readily lend themselves to technically logical statements.
[6] See Marcel Granet, *The Religion of the Chinese People* (New York: Harper and Row, 1975), chap. 4; and John K. Fairbank, Edwin O. Reischauer, and Albert M. Craig, *East Asia Tradition and Transformation* (Boston: Houghton Mifflin, 1973), chap. 3.

tion to structure and abstraction as the ultimate way of understanding the world, there are left the feelings that our perceptions give rise to. Both may be important and perhaps even coequal as Auguste Comte saw when he proposed that the good society would give equal scope to the expression of both intellect and feeling.[7]

The emphasis upon feeling and immediate apprehension that is central to the Eastern mode of approach to the perceptual world is quite foreign to us. Perhaps the way rational structure has concerned artists working in the West is best exemplified by Vitruvius, Leonardo da Vinci, Albrecht Dürer, Palladio, and the poet and biologist D'Arcy Wentworth Thompson. Vitruvius's *Ten Books on Architecture* is as much a treatise on late classical engineering as a book on architecture. In fact, engineering problems occupy him as much as problems of design. He never leaves us in doubt as to how to plan and make things. Palladio tried to put down what seemed to him to be optimal proportions and, what is important here, stated them as rules. Dürer and Leonardo both tried to evolve rules for the proportions of the human physique (which have plagued artists ever since). Intellectualized presuppositions preceded observation, and intellectual coherence and beauty were considered inseparable. These were only milestones in a continuing attempt to reduce natural forms to rational schemes that began in ancient Egypt. As far as the work of artists was concerned, Erwin Panofsky has detailed such tendencies in "The History of the Theory of Human Proportions as a Reflection of the History of Styles."[8] He shows there that such works expressed attempts to make perception consistent with rational notions of the nature of the world. In this sense, one may add, artists were not alone; they were manifesting a tendency that was in accord with what scientists were also trying to do. D'Arcy Wentworth Thompson in *On Growth and Form* (first published in 1911) went as far as one could go in trying to subsume biological forms and structures under essentially rational formulations that could be given mathematical expression. In fact he assumed that it was only a matter of discovering the mathematics, not whether it was there at all. It is not surprising that this book continued to have so much interest that it was updated in the 1970s. Western philosophy of science encourages looking at the natural world as a series of logically interrelated structures.

---

[7] Comte saw this as a masculine-feminine distinction. Until we submit both boys and girls to the same socialization and training we will never be able to say surely whether men naturally think with the head and women naturally think with the heart, as Comte thought.

[8] Printed in Erwin Panofsky, *Meaning in the Visual Arts: Papers in and on Art History* (Garden City, N.Y.: Doubleday, Anchor Books, 1955), pp. 55–108.

Eastern thinking does not ignore using a series of laws as a way of apprehending the cosmic order. Indeed, Indian thinking has always thought of Rita as the ultimate order of things and the Chinese emphasize Tao. In such conceptions there is what we have recently called structuralistic interplay.[9] In fact, in the terminology of Western epistemology one may call both closed mechanistic systems. But the idea that such rational mechanical images of the world could be all that we can ever divine about the ultimate nature of things seems repugnant to Eastern intellectuals. It is not that they were unable to deal with them. The historic Buddha, Gautama Sakyamuni (ca. 563–483 B.C.), dealt with the epistemological questions that theologies force upon us on a level of sophistication that was unmatched in the West until Immanuel Kant's critiques in the late eighteenth century. However, what is missing in the East is any stress upon the ultimate order of things as rationally apprehensible rather than as intuitively felt. From at least the fifth century B.C. in Greece rationality has been a central preoccupation of Western intellectuals. Classical thinkers were so loath to give any validity to feeling as a guide that they were not even willing to allow the question of the existence of God as a prime mover and ultimate order of things to be determined by priests. Such matters were not even a religious question. Answers were sought by rigorous, formal, logically coherent exegesis. Gut feeling did not enter into any of it.

The tendency in older Eastern thinking is to regard such formal infrastructures as ancillary and epiphenomenal at best. Essential to truth is what is felt to be true, a notion that affects all phases of Eastern cultures. We are perhaps most aware of the Eastern mode of apprehension in its effects upon religious consciousness. Where it led can be fairly termed "radical introspectionism," with controversies as sharp as any that rent Christendom in the sixteenth and seventeenth centuries. The effects of this view of the nature of reality on the artistic system have not received as much dilettante attention as religion and for this reason are less known and studied popularly. We have already emphasized that Western art is dominated by rationality and, in its American manifestations, often confrontation as well, but Eastern art is dominantly felt and empathic in the sense that Lippert originally used the term. Eastern art does not confront, it shades almost insensibly into the natural order without clearly defined universes. *The Mustard Seed Garden Manual of Painting*, the great seventeenth-century Chinese text on

---

[9] Structuralism is a viewpoint in which the rules of any system are generated by the interplay of variables within it.

brush painting, continually emphasizes the necessity of feeling form and obtaining knowledge of the external world through total empathy with the nature of things, an understanding that is intuitive rather than rational. We are told, for instance (among many similar things), to think of pines whose forms have been distorted by the wind as having the tension of young dragons and to feel the *Chi* (breath) of rocks. (The actual method of instruction was to copy and repeat exemplary works until one felt the nature of the forms being studied.)[10] Once this empathic apprehension is achieved the artist renders what he sees by a spontaneous autonomic expression of feeling. This process is often seen to require considerable meditation in order to free the artists from anything that distracts from spontaneous empathy. It is for this reason that preludes to actual work frequently involve Taoist and Ch'uan (Zen) meditations.

Such approaches to what art must express and the appropriate matrix for creative action itself may seem bizarre to anyone who holds common Western views on such matters, although it is not that Western artists never try to do the same thing. There are repeated references to retiring to the country to work so as to empathize better with the natural order, especially among the Romantics. Western artists recently have tried to ritualize such prolegomena in imitation of Eastern practice; prior to the 1950s such ideas were only known to those among us who both went to major universities and took courses in what was then called Oriental Studies, a very tiny number. These modes of approach are called Eastern by Northrop and form the basis of the critical system by which Eastern art is evaluated by its own critics, connoisseurs, and artists.

One should first consider the overall impression that the art of the East creates. The most general fact seems to be that the editorial and story content is subordinated to pattern and feeling in a way that goes far beyond anything apparent in all but a small part of the art of the West. There are conventions that are presumed to invoke certain moods and sentiments in each of the arts of Eastern

10 The copying method of instruction produces such an expertise in the copying of masters among the Chinese that there often has been substantial difficulty in authentication. Carbon-dating probably could at least establish if the dates were as represented. (See Peter C. Swann, *Chinese Painting* [New York: Universe Books, 1958], pp. 8–9.) Because the Chinese themselves seem to emphasize what a work of art expresses, rather than who did it, it is hardly surprising that they do not consider such copying dishonest. The only analogous thing I have encountered in the West is that present-day European cabinetmakers pay very little attention to when furniture was actually made but only to styles. No present-day Italian craftsman would see anything wrong with making six more "real" Chippendale chairs if one only had two in a situation where provenance was not important.

cultures. The comparative study of such conventions is a complex discipline in itself. Tableaux that try to capture a moment in a story are a very small element in this art. Even where it is presented as a narrative there is a substitution of a running narrative that expresses feeling rather than the structured story that Aristotle led us to think was so important. Even popular Japanese wood-block prints exemplify only a significant moment in the flux of sensation rather than clearly defined tales. We seldom see the equivalent of an Annunciation, a flight into Egypt, a Crucifixion, or the disporting Gentile pagan gods and heroes of Western art. It may very well be that the desire to convey the felt pattern in part explains the lack of interest in portraying nudes in the same way that Western artists do. Nudity per se bothers people in East Asia and India far, far less than in the West (except, of course, where Islamic influences are felt). However, Western nudes seem to focus not upon man as a part of an ongoing natural order, but upon the inherent power of the figures themselves. The male figures tend to convey a physical power that is in opposition to nature—aggressive, potent; the women convey a passive gentle sexuality that often invites assault and disorder, for instance, Manet's *Déjeuner sur l'Herbe*. One finds something quite different in Eastern portrayals. Erotic elements are portrayed more freely and frankly by artists whose work appeals to all levels of interest, be it that of scholars, artists, or connoisseurs. One does not have to look far for pieces that until very recently were hidden in special collections in order to find explicit portrayals of sex. There is nothing, for example, in the present West that is as openly produced and accepted as the erotic handbooks drawn by some of the great Japanese masters of the woodblock print. It appeared in some of the art of the ancient Gentile peoples (that was often hidden by museum curators), but in the long darkness of Christianity everyone's loins were covered. Later Western erotic art has been usually sick and prurient rather than playful and pleasurable; it shows an assault or a deception that seems meant to offend the moral sensibilities of the onlooker. (The example, par excellence, would be the pornographic drawings of Aubrey Beardsley.) Prurience seems absent from Oriental portrayals of sexuality in man and nature. There it ranges from a part in a cosmic dance that keeps the world itself going to a cultivated game of feeling in which there is interaction, but never assault. The Eastern cultures, unlike those of Islam and Christendom, never view the erotic as an excrescence to be veiled and hidden, but rather as an open aspect of life that is essential to the continuation of the cosmos itself. The erotic quest is not seen as something that bestializes man, but as another link that articulates him with the endless process of entropy and reformulation in the natural order.

Other aspects of this emphasis upon the totality and continuousness of nature can be seen in the manner and perhaps even the competence that is shown in the portrayal of the human figure, other living objects, and landscapes. Eastern portrayals of the human figure often do not even show the precise understanding of its structure, articulation, and motion that we expect in the work of a well-trained Western artist. Enough examples of mechanically accurate portrayals of the human figure by Eastern artists show that they were capable of thus picturing it if they saw any point in doing it any better than they portrayed other natural objects such as birds, insects, bamboo, trees, rocks, blossoms, or pines. In fact, they were perhaps even more adept than Westerners at conveying a sense of the life of such objects. Europeans really never empathized as well with the vitality of the nonhuman order until the Impressionists, even when draughtsmanship was quite accurate. It seems somehow appropriate that the French and Italian terms for still life are *nature morte* and *natura morta*. The great Dutch still lifes convey things to fill the belly; Chardin's subjects are waiting to be cooked. Only a small part of Western portrayals of nonhuman living objects show them alive, growing, and moving. It is a rarity, for example, to find Western portrayals of live swimming fish that display as much adeptness as the work of Chinese and Japanese artists show. It is not surprising. There are no creatures whose movements seem better to express the perceptual realm where flux is the central order of things.

With the portrayal of the human figure, drapery—as distinct from ceremonial clothing—is used quite differently from the way it is used from Giotto down. In Western art it is articulated to contained architectonic structures and, beginning with the Renaissance, was rarely used intentionally on human figures in any way that violated the integrity of the anatomical forms that it concealed. In Eastern art it is used mainly to convey a sense of flux, often floating about as if in water or weightlessly in air. Conflicts with underlying anatomy were hardly considered important until the work of artists like Hiroshige I who saw some Western work early in the nineteenth century. Emphasis is upon flow rather than underlying structure. In fact, the lack of concern with structure may account for the poor understanding of the theory of geometric perspective. There is little doubt that by the end of the eighteenth century both the Chinese and Japanese were able to portray drapery with fidelity to its mechanics when they had found it useful to express things that interested them. The same may be said of the treatment of depth geometrically. Indeed, there are examples in Hiroshige I of perfectly accurate geometric perspective, although even he followed his own traditions more often than not. In East Asia Western methods still remained a way of establishing depth that was subordinate to the use of atmospheric perspective. The reason seems simple enough. The use of atmospheric perspective is felt and does not introduce a distracting rational structure, as geometric perspective does. Indian artists went further. There is virtually no interest in structure, either in landscape or in the portrayal of animal and human figures. There are, however, endless friezes with paintings and reliefs of flowing "anatomyless" figures that dance out the endless flux of the cosmos. They usually show figures or depersonalized divinities that represent not persons but ideas as well as faces of Buddhas and Bodhisattvas whose strange serenity is meant to express a freedom from the bondage of individuality.

Dance forms of the East seem always treated as continuous with acting. Often there are conventionalized gestures that represent a complex system of meanings. These are often so complex and specific that one must be either to the manor born or a specialist to understand them. The lack of any clear distinction between acting and dancing is relevant to the present discussion. The merging of these forms seems in itself significant of the view that the primary character of existence lies in its constant flux rather than in its stases. (It is only the images of the enlightened ones of Buddhist iconography who ever appear static. They have escaped the prison of becoming.) This is in contrast to the dance in the West where the epitome lies in the pas de deux, where the man supports the movements of the woman, focusing upon her as something special, exquisite, and tender, through sequences that show the interaction of the pair, and in the male solo, where something titanic, even superhuman, is let loose in contrast with the delicate grace of the woman's part. In the theater of the East there is little emphasis upon such displays of individual virtuosity,[11] no matter how skillful and noted the performers may be, but upon a fluid, continually unfolding panorama.

It is in painting that this emphasis upon the flux—the undifferentiated continuum—is perhaps most striking. In East Asia we are first confronted by the fact that the preliminary preparation lies in developing a high level of fluency in calligraphy. In fact, ideally

[11] In the past so little attention was paid to individual "stars" that the highly acclaimed Indian dance company of Uday Shankar that toured the West in the early 1930s was recruited almost randomly from trained dancers.

**13**  Rationality and confrontation in Western art. Kevin Roche, John Dinkeloo and Associates, View from the east of the Fine Arts Center, the University of Massachusetts, Amherst.

The Fine Arts Center is a large structure, 646 feet long and 66 feet high in front (and higher in back). It encompasses a 2000-seat concert hall, three recital halls, a theater, studios for dance, painting, sculpture, and printmaking, an art gallery, and office-studios for each faculty member. The form and layout of the structure were dictated by a need to keep people engaged in different kinds of activity isolated from each other. The seemingly abstract forms shown in this photograph are functional—they are the shapes of the spaces they enclose. (For example, the viaduct starting from the upper left is a series of good-sized studios that keep the painters, printmakers, and sculptors isolated from the performing artists.) But these considerations are lost in the impression of a huge abstract sculpture and, like Nakashima's settee, there is no attempt to conceal structure with ornament. Unlike the settee, however, there is nothing that invites one to pause and feel it. The concrete is harsh to the touch.

Courtesy, The University of Massachusetts Archives.

the student is allowed no drawing of objects until calligraphic technique is fully developed.[12] The Western practice of starting the student on drawings of perceived objects from the very first is not part of the training routine. Calligraphy is a high art form in itself, perhaps even the highest art form. William Willets points out that in Chinese thinking the pairing of the highest art forms would be calligraphy and painting rather than painting and sculpture. The student is first taught to think of line as an expression of emotion and to consider even the writing of poetry as a visual art. The calligraphy must be appropriate to the emotional state of the poem and the images it seeks to invoke. From a mastery of calligraphy, whose techniques and aesthetics are studied deeply, one proceeds to drawing and painting. The very discipline is designed to produce an immediate response to one's feeling toward the ambient world. If one conceives of the world as being a continuum that downplays the separate existence of objects in deference to flow and spontaneity (which the most appreciated forms of calligraphy and drawing emphasize) it is reasonable to train students to work spontaneously with a soft brush dipped in thick black ink, a technique that makes errors irrevocable.

This attempt to capture flux is also seen in composition. Until the various manifestations of Impressionism in the last half of the nineteenth century, form was central to Western artistic endeavor, particularly in the visual arts. The contained static moment was often seen as the apogee. The simplest and most used basic composition was a more or less equilateral triangle, a form that emphasizes stability. Varying the sizes, positions, and axes of the triangles is alleged to create psychic disequilibria in the viewer that either make the composition disturbing or "give it life," depending, I am pretty sure, upon how you have been taught to respond. In sculpture the traditional poses portray the moments at which the motions of the figures have reached positions from which no further motion is possible. Perhaps the best examples one can give of this are in Myron's *Discobolus* and in Verrocchio's equestrian statue of the condottièro Colleoni. The former shows that moment in which the throwing arm is pulled back as far as it can go before the discus is let fly. In the latter piece the left shoulder of the condottièro is

[12] What may happen in actual instances may be an entirely different matter. There is substantial evidence that enforcing disciplined routines is more widespread among East Asians, but the high level of expertise that drawing so often displays leads me to suspect that students must often jump the gun and start to draw objects before they attain "perfect" calligraphy. There is no question in my own experience that proficiency in the control of line involved in calligraphic training would help the drawing of objects immensely.

turned forward as far as it will go and the head is turned tensely to a straining position. The horse also is notable in this regard. The left front leg is raised with the hoof turned inward as far as possible. The head is pulled downward as far as it will go. The whole body of the horse strains forward to the extreme position on the right leg.[13] Moreover, there is considerable emphasis upon containment within a defined space. Old rules spoke of maintaining the sense of the block in sculpture and even in modeling there was emphasis upon containment in composition. The mobile was certainly not based upon any novel technology, but the way art was thought about until well into this century would have made the idea of the fluid random motions of the mobile repugnant, even though a large mobile is hardly a randomly designed object but one that has to be carefully engineered if it is to work at all. The effect of this classic notion of the nature of design is implied by the Italian word for a painting, *quadro*.[14] The word emphasizes four-sidedness and separateness. In the East rational containment only appears where it serves to support some special point. The imperial compounds of Peking and Hue, for example, could hardly have failed to emphasize the apartness of the hereditary class of the imperial priesthood from the mandarins and the peasantry who were not ascribed to privilege but who had to take examinations to validate their rights to be anything but hewers of wood and drawers of water. Such exceptions, however, must be expected in complex, stratified societies. In general, containment and separation are not emphasized in Asian art. The bounded, contained composition does not appear as ubiquitously as it does in Western art. Frequently, objects are placed in a fashion that is relatively random vis à vis the shape and limits of a picture. Segments are caught that begin and end without any contained form. Such limits are less binding in Eastern art, although the placing of objects is hardly random in the best examples. But it was not necessarily the geometric structure of the matrix that was important; in fact, drawing and painting were even done upon folding fans. (These fans at their finest were

13 I am aware that some of these devices may be choices by default that are dictated by the difficulty of portraying motion and supporting motion in large figures without clumsy, distracting devices, especially in marble where an internal frame is impossible. A further difficulty is that older sculptors may not even have known what to show. It was not until high speed cameras were available around the beginning of the twentieth century that the actual transient positions assumed by men and other animals in motion were known with certainty!
14 Some of the other uses of *quadro* are significant. It can be a defined unit in a theatrical performance involving a change of scene, a description, a picturesque scene, a still from a film, a notebook, or a monograph.

only intended to serve the purpose of protecting the picture from fading when it was not being viewed, as no connoisseur in the Orient, or anywhere else, would ruin a good drawing or print by exposing it to light all of the time!) The use of the scroll has been continuous in both China and Japan. A horizontal scroll allows little possibility of a single focus or of geometric containment, but was viewed as an unfolding panorama between the two rolled-up ends. (Often the vertical scrolls as well cannot be completely grasped at a glance.) The same playing-down of geometric containment of composition in the art of East Asia goes even further in the carved friezes of India and Southeast Asia whose parades of Bodhisattvas and avatars could go on forever. Enough examples of geometrically contained compositions exist in Asiatic art to show that the artists could deal with such matters expertly when they wanted. The long traditions of Chinese "ancestor portraits" and Japanese wood-block prints should leave little doubt about this ability; however, even on small self-contained objects composition tends to play down geometric containment. The unimportance of limits is consistent with a world view that takes its essential nature to be an immediately apprehended aesthetic continuum in which there are no substantive separations in the creation itself between creation and creator. It is thus fair to say that the character of Eastern art is not involuted professional visions of an isolated class of artists, but is an expression of a critical apparatus that is derived from Eastern assumptions about the inner, final nature of reality. It is here that we come to what is the final question of this exegesis. What is the role of the artists vis à vis the cultural and social system? I will start with the answer and lead back to the question.

## BACKGROUND NOTE

This chapter is based upon F. S. C. Northrop's *The Meeting of East and West, An Inquiry Concerning World Understanding* (New York: Macmillan, 1946), chap. 9, "The Traditional Culture of the Orient"; chap. 10, "The Meaning of Eastern Civilization"; and chap. 12, "The Solution of the Basic Problem."

# 12

## The Cultural Functions of the Artist:

## Kroeber's *Configurations of Culture Growth*

THE intuitions of the artist lead him to the final logical[1] implications of the dynamics of the culture. Before I proceed to develop this assertion, some caveats must be stated. First, I am making a case on the basis of the role of the major artist in a period that is familiar to me, the last six hundred years in the West. I have some reason to believe that a similar case could be made for Chinese art, but these intimations are so fragmentary as to be nearly worthless, although painting, at least, was an expected activity of scholars, men who were often in the vanguard of thought and politics. However, even in the Western case (which I know well) there are pretty long spans where not even specialists seem to know the kinds of things I would want to know to write this chapter with complete assurance. In many other eras there were protracted periods of stylistic and technical stagnation whose art was hardly in the vanguard of anything. However, such periods turn out to be those in which the artists were servants of God-kings, priests, princes, viziers, and commissars, and as such their work expressed not their own perception and inclinations (if they were allowed to have any) but ideologies that were external to them. This leads me to recall an earlier part of the present essay, the discussion of professional isolation. For artists to follow their daemons they have to be professionally isolated from nonartists

[1] A better word than "logical" would be "structuralistic" here, but this is a term that is not generally understood outside of the context of anthropological theory.

and it even seems to help if they are ideologically alienated. It may be that outright persecution presents the optimal situation for the creative life. This seems to me a contention that really would be hard to argue from the evidence of the last century, because as many cases can be made for benign neglect as for persecution creating the fertile field for the work of the artist. However, it is certain that in at least one important instance persecution did in fact kill a promising start—I speak of the fate of Russian art from the period of 1910 to 1925. Recently bans on the showing of Russian Modern Art have been lifted by Soviet authorities and their exhibit reveals that something very lively and exciting was scotched when the modern Russian painters of the revolution fled abroad in the early 1920s. The work of the few major figures we know, such as Kandinsky, Gabo, Pevsner, and Archipenko, comprises less than a tithe of what was produced. The lessons of the past on such matters are, to say the least, highly confused. However, one thing that seems very certain to me is that the artist must have a measure of freedom and isolation. As far as the data for the West show, some cases can be made for the artist as the person who realizes the development of the fundamental tendencies leading to cultural change.

The most fruitful source of compiled data for this assertion lies in the late work of Alfred L. Kroeber. In 1944 he published a study entitled *Configurations of Culture Growth*. Shifts in interest away from the primacy of culture as the key concept of sociology make the book seem a scholarly curiosity, and even few graduate students bother to read it today. In it he considered the growth, mutation, apogees, and declines of a number of historically important cultural configurations. When one looks at it after forty years of the scholarly accretions to art history and criticism, Kroeber's various apogees look very much like what a grand-manner encyclopedist who was first educated before 1910 would have accepted as the consensus of the respected experts of his lifetime. There seems no good reason to take his specific judgments as any more than that, but his general contention that segments of activity within a culture have consistent patterns of growth, apogees, and decline deserves attention.

Kroeber in the first half of his great *Anthropology* of 1948 saw culture as having an autonomy that made it virtually independent of human agency. It was, as he put it, superorganic. This way of considering it meant that he never did come to terms with the psychological impetuses of such growths. In this respect his views were consistent with those of the two greatest mentors of sociology of the turn of the century, Durkheim and Spencer, and with his

**14**  Confrontation in the Western tradition: the Renaissance idea of *fama*. Andrea di Michele Cioni, called Andrea del Verrocchio (1435–1488), Equestrian statue of the Condottièro Colleoni. The figure dominates the small piazza in which it is located. The suggestion of power is carried through the figures of man and horse, each of which is strained to its extreme position. The surfaces of the entire piece are exquisitely finished with ornamental details that show the hand of the goldsmith, although Verrocchio did not supervise the final casting himself. But the details hardly matter. The figure against the sky confronts us; it is *fama*, the transcending of normal human limitations. It is poised in a frightening static moment.

Photograph, Author.

own great article of 1917, "The Superorganic" (*American Anthropologist*). Still an insistent question remains. What is the agency of development of at least the artistic aspect of the tendencies that underlie the all-encompassing metacultural systems of these various national historical developments? How does the artist himself figure the maturation of the cultural system in which he is embedded? Kroeber's data show that the artist catalyzes the internal development of a cultural system to its final form.

On its most naive level this can be simply the reductio ad absurdum of an overripe culture. The best case I can think of this is Cervantes's mordant look at the culture of chivalry. If one wants to see what it involves (divested of its erotic elements), it is all to be found in Thomas Bulfinch's *The Age of Chivalry* and *The Legends of Charlemagne*. This is a cosmos that is so bizarre as to be almost funny. It was a world in which bards concerned themselves with the problems of breaking a hippogriff to the saddle, without stopping for a moment to consider the plausibility of a hippogriff, a cross between a horse and a griffin (which is itself a cross between an eagle and a lion). Bulfinch, the scholarly son of the great architect, should have had trouble keeping a straight face as he put it all together in his rather loosely strung narratives. In fact, however, Cervantes had given this culture its coup de grâce three centuries earlier. Poor, battered Cervantes was born in 1547 and spent a good part of his life serving in the wars that were nurtured by such chivalrous fantasies. He lost the use of his left arm and hand in the Battle of Lepanto and thereafter was unconscionably subjected to one indignity after another. But in the last ten years of his life he had the final say of all time on such matters and died before his betters could exact an apology. He published the first part of *Don Quixote* in 1605, the second part in 1615, and he died in 1616. The broad farce of this book is what first meets the eye. An aging hidalgo who is addled by reading chivalrous romances sets forth as a knight errant with a gross, visceral peasant for a squire. It is no surprise that this quest brings only disappointments, beatings, and ridicule. If one reads it on this level alone it is hard for many of us to finish. As the book goes on, however, one may see that Cervantes became fascinated by the assumptions about the nature of reality that lay beyond the contrasting perceptions of the same appearances by the knight and his squire. One wonders if he did not see himself as Don Quixote and whether he was even envious of the ability of the rogues and peasant slaves to survive the Hamlets. Don Quixote dies a wise but broken man; Sancho Panza, his squire, has, suitably, become a rural magistrate. But whatever drove

Cervantes is only peripheral here. The book showed that even in early modern times such images of the motives of a military caste were not taken at face value and when they burst into a pyre of unprecedented proportions in 1914, three centuries later, no new resplendent phoenix could arise from the coals. The *Divine Comedy* of Dante shows the same process of the artist seeing the logic of his world and where it could lead. Dante himself never used this as its title and some older editions give it the title of *The Vision*.[2] And a vision it is, one of an ordering of things in a universal scheme that was expressed only a little while before in the great *Summa Theologica* of Saint Thomas Aquinas.[3] It should be remembered that Dante was not only a great poet and aesthetician, but that he also had major misadventures as a politician and wrote all his great works in exile. His politics led him to write the two works that establish him as an important medieval political theoretician, the Latin *Convivio* and *De Monarchia*. In them he also anticipated the denouement of the power relations that existed in medieval society as he had observed them in his lifetime. He understood the overripeness of this order and tried to resolve the internal contradictions of its hierarchical view of life on a theoretical level. He proposed a new moral vision in the *Divine Comedy*, and in the political works proposed a pattern to make it sensible, but what remains is that he knew this society was leading to decay and judgment. After he emerges from the underworld in the *Divine Comedy* he finds Jerusalem, the radiant city, and goes thence through *Purgatorio* and *Paradiso*, but what remains most cogent for posterity

[2] It seems fairly certain Dante himself did not commit himself strongly to any title. It was not fully assembled in his lifetime and thirteen cantos could not be found at the time of his death in 1321. (They turned up after he appeared in a vision to one of his sons to tell their whereabouts!) In the poem he calls it "il mia commèdia" and he describes it as a "commèdia" in a letter to his Veronese protector Can Grande. Giovanni Boccaccio in his authoritative biography (ca. 1350) calls it "the divine comedy" as a descriptive eulogy. The first printed edition in 1491 calls it *Commèdia*. *Divina Commèdia* does not appear until Giolito's edition of 1554. It is called *La Visione* in Leni's edition of 1613 and Pasquadi's edition of 1629. The Rev. Henry F. Carey (1772–1844) used this title in the first English translation in 1804–1805 (*The Vision of Dante Alighieri*) which went through numerous editions and was still in print in the 1960s. It remains the most common English translation. Henry Wadsworth Longfellow (1807–1882) called it *Divine Comedy* in his translation of 1867. References to the work as "Dante's Journey" seem to be purely descriptive, not a title. They seem to refer to a genus of medieval stories about journeys to the next world. There are surprisingly few verse translations into English (I could not find more than ten in the Library of Congress Catalogue), perhaps because of the difficulty of making a translation that comes up to the artistic quality of Dante's verse. C. H. Grandgent's introduction to the great edition of 1911 speaks, however, of "numerous translations."

[3] Dante's dates are 1265–1321; Saint Thomas's are 1225–1274.

despite his hopes, is *Inferno*, the moment after decay and judgment. He saw Armageddon, and the near future almost did not disappoint him. The fourteenth and fifteenth centuries were chronically violent.

The same push to the logic of the development of the human condition may be seen in the work of other great writers. The most vivid pictures of the callous exploitative urban world that arose out of industrialism can be found in the novels of Charles Dickens and George Gissing. The statistical works that lie behind these stories are gathering dust in libraries. The best of them is Booth's *Life and Labour in London,* dreary tomes of page after page of tables whose precise metal type press deeply into the paper. It can also be seen in Mayhew's incomparable vignettes where we see the world that swells passed by every day and hardly noticed. However, it took a Dickens and, to a lesser extent, a Gissing to tie Mayhew's floating world and Booth's tables together to show what they meant and where they were leading. Recently Barbara Tuchman, the superb historian-journalist, took all of the strands of France's Dreyfus affair and put them together to show an unbelievable string of depravities. However, what Dr. Tuchman's account lacks is any statement of the system of meanings and values that could produce such excrescences. This mentality was so enervating that the Germans beat the French thrice in seventy years.[4] But if one wants to see why France fell, the cause is told implicitly by the picture of its society shown in that massive, compellingly interesting compendium of trivialities, Marcel Proust's *The Remembrance of Things Past.* One can perhaps say that most of the other very great novelists of the last sesqui-centennial tell the same story—Tolstoi, Dostoevsky, Thackeray, Bellow, and perhaps most cogent for my generation, Kafka. It may have been possible to dismiss *The Trial, Metamorphosis,* and *The Castle* as diseased fantasies when they were published in Europe between the wars, but it is possible to say that they pictured a world cut of the same cloth as the goofy but not harmless Kaiser Wilhelm II, correcting the pacing of the orchestra as he sat beside the podium from which Edvard Grieg was conducting *Peer Gynt.* The surrealism of Salvador Dali and Max Ernst gives us the same harrowing image of a dissolution of rational, formal order. Giorgio di Chirico saw the same tendencies in different images as treeless straight stone streets peopled by figures who have featureless riveted metal ovals for heads. Even when di Chirico tried to return to an academic imagery, the fight against the decline of order and his own sense of aliena-

---

[4] In 1918 the Americans, Canadians, and British bailed them out.

tion remained insistently evident in the lonely paysages that he produced. It is the day before the holocaust, the moment before the S.S. men knock on the door. However, this compulsion of the artist to carry the culture to its final logical implications extends to the formal aspects of art as well.

Since this discussion started with reference to literary forms it seems best to take these first. The archetypal discussion of Western literary form appears in the fourth century b.c. in Aristotle's *Poetics.* Today the *Poetics* seems rather stodgy. Aristotle tells us, for instance, that, above all, poetry must be imitative of nature. He does not say how to do it and since we do not know that he ever wrote any poetry we have no way of guessing from his own work what he could have meant. (This emphasis on realism is, however, quite consistent with the fact that the Greeks colored their sculptures, a practice that now perhaps seems an unbelievable desecration considering the wonderful quality marbles available to them.)[5] The best poetry of the time that survives, I am told, certainly apotheosizes language just as much as Milton and Shakespeare apotheosized English, but it seems unlikely that it mimicked everyday speech. Aristotle's emphasis upon realism and many other particulars of the *Poetics* seem largely curiosities late in the twentieth century, and these characteristics may make it quite easy to forget that it set down standards that were to be a current in Western art for most of two and a half millennia. Art was always to be formal and contained. The artist was to follow rules and every work was to have a defined beginning, middle, and end. Each of these had definite characteristics and each served defined psychological purposes for the reader, listener, or viewer (*De Poetica* 1450b and 1451a). Aristotle says that

> all human happiness or misery takes the form of action; the end for which we live is a certain kind of activity, not a quality. Character gives us qualities, but it is in our actions—what we do—that we are happy or the reverse. In a play accordingly they do not act in order to portray the Characters; they include the Characters for the sake of action. So that it is the action in it, i.e., its Fable or Plot, that is the end and purpose of the tragedy; and the end is everywhere the chief thing. Besides this, a tragedy is impossible without action, but there may be one without Character.

---

[5] I can find no record at all of whether or not the sculptors themselves liked the practice of coloring sculptures.

Aristotle's rules formed the basis of our classic idea that form and not emotional content is important and this idea has come to dominate classic Western literary work down to our own day. In the next paragraph Aristotle even complains that the poets spoil the plots by distracting speeches that portray character. Despite Aristotle's displeasure, many artists of considerable power have had trouble excising the emotions that arise with action, but the portrayal of the psychological subtleties of the characters is seen only exceptionally in classic Western literary work. Corneille and Racine and even Oscar Wilde are more the rule than Shakespeare, O'Neill, and Albee. In the pure classic form, in fact, the Fates callously pick out the characters for ineluctable destruction irrespective of their deserts. Greek rationality—what Nietzsche called the Socratic critic who insists on order—set the ethos of Western culture. The *Poetics* was only a small part of a logically coherent organon of knowledge that was to dominate Western thinking down to this century in politics, science, and art. But logical forms, we must emphasize, are not immediately apprehended through feeling, they are ratiocinated.

It does not seem accidental that the end of the rational, formal, architectonic Western artistic tradition can be placed at the end of the second decade of this century. It was perhaps then that the underlying qualitative themes of the culture had been carried to their final implications in every field of endeavor. Our long lovefest with rationality had passed its climacteric. It was occurring in science and politics as well as in art. The two editions of Bertrand Russell and Alfred North Whitehead's *Principia Mathematica* were published from 1910 to 1927. Their work was supposed to prove to those concerned with such matters that mathematics were logical and self-consistent. Only four years later (in 1931), however, Kurt Gödel, then twenty-five, published a short paper called *On Formally Undecidable Propositions*[6] now known as "Gödel's proof" that showed—to the disquietude of the mathematical community ever since—that not only was such not so at that time, but unlikely ever to be. In 1979, Douglas Hofstader, a young theoretical physicist and logician, published a dazzling book, *Godel, Escher, Bach: An Eternal Golden Braid*, that showed that Gödel's proof gave only a hint of the much larger question of whether the same doubts about internal consistency could not be raised about the entire supposition that cognition, machines, and art had behind them rational, mechanical images. C. Wright Mills called the tendency to build

[6] The German title was substantially longer and more descriptive: "Über Formal Unentschiedbare Sätze der *Principia Mathematica* und Verwandter Systeme."

big, consistent, integrated inclusive systems in sociology "grand theory." These systems were built up systematically from scratch. "Grand" is indeed an apposite expression for the attempts of Comte, Hegel, Spencer, Marx, and even Durkheim to actualize a hope of philosophers of science that there could be an all-inclusive system of knowledge. Karl Pearson called his great book *The Grammar of Science* and positivist speculations on a "Hierarchy of Science" showed no doubt that all the missing ranks could be filled. Comte and Spencer placed sociology in what they thought was an only momentarily uneasy position at the top of the new organon of science where it waited for a perfect mathematics, a perfect physics, and a perfect biology to fulfill its destiny as the guide to human order, happiness, and perfection. All of them knew too much to expect it to come to pass Tuesday week, but they didn't think it very far off. But just before the Great War of 1914 it became hard to support such images of the ultimate nature of things and such hopes for the destiny of science. Seminal thinkers were finding maelstroms where they should have found calmly flowing streams. The most obvious break came in psychology with the work of Sigmund Freud. Order to Freud was at best a fragile social necessity imposed ruthlessly upon a violent, chaotic, hedonic id. In physics, then in astronomy, conceptions that the ultimate substratum was orderly broke down apocalyptically and romantically. Einstein's papers on relativity brought the doubts about a tidy, fixed physical order that was consistent with the seeming regularity of daily experience into the open. Werner Heisenberg went a step further and asserted that at the basis of even the phenomenal was not order but only uncertainty and differing probabilities of occurrence; and when Erwin Schroedinger asked himself *What Is a Life?* he gave the same answers about it. Einstein saw what he had done and he did not see that it was good. He was twenty-one in 1900 and a nineteenth-century man in his expectation of a grand order; he complained repeatedly that God did not play games of chance. Meanwhile others spoke of entropy and the ultimate "discreation" of the universe itself.

In politics the same dissolution of old understandings and old order was also imminent. The overripe regimes that had been built up to satisfy the demands of nationalism were everywhere about to fall apart in the hands of their stewards. But what was the ethos of these regimes? They were essentially feudal, aristocratic, and militarist. Their exemplars were neither crafty enough nor tough enough (for the most part) to deal with the corporate behemoths that the haute bourgeoisie of the industrialized countries had assembled. (In truth, the last probably seemed preferable to most observers because the power struggles of the corporate managers did not yet seem so catastrophically disruptive of everyday life. At least for the time being they were manifested only in crabby manipulations on the bourse, and this perhaps was why industrialism looked good and peaceful to Herbert Spencer and others.) Moreover, the military over-lords had made alliances with organized Christianity that were chronically uncomfortable to both. The more thoughtful Christians knew, as Richard Niebuhr was to put it later, that religious organizations often achieve worldly success by ignoring the precepts of their founders. The end of the nineteenth century saw a crisis of confidence of each in the other. Aristocrats and generals saw in Nietzsche and Schopenhauer a more plausible reading of nature's intention for man than they saw in Milton, Calvin, and Aquinas. The greater part of the bourgeoisie, as Max Weber noted in *The Protestant Ethic and the Spirit of Capitalism*, probably did not believe any of the ideologies that were so grandly purveyed to the lower orders of society. For the capitalist, all paternalistic illusions, all "heavenly ecstasies of religious fervor," indeed had long been drowned "in the icy water of egotistical calculation." I am too wary to assert, ex post facto, that the Holy Wrath and Armageddon were inevitable. This world did enjoy an Indian summer between the Great War and the Great Depression that hardly could have been expected, but the decline of the West as the nineteenth century knew it was in the works.

The decline of bourgeois culture did not take the form that Brooks Adams, Oswald Spengler, and, later, P. A. Sorokin envisioned. It was a passing of what Jean Renoir, I think more accurately, saw as the disappearance of a grande illusion—chivalry and a fellowship of good breeding that transcended transitory quarrels. On the sidelines, ready to build on the rubble were the Adolf Hitlers, the Georges Clemenceaus and, later, the now-faceless manipulators of industrial capitalism.[7] The last took their inheritance when the bomb over Hiroshima marked the end of the Armistice of 1918. Alexander Berkman at least had Henry Clay Frick when he sought a suitable exemplar of raw capitalism to shoot (and he could not have found a better one). Society was more visible than Hell itself. It was at Newport, Tuxedo Park, Cannes, Mayfair, and Palm Beach,

[7] The industrial and financial leaders of the late twentieth century seem no longer to be popularly known and visible in the way that J. P. Morgan, the elder, John D. Rockefeller, Sr., Henry Clay Frick, Jay Cooke, and Andrew Carnegie were in their day. Jean Paul Getty, whom *Fortune* noted as having the largest personal fortune of the mid-century in the United States, was hardly known outside of the oil business.

and it crossed the ocean first-class on the *Titanic* and the *Lusitania*. Its coming and goings were reported in the *New York Herald* and it received respectful obituaries in the *Boston Transcript*. But who today is usually sure to know who the present chairmen of the board of Ford or Chrysler are except their peers at General and American Motors? A visible formal hierarchical society with clear, stated codes, and identifiable leaders has simply disappeared. The ensuing anomie gave the speculators their greatest field day since the expansion of Roman power at the end of the Republic. As always it has paid handsomely to "foreclose on the rubble."[8]

Artists always seem to have been in the avant-garde of such crises. In dance, theater, painting, graphic arts, music, and literature—in all of the arts—one sees projections of the future, time and again. In the recent history of the West art has first shown the breakdown of the last vestiges of the orderly, rational, classical world. In some instances we may see such statements for the future a century and a half before the beginning of the denouement. Even Mozart—who knew all the rules well—often ignored classic order when he heeded what must have been the whispers of his own daemon (which seems to have been his usual practice in his late work). Take the six quartets of the Haydn set.[9] C. B. Oldman writes:

> They are too well known to call for detailed discussion; it is enough that they are now universally recognized as among the supreme examples of their kind. Such, however, was not the general verdict at the time. A critic of the day found them "much too highly spiced"; Prince Grassalkowics tore up the parts in a rage on finding that they really contained the "hideous stuff" that was being played before him.[10]

To these irritations to aristocratic sensibilities should be added, according to Alfred Einstein, the Hoffmeister Quartet (K. 499) and the last three sets written for the King of Prussia (K. 575, 589, and 590).[11] Einstein makes it clear that these, like much of the rest of

[8] I owe this felicitous phrase to my old college crony, the journalist John Keats. Foreclosing on the rubble is no new thing. Suffice it to say Schliemann found at least eight strata on the site of Troy. Rome built a colony on the site of Carthage within fifty years after its "final" destruction; Dresden and Coventry are now clean new cities as is Berlin, and so it goes.
[9] Op. 10 K. 387 (Sept. 1773); K. 421 (June 1783); K. 428 (June or July 1783); K. 438 (Nov. 1784); K. 464 (Jan. 1785); K. 465 (Jan. 1783).
[10] C. B. Oldman, *Groves Dictionary of Music and Musicians*, 5th ed. (New York: St. Martin's Press, 1965), 5:948, s.v. "Mozart."
[11] Alfred Einstein, *Mozart, His Character, His Work* (Oxford: Oxford University Press, 1945), pp. 172, 184.

Mozart's later chamber works, were no copybook exercises written according to the rules of the schoolroom, but serious explorations of new forms destined to be caviar to the general.[12] Mozart carried this on to other aspects of his work. His favorite opera, *The Magic Flute*, departed so far from rational, classical strictures that it only achieves dramatic coherence when one ignores the plot. Much the same kind of restlessness with formal constraint had already been noticeable in what I have spoken of earlier, the Baroque device of releasing the tension of a rigid, formal system by the ecstatic breaking of bonds. These bonds, these rules, had been established earlier in an attempt to achieve a new synthesis out of the shambles that the man-centered renaissance thinking had made of a hierarchical medieval view of the nature of the creation as infinitely small gradations from the least of the creation, to man, and through nine levels of angels to the prime, unmoved Mover. But by the last quarter of the eighteenth century these innovations of the great Baroque and classical composers had themselves become orthodoxies. By the last half of the twentieth century they had become so much a part of academic practice that it is not unusual to expect a piano candidate for admission to a conservatory to play Bach's *Three Part Inventions*. Another portion of Bach's work shows he wrestled hard with the aspect of his personality that was continually in conflict with rigidly controlled tensions of *The Art of The Fugue* and the chamber and keyboard works. The other side of him was passionately religious and kept him ever in fear and trembling before the Lord. This was expressed best in the church cantatas which were a new kind of church music that went with the religion of Luther. The words seem irrelevant; the music itself is passionate and seeks a direct apprehension of the religious state in a way that the earlier chants did not; it does not belong with the ordered, formal, intellectual outlook of scholasticism. In its editorial content one sees an analogous process at work in the iconography of renaissance painting even when it is technically at its most innovative. The clientele that keeps the groceries on the table looks for content and not the expression of the special perceptual realms of art.[13]

---

[12] Ibid, "Chamber Music for Strings," chap. 11, pp. 167ff.

[13] Indeed, we have many classic cases of this in recent popular American art. Norman Rockwell, Wallace Nutting, and Andrew Wyeth come to mind easily. They are hardly peers as artists. The principal eulogies of Norman Rockwell's art come from the Curtis Publishing Company which controls the copyrights to its reproduction. The pictures themselves are false to my own memories of the 1930s, when I came to adult awareness. They show an America whose dominant moods were cheerfulness, kindness, and optimism. The great photographers of the period caught what I saw—pessimism, despair, and fear—moods that Rockwell's pictures utterly fail to show. Rockwell showed what the editors at Curtis

In painting and other visual arts this also occurs. The most extreme case I know of lies in the Impressionism of J. M. Turner (1775–1851). Here is not the sort of adumbration that one often finds in many earlier painters whose work emphasized plasticity rather than architectonic form, but a fully realized Impressionism. Most of this can be seen in the great number of morning sketches that he did for his own satisfaction without thought of a market, but it can also be seen fully developed in a number of paintings done by him, such as the *Fighting Téméraire* and the less-known *Slave Ship* in the Boston Museum of Fine Arts. In other visual arts economic considerations limit a spontaneous expression of the artists' visions more than in painting. Dancers and composers of musical works that require large forces must almost necessarily be able to command extensive resources to realize their visions. A sculptor who hopes to carry his work beyond a clay studio model has to be able to pay founders, stonecutters, and welders, and this takes plenty of money. Even Rodin, arguing with the force of an already great reputation, discovered that it was not easy to get the town fathers of Calais to mount his monument to its martyred burghers as he intended. (A generation later, Julius Rosenwald gladly paid for properly mounting full-sized duplicates of the figures at the Rodin Museum he gave to the city of Philadelphia.) The whims of those who control the commissions are also critical. In architecture this goes even further. Expenses of execution are greater than in any other art form. One often wonders if the dictum that form follows function may not owe its popularity to the fact that it made a virtue of a necessity in operating in a monetary matrix. With the dance too, such limitations also intrude upon the artist. Until perhaps 1910 it was financially impossible to stage a large work without court or government patronage, and even today, unless one keeps to work that is close to classical styles, one must have some

---

wanted him to show. Wallace Nutting (whose photographs were, incidentally, given as premiums with *The Saturday Evening Post*) unquestionably invokes a comfortable nostalgic imagery if that is what one seeks, but when one looks at these photographs a half century later one realizes that they are visual portrayals of the lonely world of Sara Orne Jewett's *The Country of the Pointed Firs*. In both cases Curtis was selling an imagery not art. An almost sublime case may lie in the work of Andrew Wyeth. Even Wyeth's detractors concede that his paintings are technically superb, but I think it is fair to say that their imagery and not their technical quality accounts for their popularity. No attention is paid popularly to the omnipresent intimations of a lonely, psychologically disturbed world that they show.

way to be independent of box offices receipts.[14] And even the strictly classical dancer is not independent of this set of market limitations. The most rigidly classical dance still practiced stays alive in situations that avoid the market. The main exponent of classical ballet is the Soviet government; in Japan classical forms are practiced mainly by a troupe within the imperial compound in Tokyo. Other traditional Japanese art forms enjoy similar protections from the vagaries of popular taste. But all of these cases involve being forced to conform to officially approved forms. As I indicated earlier, there has been some recent relief for the artist in the United States[15] from such strictures because the public and private foundation support available to American artists is given in ways so oblique and ponderous that the system itself precludes control over the results. It may even be that letting the artist do as he wishes seems conspicuous waste to the patron and thus, if Veblen is right, honorific.

However, when one puts aside iconography and journalistic content art shows a consistent pattern of anticipation of the crises in politics, economics, and the system of stratification—who is patronized and who receives deference. Inevitably this perhaps cannot be on a level of direct editorial confrontation without violent response. When Diego Rivera painted Marx and Lenin as heroes in the lobby of the RCA building in 1934, John D. Rockefeller, Jr., personally ordered hacking it off the wall. But a more intellectualized confrontation on an iconographic level was quite acceptable as we may see in the work of Reginald Marsh, George Bellows, and Guy Pène du Bois and in some of the mordant pieces of Grant Wood—*American Gothic, The Daughters of the American Revolution,* and *The Artist's Mother*—tough old guardians of church-supper piety. On the most abstract level freedom is even greater. One can get away with anything because what is being anticipated is far outside of the understanding of all but the initiated (except where the artist must contend with crude, resident ideologists). At worst it offends those who think a painting should be a picture.

It is now appropriate to return to Kroeber's *Configurations of Culture Growth.* First, a caution must be interposed about his

[14] The cost of mounting any new production is enormous. I could find no data on what number remain on the boards. It is difficult to determine, for instance, how many ballets of Martha Graham did not stay in her repertory. For every *Oedipus* there must have been some proportion that was only shown for one season.
[15] One may hope that the crackpot economics of the Reagan administration in this area are transitory.

presentations. The paragraphs that follow give them a high level of authority. Kroeber gives importances to different artists without ever making clear how he arrived at his judgments. The first copyright of his book was from 1944. He was then about seventy-five and I remember him as a sick old man. (He died a short time later.) Which of the later artists whom he mentioned would now be accorded the importance he gave them thirty-five years ago can be fairly questioned. In the chapter on music, for instance, there is almost no mention, if any, of American music. The chapter takes no account of the fact—and he may not have been aware of it at all—that by 1940 American music was competing easily with European music for the interest of creative musicians in the West. But let us be fair to Kroeber; if one takes as a standard the actual pro gramming of major performing groups at that time, he did not miss a very big boat. (In fact, it is still a matter of some concern among musicians that the big orchestra conductors rarely have enough clout with audiences to bring avant-garde music to the public. It takes a Stokowski, Monteux, or Koussevitzsky to jam it down their throats.) When one goes further back in time and across to Europe most of Kroeber's scholarship does seem to represent a consensus that still has strong support. Recent scholarship usually gives considerably earlier dates to the origins of most of the various schools in the arts than the sources Kroeber used, but this is unimportant to the present discussion. The basic premise remains tenable—there are fairly consistent configurations of culture growth, involving slow starts, crowded apogees, and then declines.

Kroeber's book, however, has a very serious difficulty for one trying to use it with any specificity. This is the presentation itself. It is neither consistent from one chapter to another nor within any given chapter. In indicating the specific areas of culture growth he sometimes uses lists of men; sometimes maps with dates; sometimes time spans shown by lines of varying thickness (with no real consistency as to the significance of the thicknesses). To put it simply, he did not quantify his data consistently and one can doubt if he thought it important to do so, considering the work he did earlier in his life. It is useful for the present study that one can, after some interpolation, reduce them to reasonably consistent data, by finding the starts and peaks of the cultural configurations and their accompanying high art forms.

What appears from this exercise (which is shown in an appendix) is a reasonable consistency with relation to the appearance of major artists to a state of anomie and disintegration in the ambient society. The first thing that I was struck by is that the periods of major peaks were far more often than not "unserene." In literature Kroeber saw the peaks of ancient Greece at about 400 B.C., Rome at the end of the Republic. In France he saw two peaks, at the end of the Middle Ages in 1500 and at the end of the *ancien régime* from 1850 to 1940. In England Kroeber also saw two peaks. The first comes with the sixteenth and early seventeenth centuries— Jonson (1573–1637), Shakespeare (1564–1616), and Spenser (1552– 1599), with Milton (1608–1674) at the end, and the second, in the nineteenth century, but he makes no mention that, although nine-teenth-century England produced poets comparable to the earlier period, it produced no dramatists of the same stature. The first period produced no novels of note. The American peaks are given as the decades of and following the Civil War, and the 1930s.

Painting and sculpture followed similar patterns but they usu-ally ran somewhat ahead of literature. Greek sculpture by the con-ventional judgments Kroeber followed peaked at 400 B.C. but there is no question that the same critical criteria that forced a closer look at primitive sculpture has given considerably greater artistic value to the works from the immediately preceding archaic period. If we take technical virtuosity alone—which is to say skill in handling materials—the judgments he used, I think, stand up fairly well in the estimation of scholars. In France the medieval peak is at 1100 and the modern peak is from about 1875 to 1920; Italian work reaches its height in the fifteenth century; Spain in the middle of the seventeenth century; in the United States, if one considers only indigenously developed forms rather than epiphenomena of European tendencies, the peak lies in the thirty-five years immedi-ately following the Second World War to the late 1970s with its so-called Neo-Academism (or Neo-Realism).[16] Kroeber also noted that sculpture consistently seems to peak earlier than painting. I can only give a speculation here as to why. In my experience painting is, as it has been practiced in the West, essentially more intellec-tualized than sculpture. It involves a less direct kinesthetic appre-hension of form, more playing with involuted questions of the per-ception of color and light and with the creation of self-consistent perceptual universes (e.g., Maurits C. Escher and René Magritte!). Sculpture has to exist in its environment; it inevitably confronts architectural and natural features, often without defined frames. It has not been as slowed down by the involuted intellectual con-siderations that surround Western painting.

Kroeber did not consider the dance or architecture. The first

[16] At the moment of writing (1980) there is no consistently used term for the renascence of interest in traditional craftsmanship.

omission is understandable. Notational systems for the dance were not invented until late in the nineteenth century and the Laban, a truly accurate system from which a director could actually mount a performance that would at least be consistent in the relation of the steps and positions on stage of the dancer, was not perfected until the 1940s. In Eastern culture areas we know what the dances of the past were like because these countries have carefully maintained systems of training, but in other cases we know very little directly. It is of course a possibility that a choreographer could, for instance, use the portrayals of Greek vases and Babylonian friezes and relate them to the recent ingenious reconstructions of their music and make plausible guesses as to what the dances were like. However, in the absence of actual continuity of performance from the original showing, critical judgments cannot be made in the same way that we can judge *Giselle*, which was first produced in 1841 and is still performed with few significant changes from the original choreography.

His omission of architecture, however, is virtually incomprehensible. It is the most visible and most easily studied art form with respect to its techniques, history, and aesthetics. However, some observations can be made that are relevant to the present study. Architectural styles show first an innovative phase where structures are fairly modest. Later the aesthetic of this style gains "respectability" with those who can raise or provide the money to put up big structures.[17] In the innovative phases we see intimations of the wave of the future. Working around the end of the last century, Richardson, Furness, Sullivan, and Wright put up structures that grew out of their sites as if they had been dictated by a Taoist aesthetic. They were often radically at odds with contemporary tastes. Almost a century later we know that they were responding to their own daemons and that they were pained by the ruination of the land that the mogols had demanded to show that they were "voracious predators." (As William Dean Howells pointed out in *The Rise of Silas Lapham*, "Lapham's Paint" was painted everywhere on large rocks by the side of the road.) Today the work of these men is respectfully established as the antithesis of the big,

---

[17] It is not clear why aesthetic quality sometimes seems lost in the amplification of size. It is possible that it is not so much that small is beautiful, but that small things are more easily apprehended as a totality than very large things. Bramante's *Tempietto*, a tiny affair seems to come to more than Saint Peter's aesthetically. One can apprehend the Tempietto in one glance; Saint Peter's can fit the Queen Elizabeth in its aisle. Its dome seems stunning if one gets a mile away.

glass-sheathed skyscraper.[18] The tendency of the artist to anticipate new ethoses and new ways of understanding is most apparent in architecture. It is surprising that the architect can even get to first base in expressing himself as an artist. The architect has to build to realize himself as a creative man. This perforce requires that he adjust himself to those who control the means to bring his vision off the drawing board. Other artists do not need to contend with this condition. Poetry that involves a novel new vision of things can remain mute, as did Emily Dickinson's. Much of her work remained in a bureau drawer until it was dribbled out by a bizarre niece who saw some use to the poems of the maiden aunt whom townspeople viewed as mad. A century later Emily Dickinson seems curiously sane. The gossips of Amherst whom she enjoyed keeping busy now seem to have been a pack of preposterous, exotic village queers. Materially a poet needs only a stub of a pencil and a piece of brown paper. Similarly paintings like Whistler's nocturnes and Turner's morning scenes remained unsold at their creators' deaths, as did much of Cézanne's work. However, it seems that even when a certain phase of a person's work is in demand by moneyed clients this work can be kept up. I will not say "on the side" because this would assume that the central concern of the artist is to make a living. Making a living at it may, indeed, encourage him as an artist, because as indicated earlier the artist must receive response from someone in order to persist, and, if the response is expressed in economic terms, it makes the other roles he must perform in society easier. One reason why so many artists remained in relatively modest circumstances, even if rarely in permanent abject poverty, was that the clientele for their most innovative work remained small. It is only in the exceptional case that the artist achieves enough standing in his lifetime to make consumers accept what he gives them. When Joyce Cary in *The Horse's Mouth* showed the derelict old painter Gully Jimson imitating his own early popular work when he needed money to live he was showing a situation that is often paralleled in historic situations. About 1925 Picasso's dealers seem to have realized that they could sell any of the work that derived from his classic phase—a phase that did not exact the intellectual demands from either the artist or viewer that his Cubist period work did. They pushed it or at least did not

---

[18] How often skyscrapers affront aesthetic sensibility is not at issue here, and surely many, many do not.

release much else for sale.[19] In spite of these concessions to economic necessity that may be found even in the careers of the most prestigious artists, the role of the artist as the proclaimer of the ultimate implications of his culture remains.

The observation itself is hardly novel. It seems to have been realized by every historian of any consequence. It is more than the articulate character of art that makes it a good way of knowing how the most creative people saw things in the past; it also gives an abstract epitome of the changes in the most important meanings. It is true that its rarified character seldom allows one to find out much about what was happening in the kitchens and stables, but the decisions that determine the future of the world are made in the chancelleries, the law courts, and the universities, and they often come as a response to ideas that derive from the intuitive visions of the creative man. In *Huckleberry Finn* Mark Twain saw the behemoth of industrialism destroying what little seemed left of humane, concerned, natural fellowship; in England Henry James saw the endless tension in the pull between the demands of civility and insistent, raw passion. Both saw nineteenth-century society heading for a blow-up and neither was wrong. Earlier Henry David Thoreau had seen it too and had tried his doomed retreat to Walden Pond. During their lives there appeared adumbrations of what were to become full-blown tendencies in Western culture, Post-Impressionism, Surrealism, Dada, Expressionism, Cubism, and Bauhaus principles, to name only a few. The manifestations of these movements and schools provide bizarre juxtapositions, but we must realize that our normal ambient world is also filled with bizarre juxtapositions—a dean of a conservative seminary pitting his ideas against a half-modernized society; the United States against bloody but unbowed Asian peasants; the Kremlin against Afghanistan hillbillies, every last one a ragged individual. Do the faces in Expressionist pictures look any different from those of the drugged and proletarianized in developed societies who have only been offered ghettoization? Contrasts, however, seem inevitable wherever civilizations have become complex enough to be stratified.

The message is not necessarily explicit. It does not need to be Francisco Goya's horrors of war, Käthe Kollwitz's longing faces of

[19] It is not essential to the present essay to judge the validity of the contention made by some of Picasso's detractors that he showed no new vision for the rest of his life. I doubt this very much and I think that when the huge production (including the unsold and unshown works) that continued until his death fifty years later is studied systematically this contention will prove wrong. (This was written before the Museum of Modern Art show of 1980.)

the doomed, or Kafka's *Castle*, but a new vision that when carried to its logical implications heralds a different way of seeing, feeling, and acting in the day-to-day world. In *Time of Need: Forms of Imagination in the Twentieth Century* William Barrett carried on a brilliant analysis with the same implicit premise. He set himself a specific task of showing that Nihilism is the intellectuals' response to the reality of time, although he did not deal with many of the qualities of modern life that oppress others of us as much, such as boredom, intrusion, and mechanically produced sameness. But it is unfair to impute any fault to him for not doing things he did not say he was going to do. Some notice should also be given to Robert N. Wilson's book *The Writer as Social Seer*. Wilson does not discuss the deep, general discontents that Barrett sees as qualifying all experience and as ubiquitously expressed in our art, but focuses upon particular writers and the aspects of the malaise to which they felt compelled to respond. If the book had been published before I wrote the earlier chapters of this essay, I would have made extensive use of it, but in my opinion it does stand as evidence that an independent analysis moved in the same direction that I did here. (We may, of course, both be wrong.)

It is appropriate now that this essay is in its final pages to consider why peaks in art tend to precede those in science and philosophy, as Kroeber noted. I hope that I am not about to provide a denigrating note about artists. In part it is simply a matter of how the professional demand for precise methodologies slows down the work of the scientist and philosopher. The final work of the scientist—the creation of a precisely conceptualized system of understanding—does not lie in ad hoc exercises in radical empiricism. If one ignores methodological precision, a very good case can be made for witchcraft and malicious mesmerism. Much of the misfortune that attends the human condition from day to day defies any immediately observable sequence of causation, but is only expressible as probabilities based upon mathematical operations involving semi-functions, operations that give us a way of measuring how tidy or untidy things are. As Jules Poincaré would have said, witchcraft as an explanation of misfortune has convenience and simplicity. It only falls apart when one tries to relate it against an essentially positivistic scientific system and demands that one relate it to what systematic workers already believe to be generally true.[20]

---

[20] Arguments that propose "intuition" rather than expertise as a guide to action seem to overlook a good deal that I am too much a child of the first half of this century to ignore. It is forgotten that the exemplars of great intuitive thinking—Plato, Aristotle, Einstein, Newton, and Kant, among many others—knew a great

It is a fact that science has long periods of incremental growth while existing conceptual frameworks are fully exploited and needs for new understandings seem to present themselves to creative minorities. But to arrive at this point there are usually countless hours of routine, often banal work. In short, the advancement of science depends upon conceptualizations that can be articulated to precise methodologies. This is necessarily a much slower process than sensing a new shape of things that is stated ahead of the proofs at hand, which characterizes the creation of the artists. In 1850 Herbert Spencer and Auguste Comte, those pompous old humbugs, looked upon an already well-developed industrialism and saw in it the new Jerusalem. A half century earlier Blake had already asked "was Jerusalem builded here among these dark Satanic mills?" But it took until 1889 for all the data to be in for Blake's suspicion to be confirmed systematically. In that year, six years after the death of Karl Marx, Engels published the last volume of *Das Kapital*. In 1845–1846 the youthful Marx and Engels had already sensed what nineteenth-century industrial capitalism was to produce, both culturally and politically, and they put down their thoughts somewhat impressionistically in *The German Ideology*, but they were in their middle forties before even the first volume of the precisely conceptualized *Das Kapital* appeared in 1863. But even before Marx and Engels were born—in 1818 and 1820—artists had gone where their visions led them. In doing this, one can go considerably earlier than the last century to see parallels. At the end of the fifteenth century Leonardo da Vinci and Albrecht Dürer both saw the immediate world as an emergent of a minutely studied microcosm. It was not until considerably later that thinking the way they did about biology—and in Leonardo's case, geology as well—came to be safe and orthodox. In the case of Leonardo his vision was so far ahead of his time that he had no influence at all on the development of science and his scientific work remained largely private fantasy. The art that went with it long remained just as inaccessible to common understanding. Every kind of nonsense has been written about the man and his work, from transports about the smile of La Gioconda and the sweetness of Saint Anne and the Virgin to speculations about the psychodynamics of the disturbingly hermaphroditic Saint John the Baptist.[21] What is known with more certainty is that even

deal to start with, so much, in fact, that they knew that the accepted understanding of science of their times needed revision to account for what they knew.

21 Much of the speculation about Leonardo and his work is needless and silly. He is what we may call an extremely well-documented person, from birth to

his own pupils, Giovanni Boltraffio, Ambrogio de Predis, Marco d'Oggiono and Andrea Salai, tried to extract tricks of chiaroscuro from his work but never really seemed to have understood the mentality of the master. A good half century passed before the cluster of the great early biologists, physicists, and cosmologists began to see things in the same way that he had. In the meantime, he had died in France (1519), honored by Francis I, who clearly saw that there was far more to him than the "mechanicien" of his death certificate. The mysteries of nature to which he had initiated himself were buried in his notebooks (many of which are still missing). The dates of these scientists are interesting when posed against those of Leonardo (1452–1519): Niccolò Tartaglia (1500–1577); Girolamo Cardano (1501–1576); François Viète (1549–1603); Johannes Kepler (1571–1630); René Descartes (1596–1650); Pierre de Fermat (1601–1665); Giles Roberval (1602–1675); Jacob Bernouilli (1654–1705); and Johann Bernouilli (1667–1748). These figures, whom Kroeber, I think with justification, considers the great founders of modern science in the influential published form, are mainly mathematicians and physicists. However, the kind of biology that involves observation of the minutiae that interested Leonardo reached its high points in the eighteenth and nineteenth centuries and it was well for his own hide that he kept his thoughts to himself: the fifteenth century was even less ready than the nineteenth century for studies that led ineluctably to the theory of evolution. In the next century his way of looking at nature came to be generalized to the very cosmos itself. It was the century of Newton, Galileo, Leibnitz, and Halley whose visions of the cosmos were the wave of the future. Leonardo and Dürer and many other artists of the late quattrocento approached the study of the human figure and the rest of the observable world in a way that was denigrated by the institutionally validated scholarship of the time. It was perhaps precisely because nature and society as they saw it could not

---

death. We know that his drawing-room manners were impeccable; we know that the powerful people with whom he came in contact saw him as a person of great personal charm and intellect; his diaries show that he did not think the people for whom he worked were to be trusted with a complex, destructive technology; there were no women in his life, but there seem to have been no men either. The early arrest for heresy—which he got out of because the other two young men were also connected to powerful and well-to-do families—seems to have been mostly that; the implication that they were persecuted for homosexuality is implausible because little stigma was attached to homosexual attachments in renaissance Europe. They were viewed as immoral by the church, but the impedimenta of hysteria about adequacy that attends them in Anglo-Saxon cultures was absent. One suspects he caused malaise, like many bright men who fail utterly either to conceal or reveal themselves.

be studied under the theological rubrics of the learning of their contemporaries. In fact, Louis Feuer has shown in *The Scientific Intellectual* that the theological concerns that have been given so much
importance by Talcott Parsons and Robert Merton as an impetus
to the development of modern science were chronic impediments to
science and learning.[22] However, the essentially intuitive way the
insights of artists foreshadow the systematic work of the scientist
perhaps makes for its real limitation as a guide to action. The work
of the artist thus often lacks the scientific essential of duplicability.
Any understanding to be integrated with the organon of science
must be stated in such a way that the reasoning is apparent to
others concerned with the same matters, a need met only when a
standardized methodology has been formulated. But it is this very
freedom from a standardized methodology that makes it possible
for the artist to rush in where angels of science fear to tread.
Shakespeare, for example, may have sensed a great many things
about the dynamics of behavior from puppy love (*Romeo and
Juliet*) to the Oedipus complex (*Hamlet*) and the distortions of
perception that are associated with the sense of discrimination
(*Othello*), but the lack of a knowledge of Shakespeare's way of
arriving at these understandings means that his work itself does
not allow us to go beyond the gut feeling that he was right.[23] It was
almost three centuries after his death before a dynamic psychology
was stated in such a way that the things he sensed could be subjected to methodologically standardized observation.

It is also the slow effects of the need for precise conceptualization
that makes it usual for philosophical systems to come to their ma-
turity later than the artistic aspects of the culture and even later
than the scientific aspects. An older definition of the task of philosophy was the search for the common. What has been treated
under the rubrics of the academic study of philosophy has often
been a good deal more than just that, but, at bottom it has been
always at least that. Before one can engage in the quest for the
common, the special systems of conceptualization of the sciences
must be formulated clearly. Contrary to what is so often believed
even by many scholars of unassailable competence, science may

---

22 Ideology remains an impediment to science and learning. Stalin rejected
Western genetics although throughout his regime straight courses in Mendelian
genetics were taught in the Soviet Union as examples of bourgeois anathema. It
is only recently that Europeans have rejected the idea that the natural order is
an adjunct to state and church.
23 Shakespeare's own personality eludes us in any psychological terms. Legal
and parish records show us a solid citizen who was hardly distinguishable from
the generality of propertied yeomen of the early seventeenth century.

have little to do with experience. Indeed, the exact difference between a trained scientist and even a highly observant layman is that the scientist denies the value of experience unmediated by abstraction. This approach to an ultimate abstraction that can stand by itself independently of the vagaries of idiosyncratic experiences requires a painstaking subjection of sciences to an intensive technical, logical, and epistemological analysis. It is thus to be expected that the climaxes of philosophical work should be latest. It may be true, as the late Gordon Allport suggested, that there is an inherent human propensity to generalize, but logicizing is not equally inherent, as the failure of the Chinese ever to evolve a developed technical logic testifies. However, as we noted in an earlier segment of this study, once these philosophical systems are evolved they always have their effect upon the subject, technique, and aesthetics of the work of the artist. Finally we must note that in the internal dialectic of this process of isolation and self-criticism is the sense that the artist often sees further and sooner about the human condition and thought itself than the politician, the scientist, or the philosopher, not to mention the generality of us. He can do this only because, at his best, he is free of the idols, the taboos, and the rules that keep the rest of us in separate cells of our larger prisons. Because he sees things for us before we see them ourselves, it is for our own perpetuation that we must allow him to be free.

## BACKGROUND NOTE

This chapter is based upon A. L. Kroeber's *Configurations of Culture Growth* (Berkeley, Ca.: University of California Press, 1944).

His theoretical assumptions are contained in the first half of his *Anthropology* (New York: Harcourt Brace, 1948), and *The Nature of Culture* (Chicago: University of Chicago Press, 1952).

After I wrote this chapter, I encountered Christopher Small's *Music, Society, Education: A Radical Examination of the Prophetic Function of Music in Western, Eastern and African Cultures with its Impact on Society and its Use in Education* (London: Calder, 1977). Finally, the social role and vision of the artist is examined in John Wilson's *The Faith of an Artist* (London: G. Allen Unwin, 1962), and in Robert N. Wilson's *The Writer as Social Seer* (Chapel Hill, N.C.: University of North Carolina Press, 1979).

# 13

## A Summing Up

WE have come to the place to summarize the present effort. First I should make it clear that I have deliberately given little attention to popular taste. The efforts to satisfy it and create it are good-sized industries and their products have far greater immediate importance in the day-to-day lives of a far greater number of people than anything that has appeared in these pages. It seems to me to be probable that such will remain the case, for it is highly unlikely that any large segment of the laity will ever receive the training that is needed to apprehend what artists themselves regard as interesting or good, and this is just as true of Bourbon Street as Bach. For most of us, it is probably too much work for the return it gives. As I pointed out earlier, few major works of art become popular for the technical reasons that professionals and knowledgeable laymen regard as important. I am convinced that popular art has to be treated in a framework where what the audience wants is more important than what the artist himself may wish to convey. I have here followed my own prejudice that the latter is more important than the former. It has, in large measure, made this essay imply an ideal type in which "serious" art is the independent variable, and "folk" and "mass" art drift on without influence upon the work of serious artists. Such a view is just as much at odds with reality as one which views "serious" art as being a pure emergent of folk forms. Each has its effect upon the other. Ex-vacuo primitives seem few in the history of art and so do titanic figures who never touched the ground. I have, however, tried to present a prolegomenon to the sociology of art that does not take art to be purely a manifestation of an attempt of the socially powerful to support ideologies that apotheosize their own common basic personality structures and the interests of the families and strata to which they belong. Much art has been exactly that whenever societies have been complex enough to be stratified. Where modern judgments consider their tastes to have been good such work still appears good. But such work often also suffers from the limitations of its clientele as well. One of the largest palaces in Europe is the Palazzo Reale at Caserta near Naples. It was erected after plans of a Neapolitan stage designer of Dutch ancestry, Luigi Vanvitelli (1700–1773), to provide a suitable residence for the Bourbon kings of Naples—monarchs of the Kingdom of the Two Sicilies, a realm that never reached its highest glories because of recurrent famines and endemic malaria. It also gives us Queen Victoria's patronage of Sir Edwin Landseer's portraits of dogs and gillies. One can, however, also look at the great Gothic churches of France and the Palazzo Farnese as expressions of upper-class tastes, and that they were, but when this is the only thing that we can say we end up with a congeries that mainly interests students of stratification. There still remains a small portion that responds to pan-human needs, concerns, and sentiments that transcends the accidents of any particular stasis in human consciousness. A somewhat larger portion of art can be understood within the context of meanings given by the larger cultural configurations in which it occurs.

It is appropriate here to interpose comments upon an issue that I have reason to believe may trouble some readers. How persistent are the social structures in which the work of creative artists have been and are carried on? It depends upon what one means by a persistent social structure and this can refer to many things indeed. Since artmaking has been a continuous human activity, it is plausible that there is continual interaction among artists and their students. If, therefore, one takes "persistent social structures" to mean networks or relations among artists, they are easily found. Moreover, they appear to last as long as the civilizations in which they occur do not meet cataclysmic disruption. Chinese, Indian, Japanese, Western European, Russian, and Islamic traditions in the arts have been carried on from generation to generation and locality to locality and within each context the artists seem to know each others' work except for local folk forms. Whenever I looked for connections I found that I could find them. "Recent scholarship" will usually turn up not only parochial connections, but a surprising, even if esoteric, familiarity with what was being done elsewhere by serious workers. Individual international and crosscultural reputations can frequently be found as far back as any documentation is possible, and the frequent diffusion of the work of identifiable men suggests that at least the clienteles were more than local. I took no systematic interest in this question so I am not sure how much of this can be pinned down precisely. The data themselves are fuzzy. However, in China connoisseurship has a history that goes back to Han times (202 B.C. to A.D. 220), in Japan for at least a millennium, and in Europe well back into classical times. Moreover, if one considers traditions of training, performance, and craftsmanship as needing defined relationships to be kept going, there are persistent social structures, even in the context of catastrophic social and political conditions. In fact I believe highly developed forms take so long to develop that they have to have some continuity even in the face of recurrent social instability.

However, if one is looking for an institutionalized continuity of the position of the artist and of his activities, that is another matter. It is true that there are various national academies of arts and artists, but they are at best a series of Holy Roman Empires—they legitimize the establishment and seek, usually unsuccessfully, to inhibit the growth of new forms. They always lack what is a sine qua non for institutionalized position—clear-cut rights to make specific demands of politically organized society. From a logical standpoint, not being able to find something is no proof at all that it does not exist. Even with this caveat, one might doubt any strong institutionalized structures in the arts for a quite different reason. Whenever institutionalization takes place it occurs in a context of suppressing controversy over the control of property, especially property that is strategic in the ultimate power structure of the society— who bosses whom. In the arts this remains a professionally isolated control of academies, galleries, orchestras and the like; and I outlined the way they can push the production and diffusion of art in defined directions. But we find almost nothing if we are looking for something analogous to the way that the government and banking set institutionalized limits upon the actions of one another because there is a perpetual struggle for the control of strategic property that has to be contained. John Strachey's coming struggle for power never came because it was already there. In politically important countries only the nominally Marxist societies of the Soviet Union and the People's Republic of China have continued to follow Bulwer-Lytton's dictum that the pen is mightier than the sword and seek to contain the artist as a pillar of the state. In the West this has not become the case because the artist is regarded as little more than a decoration without any obvious role either in supporting or subverting the system of power in the society. The actual case is quite different. There is not a single major art whose basic qualitative character has not suffused our entire culture. We see and analyse the world around us in terms that have been laid down by artists, from our perceptions of motion, form, and color to our politics, philosophy, and sociology. I found nothing clear when I looked for the "functional integrations," coordinations of activity, and intrusions of the force of politically organized society to establish rights and duties that mark activities that are believed to be important enough to institutionalize. I do not know, however, if I missed the cues that another would have seen easily.

Other readers may find fault with me for not considering continuing art markets. If I had concerned myself with connoisseurship there might have been no justification for by-passing them. I have considered attempts to satisfy the wants of consumers as a ubiquitous imperative for artists, no matter what the media are. Only teaching seems to provide a by-pass, but even here students want one kind of training and not another. However, whenever one considers markets for art that is already produced one finds oneself mired in sour Veblenian analyses of the symbolic systems of elites that lead them to favor one thing over another and, inevitably, the accuracy of their guesses as to unearned incremental changes in market value as well. (In a final sense, art speculation is an attempt to guess what ultimately the super-rich will want long before they are aware of it themselves.) Such considerations impinge on art-making as an on-going activity, but rarely entirely dictate the final form that it takes. At least in recent Western experience, artists and their clients seem to have had relationships to each other characterized by distrust at its most cordial, and profound alienation at its worst. Collecting is not necessarily motivated by an appreciation of the works for their own sake. The Puritans thought the art collection of Charles I to be replete with vanities, but they made no bonfire and treated it as though it was worth something.

Connoisseurship—knowing what things are and why they are desirable—is another matter entirely. Prestige of possession, market values, and capital gains, and the like are secondary if not actually irrelevant to the motives of the connoisseur. Often the influence of the works themselves upon people with the means to buy them changes their attitude toward them profoundly. Joseph Widener built up a collection of paintings that so dominated him that he gave it to the nation because (like many other collectors) he felt that it had a life of its own and should really be public property. He is said to have wept when he looked at the pictures on the last night that they were in his house. Andrew Mellon, the stiff-necked old financier, paid a monstrous ransom for a collection of pictures that Lord Duveen had put in an apartment above him.[1] Here one can easily make not only crossnational comparisons between European and North American countries, but readily document studies of such activity in China, Japan, Korea, and Czarist Russia as well. However, connoisseurship remains largely ex post facto to the way the artists respond to their society and to their social role.

I have also shied from trying to generalize about the great public collections of art. Inevitably they reflect the tastes of donors and curators. It is only perhaps in the last seventy-five years that being a curator has moved from mountebankery and aristocratic sinecures to an independent expertise. The curators of the better museums, impresarios of the performing arts, dealers, and even some publishers have the clout to bring the tastes and judgments of experts to those who have the means to support artistic activities. (It does not hurt, of course, to be at ease in a drawing room, as Thomas Hoving and Philippe De Montebello of the Metropolitan Museum of Art testify.) Two common assumptions seem entirely gratuitous; the first is that the very rich can impose stale, idiosyncratic judgments upon the entire society. Such efforts have a way of dying with their patrons, sometimes, indeed, before, as the demise of Huntington Hartford's Museum of Contemporary Art testifies, as does also the short life of the French academic styles favored by Louis XVIII and Napoleon III a century earlier. The record is that rich collectors often do know what they are collecting. For every Isabella Stewart Gardner who immured herself in a Venetian palazzo in the fens of Boston and collected so indiscriminately that one can only say that she spent a great deal and had no coherent taste, there is a John G. Johnson, an Albert C. Barnes, or a J. P. Morgan, Sr., who knew perfectly well what he was collecting.[2] There is no way to tell the ratio of good collections to junk among

---

[1] Duveen played a carefully calculated game. He gave Mr. Mellon a key to the apartment and is said to have instructed the caretaker who watched the apartment to make coffee for Mr. Mellon. Mr. Mellon came in at night, drank the coffee, and looked at the pictures for hours on end. He bought the pictures and built the National Gallery to house them.

[2] Even Mrs. Gardner had some restraints upon her idiosyncracies. She bought from very expensive sources with good advice—Bernard Berenson's among others. J. P. Morgan employed experts. Johnson and Barnes may be the most interesting of all. Johnson was a rich corporation lawyer who knew old masters expertly enough to by-pass the major dealers of his day; Albert Barnes was a contentious chemist who invented, sold, and made the world supply of Argyrol (himself; alone; at home; by a secret process) and wrote an important treatise, *The Art in Painting* (New York: Harcourt Brace, n.d.).

such donations. Only the best collections survive "going public" intact.

Equally important is that not only do artists respond to the demands of markets, but they have often created them as well. Perhaps the most striking case in the West lies in the development of Mannerism in Italian painting after the deaths of Michelangelo (1564), Leonardo (1519), and Raphael (1520). These three were far more than primi inter pares; they were clearly far better than any of their contemporaries. Yet their extreme popularity may have accounted for the period of sterile imitation in Italian painting (outside of Venice) that set in in the sixteenth century. Their own successes in getting their styles accepted range from Michelangelo's protean, titanic battles with Julius II to Leonardo's subtle patient conversion of his patrons to his mysteries. Yet, for good or bad, it took better than two hundred years for many people in central Italy to paint in a way that ignored their precepts. I have not dealt with this area because I tried to confine myself to considering only those variables that relate to how the social structure in which the artist works and the values he derives from the culture affect the forms and qualitative aspects of his art.

I wrote this essay with a disturbing realization that the rubric "Art" covers a variety of things. If one takes it to mean the varying manifestations of a creative, panhuman daemon it would cover a great deal more than what has historically been considered art in the West. Such a meaning could also cover nice mathematical proofs, the new cosmology, relativity, molecular biology, and even D'Arcy Wentworth Thompson's study of the mathematics of growth and form. I have therefore kept to forms in the world of perception that require the agency of the creative man to be realized. It is for this reason that I proceeded from the quality of appearances of the world that man creates when he seems to be responding to aesthetic rather than utilitarian needs. It may well be that Talcott Parsons's *The Social System* seems an ultimately unsatisfactory book, not so much because it is needlessly weighty, but because it fails to give any importance to the ever-present aesthetic component in determining the forms that human culture takes. In this sense his sociology was even less than what Auguste Comte left ninety years before.[3] Comte had at least moved clumsily toward realizing the need for considering the aesthetic component as one of the things that civilizations express when he gave feeling and sentiment a role equal to that of the intellect in the stages of the evolution of civilization.

[3] Comte died in 1857; *The Social System* was published in 1951.

In an effort such as this there was no closed formal conceptual framework that gave one an obvious place to start. The Victorians were fond of saying that art is long and life is short. Even the sparest line drawing of Picasso marks a stage in a development of technique that was already highly advanced twenty-five hundred years ago and will probably continue in directions that we can hardly imagine at this moment. The futurologies of the past always turn out to be dated because they were always based on the perceptions of their presents. In the absence of either the logical or the temporal containment that would have made it better to start at one subject than another, I began these pages with a recurrent and obvious evidence of an aesthetic component in civilization wherever it occurs—the varying qualitative character of the appearances of cities. A start could have been made from any number of other manifestations. One could easily, for example, have compared the zoological gardens of London, New York City, and Philadelphia, and related them to the Gothic Revival as it was manifested in nineteenth-century ornamental iron work, in plant conservatories, and in parks. This stylistic consistency is not accidental, but I know a good deal about urban sociology and nothing about zoos (although I am sure someone has done some historical sociologizing about why and how menageries came to be called zoological gardens). Cities were, I think, a very good place to start for reasons that have long been understood by archaeologists and historians. Civilizations, those varying, specialized, complex manifestations of culture that go beyond meeting common necessities, have always been a product of urban life and have always been most easily seen in cities. It is here that human life itself seems to be manifested in its most intense form. If we are to follow our prejudice that art is the most intensely felt aspect of human life, it is reasonable to go to the manifestation that gives the clearest image of it—the quality of cities. It seemed better to start with them than with those monasteries of upper-class tastes and scholarly involution, the art museums, although one must admit that the latter have their function in enabling one to compare style, technique, and quality. Nevertheless, the problems remained of limiting the universe of discourse of the study. To speak of the creative as being at the basis of art can include a great number of disparate things from new, exquisite cruelties, through the unpeopled afternoons of Cézanne's lonely paysages, to the tidy elegance of Aristotle's works in logic. "Creative" seems to be a word that covers far too much. I have thus confined myself to those aspects of the world of appearances that show differences that seem only to be accountable through a way of perceiving and interpreting the world that arises from what we must call an aesthetic component in the human psyche, what Georges Gurvitch called the noetic mind. The qualitative differences in the expression of this panhuman creative aesthetic component we term style. Only peripherally have I concerned myself with art as the constant expressions of the stages of intellectual development of the societies where they are found. One could have taken either the aesthetic component or the intellectual substratum of art as the independent variable; here I have taken the aesthetic component.

As style emerges the technique necessary to express it develops hand in hand. This leads to a professionalization of technique that is the main condition that separates the work of professionals from that of laymen. The professional practitioner in any field is inevitably separated from laymen in following his calling, and, with this separation, he looks odd in the eyes of the world. This is likely to occur for any professional qua professional, but the lay expectation that all art must be easily apprehended by anyone introduces a burden upon the artists that few other professionals are expected to suffer. As is the case in many other fields, the isolation of the artist with his fellows results in a development of special ways of viewing things that often makes what interests artists appeal only slightly to most laymen, or even be utterly incomprehensible. Nevertheless, the artist does not even control recognition by his fellows, let alone the living that must ultimately come from the public at large. He has to come to terms with the expectations of those who control access to the attention of others.

Art, the work of the artists, thus even on this level becomes a socially constrained pursuit. The creative elaboration of activity beyond economic and hedonistic needs is ubiquitous and its very universality among humans suggests that it is an inherent human need. However, the difference between art—exciting creative work—and craftsmanship—the capacity to produce what one intends—continues to elude me, even after some sophisticated training and a good deal of reading. I am still unable to find better terms for the characteristics of the works of artists that excite me aesthetically than either empathic power or significant form. I am sure that this characteristic is dependent upon sharing that common system of meanings which Émile Durkheim called the collective consciousness. Styles themselves seemed to be a part of the collective consciousness. Their development and decline seemed to be related to the extent to which they provided a medium for meanings that remained important to large segments of the societies where they were manifest and to the fortuitous appearances of major artists to exploit all the possibilities for growth and development within their limits. Great artists have always seemed to have pushed styles to their limits, but they also evoke meanings that are universal and beyond the accidents of time and place. They present universally understood cues that evoke universal experience. Yet I remain uneasy with the idea of universal experiences. A close look has too often shown me not universality for all mankind, but at most only for most people in an era of civilization. This is another reason why I gave so much attention to cultural systems.

I then considered the organizational aspects of the professionalization of art. This process fosters the developing of a set of meanings that are not necessarily understood by the majority of laymen. Moreover, we noted a constant influence of ambient technological, demographic, and spatial factors. The demographic variable seems not to have been given the force which it is due here or anywhere else. The ideologies that legitimize systems of stratification were also given no explicit attention. I omitted the latter mainly because it has been done unexceptionably well elsewhere,[4] but also because I have tried to keep art and culture the independent variables.

I have also noted a set of limitations that occur whenever a field becomes professionalized—the influence of a taught tradition and the organization of schools to maintain it. There is no question in my mind that schools not only teach neophyte artists to write, paint, sculpt, dance, or perform and write music as professionals do in their own society, but for the most part the curricula themselves discourage responses to influences external to the training systems as well as attempts at trying anything that is markedly new. Only a very small number of the most able students ever enjoy the careful coaching that encourages them to develop the new forms that they see for themselves. For the rest, unless they rap with other students, it stops with Czerny.

I went on to consider the consistently experienced, extraprofessional influences that shape and limit the work of the artist. It seems fair to say that the most important difference between "studio" art and art produced for a mass market lies in the unabashed subordination of the impulses and explorations of the artist to considerations of profit in the latter. There is no logical necessity that popular art be bad art, and indeed there are more than a few cases where popular art has been respected by professionals, but it has been rarely for the same reasons that it has been popular. Fred Astaire was to his audiences a vital, sexy young man who gave them brief moments in a radiant city amid the ugliness and banality

4 E.g., Arnold Hauser's *The Social History of Art* (New York: Knopf, 1951).

of the Great Depression, but when Mikhail Baryshnikov saw his films forty years later, he saw a dancer whose technique and artistry seemed unbelievably good even to him.

We saw that there is in any civilization a growth of classes of critics who take upon themselves the roles of arbiters who enforce their values and standards and make them those of the artistic and literary productions of their time—or at least they try. The personae of these gaolers of the culture range from policemen, bureaucrats, and priests, through to specialized professional critics and art historians, to the artists themselves. Except for the last group, they rarely serve to encourage the artists to carry their work into new realms of consciousness, motion, and perception itself, but simply reinforce the intellectual prejudices and institutionalized interests of the critics themselves (which may be at odds with what the artists themselves want to do). Friction and tension seem inevitable—the artist is trying to push forward; the critic tries to hold back. Whistler's battle royal with Ruskin not only added a new intensity of vituperation to such controversies, but epitomized a process that is inevitable whenever the standards by which art is judged fail to fit what artists want to do.[5] The intellectually coherent standards of professional critics come after the art itself is produced if there is a body of acknowledged good work from which the critics are able to derive their standards. However there is another kind of professional criticism that is applied to all art, even before the emergence of the distinction between artist and critic, the critical apparatus that the artists themselves bring to their work.

I went on to consider the dynamic aspects of cultures that seem to give form and direction to this common critical apparatus that determines the basis of the judgments of the professional critic and the artist as the constant critic-in-residence of his own work. I avoided the history of aesthetics because technical work in aesthetics has been articulated to learning theories which were in turn articulated to epistemology. Much of it was formal and rational and the dream of understanding our responses to art in such terms is not new and is by no means dead. It may indeed be about to enjoy an unprecedented vogue; witness Douglas R. Hofstader's *Godel, Escher, Bach: An Eternal Golden Braid* and George Stiny and James Gips, *Algorithmic Aesthetics: Computer Models for Criticism and Design in the Arts*. In addition, Hofstader's private world turns out

[5] The wide publicity that mass newspaper printing gave to their controversy made what previously would have been a catty below-the-salt argument into a cause célèbre.

to be very urbane and often extremely funny. However it also turns out that his favorite painter is Maurits Escher and the Bach in which he is most interested is the Bach of *The Art of the Fugue* (which is so "abstract" that it was written without instrumental scoring) and not the passionate church cantatas. Stiny and Gips obviously could not tell anyone why one responds to anything but only how a computer can tell us to what extent the work in question conforms to the standards programmed into it (which limits art to the intellectual and affective limitations of computers). It is, of course, a remarkable intellectual exercise, but I may not be the only one to miss the pictures. Attempts to intellectualize the core of art in such terms may seem no more satisfying than their predecessors. Bad as the term may be we may be pushed back to what Clive Bell called "significant form"—"a combination of lines, colours and forms that move us aesthetically"—a definition that would take little effort to generalize to arts other than painting. Various examples of significant form were given to us by both Roger Fry and Clive Bell, but we are left with an odd feeling that it's there when artists and critics say it's there—a methodology that seems curiously unsatisfactory to those of us whose confidence in our intuitive intellectual gifts was destroyed by logicians before we reached twenty. Nevertheless, if one is familiar with a fair sample of the best art in the West and a smaller part of the work of other civilizations and primitive societies, there is still an inescapable feeling that Fry and Bell were stumbling toward something essential. These aspects were left to one side because I felt they could be termed sociologic only in the sense that they represented the ways that collective opinions in the society itself define how one approaches such matters. It was my curiosity about what lay at the basis of such collective opinions that turned my attention in the last part of this essay toward a group of writers who concerned themselves with the dynamics of cultural systems.

Several score of writers could have been selected if I had wished to make one far-fetched case after another. Indeed I have omitted some very important writers who concerned themselves with the sociology of one medium or another. Max Weber, for example, wrote about music in the way he wrote about many things, too technically for laymen, but too bound to his own readings of things to interest professionals in the fields themselves. In a sense this is perhaps always a difficulty in writing about the sociology of anything at all; the sociology of it always seems to deal with peripheral nuisances (if not downright banalities) to the professionals themselves. The arts are no exceptions.

The writers who were taken dealt squarely with the arts themselves. They were not always sociologists but they all wrote about sociology because they were all concerned with the general forces rather than the historic accidents that determine the quality of the human condition.

It was a quest for some basis for the underlying assumptions of critical systems that caused me to start the last section of the present essay with Friedrich Nietzsche's *The Birth of Tragedy.* Nietzsche saw three constant recurrent elements in ancient Greek drama:[6] an element of the dream on the one hand, and a constant element of sensual excess and intoxication on the other. Both were tempered by rational cognition. He called them Apollonian, Dionysian, and Socratic. These three tendencies seem to have dominated cultures almost universally and they seem even to be terms that enable us to label cultures meaningfully. Artists themselves have been either implicitly aware of or influenced by the interplay of these qualities from the Old Kingdom to the present as Panofsky's wonderful historical study of human proportion in art shows. Moreover it was a start that kept us from naive psychologizing, bad biology, and fuzzy epistemology. It carried the essay to things that were most easily regarded as needing to be placed in a social context to give them meanings sufficient to explain the phenomenal manifestations of art.

It was an easy step to go from Nietzsche to Pitirim A. Sorokin and Thorstein Veblen. Oddly I can find no evidence that Nietzsche had any influence upon Veblen,[7] and I know first hand that Sorokin held Veblen in contempt. Nevertheless, each developed ideas about the dynamics that carried further Nietzsche's readings of the elements that culture expresses. Veblen called nineteenth-century Western culture "barbarian" and saw it in clear antagonism to the aesthetic, intellectual components of the varying expressions of human collective consciousness. Sorokin went a step further and put forth a scheme in *Social and Cultural Dynamics* in which he related this to a question of whether or not we had any right to believe that there was any real world that existed independently of our sensations of it, or whether there was no more than a fragile consensus as to the meaning of sensation itself, and whether ideas themselves were the reality. Unfortunately Sorokin only considered the editorial and iconographic content of man's creative work in

[6] Ancient Greek drama is a rubric that covers a span of several centuries. Nietzsche wrote about the period around 400 B.C.
[7] Veblen used German sources easily; I believe it to be highly unlikely that Veblen did not know of Nietzsche's work.

order to explore the exciting hypothesis that the differences in the expressions of the arts may be due to the extent to which the creative artist is guided by his conception of the final nature of reality. Much of the difficulty Sorokin's work presented to thoughtful readers lay in its failure to make a set of simple but important distinctions that Erwin Panofsky made in his "Iconography and Iconology: An Introduction to the Study of Renaissance Art" (in his *Meaning in the Visual Arts* [1955]). These were between "primary or natural subject matter"—"the objects themselves"; "secondary or conventional subject matter"—the conventions of meaning; and "intrinsic meaning or content"—"the underlying principles that reveal the basic attitudes of a nation, a class, a religious or philosophical persuasion. . . ." Sorokin never considered the last level at all. As far as I can make out he really did not have the command of technical epistemological questions necessary to deal with it (and I say this as a person who is proud to have been one of his students). Moreover, his training as a lawyer often led him to take a legalistic view of evidence so that he tended to confuse appearance with meaning.

These difficulties led me to bring in portions of the analysis of the comparisons of the dynamics of Eastern and Western cultures put forth in F. S. C. Northrop's *The Meeting of East and West*. Northrop (who knew Sorokin's work) went a step further in considering the ontological aspects of culture. Northrop pointed out that the essential differences in the cultures of the East and West lie in whether the world is viewed as being composed of discrete, separable, atomistic parts or as fundamentally a continuum that only seems to have separateness in the world of appearances. He saw with it a contrast of formal, rational elements and a primacy of feeling. Either set of alternatives—if they are indeed alternatives—gives us a different kind of style and form. Northrop's views helped better than any others I encountered in explaining not only why styles develop, but why they go stale. As meanings become more precisely understood or formulated, variety in their expression is lost and the artmaking process becomes routinized and serves to inhibit creative expression. Moreover the systems of meaning that give comprehensibility to the praxis of history no longer seem adequate. It was not bad training or laziness that made later classical art decline, but the dominant meanings its techniques were evolved to express were no longer important forces in the society of the later Gentile ancient world. This process occurred repeatedly in the West and Near East, and the more I have learned about Far Eastern art with relation to the history of the societies it was evolved to express, the more this seems to apply there as well. (I did not even try to relate this tendency to decay to the art of Hindu India which remains, by and large, terra incognita to me, although I have read a fair amount about Indian religious systems.)

I was thus led to a final set of considerations. How do these systems of style develop? Sociological literature on the growth and development of cultural systems left over from the century prior to 1935 tended to view the cultural and social systems as lacking any independent development, but as ultimately expressing some other set of variables such as race and ethnicity, markets, demography, religion, or political ideology, to name only a few. It was possible to take any one of them and consider it the independent variable with different degrees of success in arriving at explanations that have what Poincaré called "convenience and simplicity." These ranged in scholarship and urbanity from Alexis de Gobineau's *Essay on the Inequality of Races* to Max Weber's studies of the interplay of religion and the growth of economic institutions. It seemed wise to go to some work that did not commit itself to a primacy of any one institutional complex or area, but to several different ones that appeared, by and large, to have an importance everywhere—such as literature, painting, sculpture, music, science, or philosophy. Here again I went to a big, admittedly flawed classic, A. L. Kroeber's *Configurations of Culture Growth*. Where Sorokin got into trouble trusting graduate students, Kroeber got into trouble trusting only himself. It was the fate of his work too that the specificities upon which so many of his judgments were based would fare badly at the hands of experts, but he seems to have known so much that most of these errors balanced out in the aggregate. The assumption remained intact in the balance. It was that in each field he studied there would be phases of growth, development, climaxes and repetitions, and declines. From his study emerged a generalization of which Kroeber himself seemed unaware: where intuition was most important, development was most rapid and where technically precise conceptualization was critical— as in the philosophy—the course of development was slowest. The arts reached their peaks earlier than any other activity. In the light of this it seems no surprise that so many observers have seen artists as the eternal avant-garde of the inner dynamics of the culture. It also seems to me to imply that wherever the role of the artist is understood, artists are going to be objects of suspicion among the mentors of stability, particularly when they are free to go where their daemons take them.

Plato knew what he was about: he proposed keeping an eye on the poets.

Appendix

Culture Growth Cycles
in the Arts, Science, and Philosophy,
Standardized from Data Relating to Periods
Studied by A. L. Kroeber
in *Configurations of Culture Growth*
(all dates A.D. unless indicated as B.C.).

| CULTURE AREAS AND DURATIONS | SCULPTURE | | PAINTING | | LITERATURE | |
|---|---|---|---|---|---|---|
| | Earliest | Peak | Earliest | Peak | Earliest | Peak |
| Greece | 800 B.C.[2] | 450 B.C. | 540 B.C. | | 1000 B.C.[3] | 400 B.( |
| Ancient (585–270 B.C.) | | | | | | |
| Attic | | | | 455 B.C. | | |
| Ionian | | | | 420 B.C. | | |
| Thracian | | | | 360 B.C. | | |
| Alexandrine | | | | 360 B.C. | | |
| Roman | | | | | | |
| Pagan (1–450) | | | | | | |
| Christian (200–525) | | | | | 240 B.C. | 0 |
| Medieval | | | | | | |
| Early Scholastic (1033–1154) | | | | | | |
| High Scholastic (1245–1308) | | | | | | |
| Northern Europe | | | | | | |
| France 1st development | 1000[5] | 1325 | 1590 | 1649 | | |
| 2d development | 1500 | 1810 | 1650 | 1710 | 1000 | 1500 |
| 3d development | 1784 | 1917 | 1710 | 1917 | 1650 | 1850 |
| Britain | | | | | 1850 | 1940[9] |
| Germany | | | 1300 | 1500 | 1750 | 1800 |
| Italy | | | 1266 | 1550 | | |
| Mathematics | | | | | | |
| Anatomy | | | | | | |
| Physics/Astronomy | | | | | | |
| Late Medieval Cycle | | | 1266 | 1455 | 1183 | 1375 |
| Renaissance Cycle | 1323 | 1505 | 1430 | 1592 | 1432 | 1540 |
| Baroque and Later Cycle | 1550 | 1822 | 1502 | 1778 | 1540 | 1750 |
| Modern | | | | | 1685 | 1938 |
| Switzerland[12] | | | | | | |
| Euler 1707–1783 | | | | | | |
| Bernouilli Family | | | | | | |
| Netherlands | | | | | | |
| Belgium | | | | | | |
| Holland | | | 1370 | 1580 | | |
| Egypt[13] | 3315 B.C. | 2500 B.C. | | | | |
| India | 1200 B.C. | 500 | 200 B.C. | 750 | | |
| Buddhist | | | | | 477 | 1200 |
| Brahman | | | | | | |
| China[14] | 800 B.C. | 900 | 300 B.C. | 1127 | 500 B.C. | 0 |
| Japan | | | 1300 | 1420 | 1500 | 1900 |
| Wood-block prints | | | 400 | 1800 | | |

It must be emphasized that Kroeber made no serious attempts to treat any of these culture areas and activities exhaustively. Many of his lacunae simply reflect a lack of interest or idiosyncratic judgments. Much of his troubles with the entire work probably could have been avoided if he had collaborated with specialists.

Notes to the table derived from Koeber's *Configurations of Culture Growth:*

1. Kroeber was clearly unsympathetic to anything but eighteenth-century German music.
2. This date is tenable if work from Knossos is considered Greek.

| DRAMA | | MUSIC[1] | | SCIENCE | | PHILOSOPHY | |
|---|---|---|---|---|---|---|---|
| Earliest | Peak | Earliest | Peak | Earliest | Peak | Earliest | Peak |
| 625 B.C. | 450 B.C. | | | | | | |
| | | | | 600 B.C. | 310 B.C. | 585 B.C. | 320 B.C. |
| | | | | 70 | 79 | | |
| | | | | | | 1 | 250 |
| | | | | | | 200 | 410 |
| | | | | | | 1033[4] | 1097 |
| | | | | | | 1245 | 1325 |
| 1300 | 1650 | | | 1517 | 1790[6] | 1588 | 1715[7] |
| | | | | | | 1689 | 1794[8] |
| | | | | | | 1760 | 1941 |
| | | | | 1510 | 1689 | 1548 | 1730 |
| 1550 | 1615 | 1480 | 1915 | 1407 | 1630 | 1679 | 1804 |
| 1474 | 1883 | | | | | | 1782[10] |
| | | | | 1450 | 1506 | | |
| | | | | 1540 | 1570 | | |
| | | | | 1560 | 1690 | | |
| | | 1480 | | | | | |
| | | | 1680 | | | | |
| | | 1680 | 1893[11] | | | | |
| | | | | | 1783 | | |
| | | | | 1654 | 1748 | | |
| | | 1500 | 1650 | | | | |
| | | | | 1612 | 1667 | | |
| | | | | 1539 | 1732 | | |
| | | | | | | 100 | 1000 |
| | | | | | | 100 | 500 |
| 300 | 600 | | | | | 100 | 750 |
| 1127 | 1368 | | | 500 B.C. | 1000 | 604 B.C. | |
| 1600 | 1750 | | | | | | |

3. Kroeber only considers poetry in Greece; 1000 B.C. seems the best approximation of the date of Homer.
4. Kroeber treats Scholastic philosophy without regard to culture area, a practice that is still common except among specialists.
5. Gothic.

6. Renaissance and Enlightenment.
7. Mersenne, Malebranche, Gassendi, Pascal.
8. Montesquieu, Voltaire, Rousseau, Condorcet, Turgot.
9. This is an interpolation that is not in Kroeber.

10. The fragmentary data that Kroeber gives upon this simply reflects the fact that modern Italian philosophy has never been an object of serious study in northern Europe and the United States, and this seems likely to remain the case for sometime. The date given represents the peak of Vico's work.

11. Kroeber seemed not to recognize Puccini, Respighi, and other Italians of this century.

12. Kroeber's information on other areas is fragmentary.

13. Kroeber does not distinguish the Old Kingdom from the New. He ignores later developments in painting. Moreover, recent scholarship has tended to destroy the idea of a national continuity of ancient Egypt.

14. There are two major pulses. The first culminates in the Tang; the second ends with the end of the reign of Chien Lung in 1796. Kroeber gives no systematic attention to the second pulse which was a period of very high craftsmanship when, in the opinion of some connoisseurs, the craftsmanship became an end in itself to the detriment of artistic quality.

# A GENERAL NOTE
## ON BOOKS ON
## THE SOCIOLOGY OF ART

The sociology of art is not enough of a recognized speciality to be accorded a separate category in the Library of Congress catalog, where it falls under the subject heading of "Art and Society." What is given there seems to mark it essentially as a residual classification. Actual general treatises are, in fact, a rarity, although a bibliography of everything relevant to the subject would probably go to several hundred pages. Specialized studies that apply the methods and concepts of sociology to the study of art forms are another matter. There it becomes more than a specialty for one man to encompass. Little of the literature ever really clears up the differences between the audiences and consumers, the product itself, and the artists. A clear separation of these universes of discourse is found nowhere. The field remains largely undefined. My own inclination has been to treat the various arts as distinct, professionally isolated activities that emerge as expressions of the total cultural system that are analytically separable from other aspects of the social system. I am aware that such a separation is probably not possible for any profession. This isolation is an analytic convenience and not a historical fact. Europeans have been at the subject for over a century, including Karl Marx and Herbert Spencer (*Principles of Psychology*); Hippolyte A. Taine, *History of English Literature* (New York, 1886); Max Weber, *The Rational and Social Foundations of Music* (Carbondale, Ill.: Southern Illinois University Press, 1958); Levin Schücking, *The Sociology of Literary Taste* (1923; reprint ed., New York: Grove Press, 1944). Charles Lalo, *L'Art et La Vie Sociale* (Paris: G. Doin, 1921), to which James Barnett attaches considerable importance, is as yet untranslated. The following are what seem the works most relevant to the present effort published between 1950 and 1975 (with an exception being made for the first effort I found to define the field in English, A. S. Tomars, *Introduction to the Sociology of Art*).

Bowman, John F. *Issues in Art: A Survey of Controversies on Art in Society.* Dubuque, Ia.: W. C. Brown Book Co., 1965.

Burland, Cottie A. *Man and Art.* London and New York: Studio Publications, 1959.

Canaday, John E. *Culture Gulch Notes on Art and Its Publics in the 1960's.* New York: Farrar, Straus and Giroux, 1969.

Cooper, Charles Wilson. *The Arts and Humanity: A Psychological Introduction to the Fine Arts.* New York: Philosophical Library, 1952.

Deinhard, Hanna. *Meaning and Expression: Toward a Sociology of Art.* Boston: Beacon Press, 1970.

Dunham, Barrows. *The Artist in Society.* New York: Marzani and Munsell, 1960.

Duvignaud, Jean. *The Sociology of Art.* Translated by Timothy Wilson. London: Paladin, 1972.

Finkelstein, Sidney W. *Art and Society.* 2d ed. New York: International Publishers, 1947.

Gimpel, Jean. *The Cult of Art: Against Art and Artists.* New York: Stein and Day, 1969.

Gottschalk, Dilman W. *Art and the Social Order.* New York: Dover, 1962.

Gowans, Alan. *The Unchanging Arts: New Forms for the Traditional Functions of Art in Society.* Philadelphia: Lippincott, 1971.

Greenberg, Clement. *Art and Culture: Critical Essays.* Boston: Beacon Press, 1941.

Haskell, Francis. *Patrons and Painters: A Study in the Relations between Italian Art and Society in the Age of the Baroque.* London: Chatto and Windus, 1963.

Hauser, Arnold. *The Philosophy of Art History.* New York, 1959.

————. *The Social History of Art.* London, 1951.

Kavolis, Vytautas. *Artistic Expressions: A Sociological Analysis.* Ithaca, N.Y.: Cornell University Press, 1968.

————. *History on Art's Side: Social Dynamics in Artistic Efflorescences.* Ithaca, N.Y.: Cornell University Press, 1972.

Mandel, David. *Changing Art: Changing Man.* New York: Horizon Press, 1967.

Miller, James E., and Paul D. Herrings, eds. *Arts and the Public: Essays by Saul Bellow and Others.* Chicago: Chicago University Press, 1967.

Mukerjee, Radhakamal. *The Social Function of Art.* Westport, Conn.: Greenwood Press, 1954.

Myers, Bernard S. *Art and Civilization.* New York, 1957.

Read, Herbert E. *Art and Society.* 2d ed. New York: Schocken Books, 1966.

————. *The Grass Roots of Art: Lectures on the Social Aspects of Art in an Industrial Age.* New York: Wittenborn and Company, 1947.

Rookmaaker, Hendrik R. *Modern Art and the Death of a Culture.* Downers Grove, Ill.: Intervarsity Press, 1970.

Tomars, Adolf S. *Introduction to the Sociology of Art.* Mexico City: privately printed, 1940.

Valentovich, Georgil. *Art and Society and Other Papers in Historical Materialism.* New York, 1974.

Wilson, Robert Neal. *The Arts in Society.* Englewood Cliffs, N.J.: Prentice Hall, 1964.

Wolff, Janet. *Hermeneutic Philosophy and the Sociology of Art: An Approach of Some Epistemological Problems of the Sociology of Art and Literature.* London: Routledge and Kegan Paul, 1975.

————. *The Social Production of Art.* New York: St. Martin's Press, 1981.

# Index

Abstract Expressionism, 43, 71, 115; adumbrations of, in Whistler, 11; as nonarchitectonic, 35

Anatomy and physiology, ancient Greek knowledge of, compared, 53 n

Anatomy, peaks in science of (Kroeber), 170

Apollonian mode, 99–103, 184

Archeologists' view of art and artifacts, 13

Architecture: and aesthetic vs. spatial considerations, 69; as a confrontational expression of personality and culture, 72–73, 126; decorative features of, 69; development of skyscraper style in, 70; and ethos, 60, 118; Kroeber's omission of, 164–65; modern high-rise, 68–70. *See also* Churches and cathedrals; Gothic churches; Palaces

Architecture, Renaissance, 60, 61

Aristotle, 179; conception of personality in, 53; *Poetics* of, as source of classic standards, rules, 155–56

Art: as the abstraction of changes in meaning, 167; amplification of experience and understanding in, 42–43; anticipates social change, 159, 162; avant-garde, and the evolution of collective consciousness, 4; branches of, discussed, 3; and confined space, 26; as a constant human activity, 4; containment vs. breaking of bonds in, 25; difference of, from other symbolizing activities, 19; established

examples of, chosen, 2–3; evocation of common experience and problems in, 40, 42; and expansive spaces, 25; experimental, as subsidized by colleges, 84; as expressing meanings of cultural configurations, pan-human needs, the tastes of its clientele, 174; as expression of universal concerns, 46; expression of emotional states in, and clarification vs. homiletics, 45, of freedom in, 24–25, of subjective experience in, 43; forms failing to express meanings, 52; human need for, 19–20; impossibility of purely ideational, purely sensate, 115; and nature in opposition to, 123; as not necessarily explicit, 167–68; peaks of development of (Kroeber), 164; peaks of development of, as preceding peaks in science and philosophy (Kroeber), 168; sentimentally adopted, and the artist's intentions, 78–79; technical aspects of, as appealing to other artists, 78–79; as a universal symbolizing activity, 19. *See also* Architecture; Dance; Drama; Music; Painting; Sculpture

Art, abstract, 123

Art, Baroque, and breaking of formal containment, 25

Art, Carolingian, 28

Art, Eastern: aesthetic continuum in, 148; as dominated by feeling, 140; emphasis upon visual pattern and feeling in, 141; portrayals of natural objects, landscapes in, 143; selec-

Acknowledgment is made to the following publishers for permission to
reprint material under copyright:
To Doubleday & Company, Inc. for excerpts from *The Birth of Tragedy
and the Genealogy of Morals* by Friedrich Nietzsche, translated by
Francine Golffing. Copyright © 1956 by Doubleday & Company, Inc.
To Houghton Mifflin Company for excerpts from *Patterns of Culture*
by Ruth Benedict. Copyright 1934 by Ruth Benedict. Copyright ©
renewed 1962 by Ruth Valentine.

Library of Congress Cataloging in Publication Data
Manfredi, John, 1920–
The social limits of art.
Bibliography: p.
Includes index.
1. Art and society.   2. Culture.   I. Title.
NX180.S6M35   1982   700'.1'03   82-8661
ISBN 0-87023-372-6       AACR2